An Introduction to Christian Apologetics

An Introduction
to
Christian Apologetics

A Philosophic Defense of the
Trinitarian-Theistic Faith

by
EDWARD JOHN CARNELL, Th.D., Ph.D.
Professor of Apologetics, Fuller Theological Seminary

AUTHOR OF

A Philosophy of the Christian [illegible]on,
The Theology of Reinhold Niebuhr,
Television — Servant or Master?
ETC.

FOURTH, REVISED EDITION

WM. B. EERDMANS PUBLISHING COMPANY
Grand Rapids 1952 Michigan

Set up and printed, March, 1948

Fourth edition, revised, November, 1952

PRINTED IN THE UNITED STATES OF AMERICA

— *This Book* —

AN INTRODUCTION TO CHRISTIAN APOLOGETICS

by EDWARD JOHN CARNELL

was awarded

First Prize

in the

EERDMANS EVANGELICAL BOOK AWARD COMPETITION

— 1948 —

To all, everywhere,
who earnestly contend for the
Faith which was once for all
delivered to the saints

Preface to the Fourth Edition

The first draft of this work was composed when I was hip-deep in sticky academic problems as a graduate student. Mature counsel urged me not to rush into publication, but against the advice of my elders I submitted the manuscript for examination. I knew that dangers attended such a venture, but I felt willing to take the risk. Happily enough, the passing years have confirmed the soundness of my decision to write. I am grateful for this outcome.

This is the foundation thesis upon which this system of Christian apologetics is built: In the contest between the rational and the empirical schools of thought, a Christian must pitch his interests somewhere between the two extremes. If he surrenders the *rationes aeternae* (the norms by which we judge), he ends up in skepticism; if he withdraws from a respect for the data of sense perception, he ends up with a high and dry philosophy. I have not retreated one millimeter from this conviction.

Perhaps the largest tactical mistake I made was in omitting an introductory chapter on the exact meaning of apologetics. I took it for granted that Christian students were already carefully versed in the basic disciplines of the theological encyclopedia. I erred in this opinion.

Let me here inject a working definition of apologetics. *Apologetics is that branch of Christian theology which answers the question, Is Christianity rationally defensible?* When critics hurl objections against either Christ, salvation, or the truth of the Bible, it is the task of apologists to arrange answers. Suppose, for example, a student refuses to believe in the resurrection of Christ, insisting on the "evidence of science" that miracles are impossible. Is there nothing that the Christian can do? Must he sit by idly and allow skeptics to ridicule his faith? The church has risen to the challenge by commissioning apologists to answer critical objections.

The purpose of apologetics is at least twofold. First, to bring glory to God. Just as we would defend the words of our earthly father, so we defend the words of our Father in heaven. Secondly, to remove from critics any excuse for not repenting before God. Men who refuse Christ because of presumed "logical errors" in Christianity are men with a self-righteousness in the area of knowledge. They are resting on props which must be pulled away.

This leads to three further implications. First, one must disabuse his mind of the thought that one is "apologizing" for his faith, as if he is ashamed of it. Just the opposite: being *sure* of Christianity's truth, he defends it against the charges of unbelievers. Secondly, technically speaking one never "argues" another into becoming a Christian. We gently refute error; then we preach the gospel, for men are saved by the power of the gospel. Thirdly, when one defends his faith, he is not in competition with the Holy Spirit. The Spirit of God draws men *through* the convicting power of evidences. "How are men to call upon him in whom they have not believed? And how are they to believe in him of whom they have never heard? And how are they to hear without a preacher?" (Romans 10:14) The great church father, Augustine, did not forsake his pagan confidence in Manichaeism until *after* he was satisfied with the rational superiority of Biblical Christianity.

One of the illusions I formerly nursed was the supposition that *all* Christians ought to make peace with a system of apologetics. Again, I erred. Apparently God places different types of minds and interests in people. Experience has assured me that there are both apologetic and non-apologetic minds among Christians — those, on the one side, who are troubled with rational objections to the faith and demand answers, and those, on the other, who are not. I am of the former construction. My heart cannot believe what my mind rejects as false.

It is not my intention to criticize those who by-pass a defensive statement of Christianity in favor of a direct, intuitively grasped acceptance. Let every individual stand or fall before his own master. My concern is to encourage those who, like myself, feel a burning within them to know if Christianity can be accepted with the consent of all our faculties. It is to this company, and to them alone, that I commend the reading of this work. It is to them that I pose the question: *If Christianity is not worth defending, what then is?*

The reactions of an author to his first published book are interesting. The first edition inflates his academic pride. He removes himself to a secluded corner and there he gently fingers the new book, warm from the presses, while modestly assuring himself that he has made a "great" contribution to contemporary literature.

By the time the second edition appears, however, his mood has strikingly changed. The book has not disturbed as much as one acre of real estate, let alone moving the world. Even the author's best friends have not troubled themselves to read the publication. And more than that, critical book reviews have dutifully exposed a string of minor inconsistencies in the first printing. No longer anticipating fame and renown from his work, the author is content just to come out even.

When the third and fourth printings arrive, a mature, steady contentment settles in, sort of a compromise between the ambition of national prominence and the resignation of complete obscurity. These later editions are accepted by the author as a token proof that he has succeeded in stating convictions which a few at least have found helpful. He now accepts this as enough, realizing that the world is too vast, too complex, to be troubled much by the ordinary stream of books which flow from the presses.

Edward John Carnell

Pasadena, California
Sept. 1, 1952

Preface to the First Edition

The task of any philosophy of life is to construct an adequate explanation for the whole course of reality. Conservative Christianity, commonly referred to today as 'Fundamentalism,' is a philosophy of life, and it competes to explain such questions as where the universe has come from, what its present meaning is, and what is the direction in which it is gravitating. Having subscribed *ex animo* to Biblical Christianity we now have the burden to make good the command of the apostle Peter, "Always be prepared to make a *defense* to any who calls you to account for the hope that is in you" (I Peter 3:15). The aim of this volume is to discharge the obligation which this verse lays upon us by showing how Christianity is able to answer the fundamental questions of life as adequately as, if not more adequately than, any other world-view.

We shall attempt to show the truth of conservative Christianity in this manner. First, we shall expose the basic predicament of man, both practical and theoretical; this will serve to lead us into a thorough discussion of the problem of the one within the many, the foundation upon which the entire volume is constructed. Secondly, we shall clear the ground for the laying of this foundation by facing such basic problems as the nature of truth, the definition of faith, the validity of the conservative hypothesis, and the nature of proof. With this finished, we shall begin the third project, the scaffolding of the superstructure. Over the space of four chapters we shall face and attempt to solve the intricate question of starting point. Fourthly, and finally, with the scaffolding completed, nothing will remain but to finish rearing and adorning the superstructure. This will be achieved by our drawing out implications for Fundamentalism from such problems as Biblical criticism, common ground, the relation between conservative Christianity and the empiricism of the scientific method, the nature of miracles, the nature of natural law, philosophy of history, the thorny question of evil, the ethical one and many, and immortality and resurrection. In the conclusion we shall attempt to show that the building is ready for occupancy.

Over and above, and in addition to, these theoretically conceived aims, a practical motive animates our work. We are assured that men are as much in need of God today as, if not more than, ever before in the history of human life, and that the highest act of philanthropy that we can engage in, in the twentieth century, is to lead men to a saving knowledge of the Man of Sorrows.

Our defense of Fundamentalism is all the more challenging at this hour, because, to the modern mind, the vitality of Christianity's theology seems effete, and its basic doctrines appear, in the light of the scientific method, to be but figments of superstition and imagination, gratuitously assumed by timorous supernaturalists. Among the contemporary intelligentsia, therefore, the antecedent probability of conservative Christianity is very low. But the Fundamentalist is assured, however, that the modern mind succeeds in ridiculing conservative Christianity only because it assigns to the latter certain propositions which the system itself does not require.

Seasoned philosophers will be disappointed by our efforts, for we have here elected to appeal to college seniors or their equivalent. The depth to which we go into problems, therefore, is conditioned by this goal. A more technically conceived volume must be drawn up to satisfy the precise mind of the philosopher. That will appear in due time. To aid the untutored in their grasp of philosophy, we have drawn up a glossary of the major terms which we use in the work.

As is natural, we have been forced to set Christianity over against other systems of philosophy; the truth of any proposition necessarily involves the falsity of its contradiction. In so doing, however, we have tried to keep before us the admonitory words of Paul, "Let all that you do be done in love" (I Corinthians 16:14). If we have failed to fulfill this standard, it has been more from a weakness of the flesh than from unwillingness of the spirit.

The author acknowledges an incalculable indebtedness to his former professor, Dr. Gordon Haddon Clark of Butler University, whose spiritual kindness, fatherly interest, and academic patience made the convictions which stimulated the penning of this volume possible. For the many shortcomings in the final text, however, the author assumes full responsibility.

Edward John Carnell

March 1, 1948

Contents

PART III. Implications of the Christian World-View

CONCLUSION

Part I

THE NEED FOR A CHRISTIAN WORLD-VIEW

Chapter 1

The Practical Human Predicament

How then can man be just with God? Or how can he be clean that is born of a woman? Behold, even the moon has no brightness, and the stars are not pure in his sight. How much less man, that is a worm! And the son of man, that is a worm! —*Job*

THE fact that man is both soul and body makes for happiness and misery. On the one hand there are pleasures. Those of the body come from proper emotions, while those of the mind come from reflection, memory, and anticipation. Plato rightly names the latter set as the better, for the transitional character of emotional delights vitiates their candidacy for the office of being the higher good. On the other hand, both body and soul afford man untold pain and misery. All who have submitted to the plying of the scalpel or to the grinding of the drill willingly testify to the reality of physical pain, both as to its intensity and severity. But the sorrow of the soul is a malady more to be dreaded by man than physical discomfitures. Many are the amputees who have endured the removal of a limb without the palliation of an anesthesia, simply because the will, dictated to by a faith-filled soul, determined that life was worth living; while others in the prime of health, replete with wealth and goods, have resorted to suicide to escape the demands which society placed upon them during their three score years and ten. In other words, severe as physical pain is, if the soul sees tranquility ahead as its possession, it is enabled to bear the burden with hope. Peace of mind is the highest form of human happiness.

1. The Sources of Soul-Sorrow

Qua body man is an animal, while *qua* spirit he is a celestial being. As a creature of time and space, man is limited by death; while as a creature of spirit, man is able to live eternally. Meditation upon these conflicting realities is a basic cause of soul-sorrow. The pressure which results from the consideration of what man is as an empirical self and what he ought to be as an ideal self creates friction. The friction, if severe enough, brings suicide.

A. The Problem of the Body

Solomon, wisest of mortal men, expressed the problem of the body well. "For that which befalls the sons of men befalls beasts; even one thing befalls them: as the one dies, so dies the other; yea, they have all one breath; and man has no preeminence above the beasts: for all is vanity" (Ecclesiastes 3:19). The body is an incredibly precise organism, a wonderful masterpiece of art and symmetry. One need only reflect casually upon the mystery of his beating heart to appreciate the Davidic utterance, "I will give thanks unto thee; for I am fearfully and wonderfully made!" (Psalm 139:14).

But the marvelous frame of man is also a source of human woe. Men are born into the world without covenant or consultation and are obliged to make the best of the body which is issued to them, regardless of its condition. We are all born 'not quite perfect.' Disfiguring birthmarks, harelip, cleft palate, crossed eyes, knock knees, club feet, or poorly aligned teeth make us self-conscious and inferior. Fortunately, reconstructive surgery can intercede in these cases. But what of the weak hearts, the congenitally crippled, and the cancerous? Without fear of confutation, we may assert that these are a source of sorrow. The end of this sorrow is death. From the time that man purchases his first pair of glasses to strengthen weak eyes till the physician nods his head to indicate that nothing more can be done to save the body, the reality and fear of death are ever before man. This is a source of anguish.

B. The Problem of the Universe

Not only is the body incompetent to act as a vehicle to bear up the eternal ideals of the soul, but the universe which makes up the environment for the body is so viciously set against man that the latter's situation seems aggravated almost to hopelessness. Let us trace some of the scientific discoveries which have contributed to the situation.

1. With the discovery of the telescope by Galileo in 1609, the boundaries of reality were pushed out to infinity. In relation to this vast expanse, man appeared to be nothing. "Science has made it impossible . . . to believe in a loving Father Almighty. The vastness of the universe that modern astronomy discloses is appalling in its emptiness of anything that even suggests a Father's care for human beings."[1]

2. The next step was the mechanical universe. Conceived by Descartes, and perfected by Spinoza, the notion that the universe is a vast machine is yet an axiom of science. "Modern science has been characterized by the abandonment of teleological interpretation for description and explanation in terms of natural law."[2] Man was now reduced to a cog in a vast, purposeless machine.

> Purposes gave way to mathematics, human will and foresight to immutable and inflexible mechanical order. Throughout the whole . . . stretches of infinity, in stone and plant and animal, nowhere in this universe was there another being like man, nowhere a being who felt and suffered, loved and feared and hoped, who thought and knew. Man was alone, quite alone, in a vast and complex cosmic machine. Gone were the angelic hosts, gone the devils and their pranks, gone the daily miracles of supernatural intervention, gone even was man's imploring cry of prayer . . . man became . . . a mere part of this vast machine; its finest flower, perhaps—perhaps a cosmic accident and mistake. To that eternal cry of the soul, 'Why?' the answer came, *Ignoramus*—nay, *Ignorabimus*.[3]

---

1. Roberts, *The Problem of Choice,* p. 404. See this work for a solid defense of teleology.
2. *Twentieth Century Philosophy,* (Runes, ed.), p. 120.
3. Randall, *The Making of the Modern Mind,* p. 227. See this excellent section for an unabridged account of this development of science.

If the whole has no purpose, can there be purpose in any part?

3. Evolution joined with astronomy to explain man's place in an ateleological universe. In 1871 Darwin published his *The Descent of Man,* in which proof was offered for the biological evolution of man.[4] Being no longer a crowning act of creation, man must now swallow his pride and meditate upon the fact that he has oozed from the slime along with the beetles, snails, and weasels. But the latter creatures are more fortunate than man, for he is aware both of his ignoble ancestry and of his dreaded end, death. Thus we have a further commentary on what Pascal has referred to as the misery and grandeur of man.

4. Climaxing science's interpretation of the universe in its relation to human values is the second law of thermodynamics, according to which the amount of *available* energy in the universe is diminishing. In time all energy will be evenly distributed. and hence, useless. This means that the world some day will be unfit for life. In the light of such wholesale slaughter, there is to be realized in life what Shakespeare confined to the stage. What is life?

> It is a tale
> Told by an idiot, full of sound and fury,
> Signifying nothing.[5]

In short, modern man appears to be but a grown-up germ, sitting on a gear of a vast cosmic machine which is some day destined to cease functioning because of lack of power. Is Solomon to be ignored when he says, "I have seen all the works that are done under the sun; and, behold, all is vanity and a striving after wind" (Ecclesiastes 1:14)?

---

4. We do not here approbate organic evolution. We merely report that there are those who do. For a Christian attitude toward evolution, see *infra,* Chapter XIII.

5. *Tragedy of Macbeth,* V.v.

II. The Nature of Soul-Sorrow

The core of man's dilemma is the problem of relating his insatiable desire for self-preservation to the realities of a death-doomed body and an impersonal universe.

A. The Union of the Real and the Ideal

In thought man can transcend the contingencies of time and space. He can dream of a better body and a better universe than those which exist in reality. Meditation upon the union of the real and the ideal brings misery.

Man appears to be literally suspended between heaven and earth, between the ideal and the real, between the desirable and the actual. He longs for a strong body, but the lethal germs cut short the hope. He prays for another day to live, but the scythe of death cuts him down. He trusts in marble monuments, only to have the earth beneath them buckle and crumble. Whatever man achieves, the universe seems determined that the weeds of time and indifference cover it over. Every cultural expression has the same verdict written over it: This is doomed to decay! What sense is there in such a universe? And who is responsible for this monstrous situation?

> Therefore is my spirit overwhelmed within me.
> My heart within me is desolate.[6]

The failure to be able to unite the real and the ideal presses home to man a strange impelling sense of the futility and absurdity of life. There is no castle that man can build which will last forever, for regardless how deep the foundation, how thick the walls, how immense the superstructure, the same decree of decay is written over it as is written over everything which man undertakes.

B. The Fear of Death

The incongruity between man's desire for life and the reality of physical death is the most maddening problem of

6. Psalm 143:4.

all. Although he sees the handwriting on the wall, man yet refuses to think that death is his final destiny, that he will perish as the fish and the fowl, and that his place will be remembered no more. Man wills to live forever; the urge is written deep in his nature.

The nature of soul-sorrow from the fear of death is plain. It is that spiritual uneasiness which is left in the heart of man when he lines up the ideals that he longs for with the reality of things as they are. Man longs for eternal life. That is the ideal. He will die soon. That is the real. The gross incompatibility between these two sides of man makes the piecing together of life's jig-saw puzzle a staggering assignment, indeed, and not a few are those timid souls who, seeing only a slight chance of success, succumb to disappointment, anxiety, despondency, desperation, and melancholy.

III. The Cure for Soul-Sorrow

Man can elect to take one of four paths as he seeks to wend his way through the labyrinth of human sorrow. Let us examine these.

A. The Four Alternatives

1. One can leap off the side of a cliff if he so chooses, but somehow he instinctively rejects this course of action. Not only is the suicide a coward, but also the act itself cuts across man's basic urge to live. Man is too much of a problem-solver to dismiss the dilemma of life by blowing out his brains.

2. One can ignore the problem and go on living as if life had meaning, but goodness knows why! This avenue is the one which the many tread, indeed, for few are those who candidly face the question of existence for exactly what it is worth. But more serious minds reject the notion because it is but an ignoration, not a solution, of the problem. It may be that indifference to the issue is the one state in which man must not be found, for the stakes involved in life and death

may be high. "For what does it profit a man, to gain the whole world and forfeit his life?" (Mark 8:36)

3. One can admit that, since we know on good rational grounds that the universe is unfriendly to our values, the only manly thing to do is to make the best of a bad situation. There is no virtue in playing the role of a whining child and making the problem worse than it is. This is the way of the pessimist, a route becoming more and more popular to the modern mind. Bertrand Russell calls it 'confident despair.'

One cannot dismiss this alternative with a sigh, for, as common sense tells us, if the universe *is* unfriendly to our values and ideals, then we *must* — if we are honest with the facts and if we still desire to keep living—be stoic and put up with an unfortunate arrangement for which we are not responsible. On this view, however, no real reason can be advanced to dissuade people from committing suicide. This may appear to be only an insignificant point, but a little reflection will show that open suicide will make for the destruction of society itself. We shall have more to say about this later.

4. The final alternative is to question seriously the validity of the pessimistic interpretation of the facts of the universe. The conservative will elect to follow this course of action, for he is convinced that the universe makes enough sense and gives enough hope to man that the latter need not descend to a straw-grasping, 'confident despair' interpretation of the course of reality. If the Christian can succeed in establishing this view of things, he will have restored hope to man.

B. The Ingredients of the Cure for Soul-Sorrow

Man's whole trouble is that he cannot find a proper meaning for life. A pessimistic meaning of the universe yields anxiety and despair in the soul. The cure for soul-sorrow, then, is that meaning of life which can restore man's faith in things.

1. The first ingredient which the cure must have is the hope for personal immortality. Man's uncompromising desire

for self-preservation forces him to reject as insufficient any meaning to reality which excludes the possibility of personal immortality. Death is man's sword of Damocles, and until it is removed, complete happiness is unattainable. This is the reason why all the classic philosophers have been content to think in but one dimension. This dimension is immortality, for the soul of man was made for eternal felicity and will not rest until it rests in this eternity.

It is in the light of this context that the Christian will press home the promises of Christ's gospel. "For God so loved the world that he gave his only Son, that whoever believes in him should not perish but have *eternal life*" (John 3:16). How one may intelligently hold to this hope in the light of the impending death both of the body and of the universe, is a question which we shall face later on. At this point, let us rest in the fact that man needs immortality to be happy.

2. But immortality cannot be secured until man has made peace with his universe. If the universe is not such as will bear up the possibility of immortality, the actuality of it can never be established. In addition to our hope for immortality, then, we must have a rational view of the universe to serve as a frame of reference in terms of which immortality can be made meaningful. By 'rational' we mean 'logically intelligible.'

Let us be clear that a rational view of life is the least that a rational man will settle for. The Christian may claim no exemption from this rule. Either Christianity is logically intelligent, or it is meaningless. There is no *tertium quid*. If the possibility of immortality is the first ingredient, the actuality of a rational view of the universe is the second.

3. Granted that we *need* immortality. Granted also that the satiation of this need is contingent upon a rational view of

the universe. Yet, is there not even a more basic problem than these? The *fundamental* question is, What is truth? Until we know what truth is, we shall be unable to recognize a rational universe when we see one.

The necessity for truth is obvious. Man, in his zeal to establish immortality, is tempted to construct artificial world-views which make for the hope of eternal life. This hope-at-any-cost gesture is fatal, however, for it commits the fallacy of thinking that wishing will make it so. Unless there is some check on proposed rational systems, therefore, they will so abound in number and style that man will be left without a criterion by which to distinguish the worthy from the unworthy.

In sum, without hope, nothing has real meaning. Without a rational view of the universe, hope cannot be secured. But without a knowledge of what truth is, a rational universe cannot be recognized. In due course, we shall attempt to show that Christianity — and Christianity alone — can make peace with three conditions *sine qua non** for human happiness.

IV. Recapitulation

Man is a creature who is both in the process of history and who yet transcends history at every point. This involvement and transcendence is the cause of that friction in the soul of man, which, if unchecked, results in pessimism and suicide. What plagues man is death. He is never sure but that his existence is analogous to the sheep in the fold which receives food day by day, but which, in the end, is slaughtered and eaten. But man cannot even be dumb when he goes to the slaughter, for he is a rational being. He lives in an ideal as well as an actual world. The only solution to his problem is to set up a veracious interpretation of the universe in which the real and the ideal are united in such a way that personal immortality is rendered possible.

* Students unfamiliar with philosophic terms are urged to check the glossary on page 363.

A. The Problem

Oscar Hammerstein II has given a classical statement of the practical human predicament in his lyrics of *Show Boat.*[7]

> You an' me, we sweat an' strain,
> Body all achin' an' racked wid pain.
> 'Tote dat barge!' 'Lift dat bale,'
> Git a little drunk an' you land in jail.
>
> Ah gets weary an' sick of tryin',
> Ah'm tired of livin' An' skeered of dyin',
> But ol' man river he jus' keeps rollin' along.

Not only do those who lug bales of cotton look for "dat stream called de river Jordan," but so do all men who face the loneliness and separation of death's call.

B. The Solution

Jesus Christ has given the immortal answer to the practical human predicament.[8]

> Come to me, all who labor and are heavy-laden,
> And I will give you rest.
> Take my yoke upon you, and learn from me;
> For I am gentle and lowly in heart,
> And you will find rest for your souls.
> For my yoke is easy, and my burden is light.

Both the statement and the solution of the problem are now before us. What is obviously lacking, however, is the clarification of the connection between them. Showing this connection will occupy us in the succeeding chapters.

---

7. From *Ol' Man River*, copyright, 1927, by T. B. Harms Co., New York. Used by permission. So severe is the practical problem here that the muddy water of the Mississippi is thought to be in a more enviable condition than man!

8. Matthew 11:28-30. The practical predicament, as we shall observe below, is really the by-product of a more basic and searching dilemma, *the predicament of sin.* If it were not for man's antecedent rebellion against the law of God, there would be no practical human predicament at all. All evil is either sin or the punishment for sin. But since the unknown can be learned only through the known, we shall proceed to understand man's sinful predicament by first comprehending the practical and theoretical predicaments in which he is involved. By understanding man's problem as he faces his universe, his predicament as he faces God's demands will become more intelligible. Our order of enquiry, therefore, is pedagogical. It is not to be supposed that the practical predicament is more of a problem to man than his sinful involvement.

Chapter II

The Theoretical Human Predicament

Happy is the man that finds wisdom, and the man that gets understanding. For the gaining of it is better than the gaining of silver, and the profit thereof than fine gold. She is more precious than rubies, and none of the things you can desire are to be compared unto her. — Solomon.

Christ the wisdom of God. — Paul.

IF the practical problem of man is dispelling the fear of death through a successful union of the ideal and empirical worlds, the theoretical problem is the location of a rational connection between these realms. Philosophically this difficulty is known as the problem of the one within the many. The many are the particulars of the time-space universe while the one is the logical or teleological connection between them.

Let us illustrate this problem of the relation between the one and the many by pointing to Luca Signorelli's famous painting, Head of a Youth. If one is to see meaning in the picture, he must not stand too near the canvas or too far from it. If one puts his eye right up to the painting, all coherence in the picture is lost. The black of the hair will appear to be blackness without meaning. But if one moves away from the canvas too far, all he can see is a vague speck on the horizon. He sees the whole, but the whole has no meaning because it lacks the support of the parts. One must come sufficiently close to the picture to see the parts and yet stay far enough away to see the connection between the parts.

In like manner one cannot see the rationality of the universe unless he keeps close enough to it to see the parts of the universe, and yet far enough away to have a perspective to see the whole as a universe. If we have only a microscopic view of the world, we are in the same plight as the myopic ant who walks across the top of a chair. What it traverses is but a series of flat surfaces and not a chair at all, for it has no perspective to see the whole. If we have a telescopic view of the universe, we have a picture of the whole, indeed, but our point of view bears no relevance to the human situation.

I. Transition to the Theoretical

As tons of blueprints must be drawn up to float one battleship, and as an intern must spend years memorizing those abstractions which make up medical nomenclature so that he can distinguish the spleen from the stomach in a practical situation, so also the philosopher is required to dip deep into abstract theory before he can produce a practical solution to the problem of the one within the many. If it takes two years to build a battleship, there is little wonder that it requires centuries to construct a rational view of the universe.

To aid the beginner in his digestion of the theoretical, let us give two down-to-earth illustrations of the relation between meaning (the one) and fact (the many). By means of these illustrations we will show that one cannot even gossip successfully without employing certain philosophic principles.

A. The Problem of Significant Speech

The problem of the one within the many begins when we open our mouth and speak. In other words, in the simple act of predication. Predication is that act of the mind wherein a predicate is assigned to a subject, as 'The paper is white.' The finished relationship is known as a 'proposition.' When affirmed by the mind, the proposition is referred to as a 'judgment.' All propositions may be analyzed into three parts, subject, predicate, and copula. In our illustration the parts would be 'paper,' 'white,' and 'is,' respectively. Now, absurd as the suggestion may first be to the reader, this simple gesture of predication involves a problem which literally bristles with difficulties. Briefly, how can the one (the predicate) refer meaningfully to the many (the subject)? The predicate term is a universal term, that is, it refers to more than one particular. 'White,' for example, is that achromatic color bearing the least resemblance to black. When we say, 'The paper is white,' actually we are saying, 'This particular instance of paperness is a case of, or may be subsumed under, the general class-concept, whiteness.' But what is this strange thing, 'whiteness'? Is it not evident that there are no two things in nature exactly alike? How then can we meaningfully use the term 'whiteness' to refer to many particulars? If one is to be meticulously accurate a proper name must be given to each individual object in reality. But this is impossible, for the grains of sand in the Sahara would certainly use up all of the names we could conjure up in a lifetime.

Without pressing this further, for this is not a textbook in formal logic, let it be known that we solve the problem of speech by dividing the particulars in reality (the many) into teleologically related class-concepts (the one). By this expedient we can carry on meaningful conversation. Everything which may be subsumed under the general class, 'furniture for lighting,' we call 'lamp.' By defining 'man' as 'a sentient being capable of worshipping God,' we have set this class-concept (man) over against other class-concepts. This is known as the 'connotative definition.' Through this definition we set man apart from horses, fleas, and pollywogs which cannot worship God, and from rocks, trees, and axes which are not sentient beings.

It might pay the reader to meditate upon this problem of predication when next he walks through the woods alone. If he will pursue it, he will find here an illustration of the problem of the one within the many.

B. The Problem of Significant Action

One may refuse to speak, but he cannot elect not to act, for determination not to act at all is itself an act. Let us here indicate how meaningful action, like meaningful speech, depends upon a solution to the problem of the one within the many. Let us use Socrates as our paradigm here.

With the rise of the skepticism of the philosophers, the people of Greece turned from virtue to vice. Laws were disregarded, contracts were broken, and the gods were despised. Here, again, we see the relation between the practical and the theoretical. Philosophy may not bake bread, but it has a strange power for making people do things. "In the younger and hotter minds this skepticism frequently took the socially disruptive form of the supposition that the only measure of truth and right for any individual is self-interest—the appeal of an idea or a proposed act to him at the time it presents itself."[1] This is known philosophically as 'ethical relativism,' where every man acts as he thinks right in his own eyes.

Concerned to rectify the situation, Socrates journeyed early to the market place to interrogate men about their souls, promising that if they would faithfully follow the Delphic epigram, 'Know thyself!' they would be led into normative ethical action. Man's trouble is his ignorance. Ignorance is the source of vice. "When a person supposes that he knows, and does not know; this appears to be the great source of all the errors of the intellect."[2]

The brilliance of Socrates lay in his conviction that morality is an art, and that like all arts, it must be ruled by standards if actions are to be meaningfully thought of as good or bad.

> For every moral judgment, every judgment with such predicates as just, unjust, temporate, intemporate, right, wrong, involves such a claim to ethical knowledge; yet this claim is found to be invalid and baseless as soon as those who confidently use such general terms are called upon to define or explain them. The aim of the Socratic interrogation was, therefore, in the first place, to awake a consciousness that knowledge was wanting, and that without it men were like

1. Burtt, *Types of Religious Philosophy*, p. 39.
2. *Sophist*, 229b.

> vessels without a rudder or steersman; and, secondly, to teach them the method of reflection and investigation by which alone such ignorance could be removed.[3]

Observe what is transpiring here. The criterion for good conduct is the one which provides a standard of classification for the many. Apart from this relation between the one and the many, *significant* moral judgment is impossible.

Socrates, however, failed in his mission, for from the 'Know thyself!' dictum, there came Cynics, philosophers who, having known themselves, decided that everything which was not an immediate satisfaction of some primitive want in man was superfluous. All culture, wealth, and refinement were thus excluded from the life of a virtuous man. In this context Diogenes achieved his immortality by rejecting social conventions and by going through the streets looking for an honest man.

The reason why Socrates failed was that he did not provide *content* for those criteria which he so clearly saw were necessary for ethical living. To instruct men to look within is quite futile. Every homicidal maniac claims that his conscience is clear. "To tell men, therefore, to look within for an authoritative guide, and to trust to their irresistible convictions, is to give them a guide which will lead them to destruction."[4]

> Socrates had defined virtue, the fundamental ethical conception, as insight, and this in turn as knowledge of the good, but had given to the concept of the good no universal content, and in a certain respect had left it open. This made it possible for the most diverse conceptions of life to introduce their views of the ultimate end (*telos*) of human existence into this open place in the Socratic concept.[5]

This completes our second illustration of the one within the many. Let us now advance to the over-all problem as it pertains to a rational view of the universe.

---

3. Caird, *The Evolution of Theology in Greek Philosophers,* I, pp. 69-70.
4. Hodge, *Systematic Theology,* I. p. 102.
5. Windelband, *History of Philosophy,* p. 82.

II. The Problem of the Many

The assignment of the philosopher is huge. He has to make sense out of the whole of reality. The problem of philosophy, therefore, is the problem of predication on a large scale. Whereas, in simple predication one class-concept is joined to a particular entity, in a completed philosophy of life a network of universals and the totality of reality are joined. Let us here carry out our illustration of the portrait, showing the difficulties which attend those who maintain too close a view of the universe, and the problems which attend all who maintain too distant a perspective.

Since ancient Greece was literally the kitchen in which most of the philosophic menus were cooked up, let us turn back to that land of philosophers for the most bald presentation of the problem of the one within the many.

> When Heraclitus declared that all is Becoming, and Parmenides said that all is Being, the problem which has ever since harassed the minds of countless thinkers was stated in all its stark simplicity. If Being is and Becoming is not, how can the many and changing be? If Becoming is and Being is not, how can unity and stability be? Man can neither reasonably doubt experience, which testifies to change, nor deny intelligence, which reveals at least *some* permanence in things.[6]

A. Example of Coming Too Close to the Universe of Change

The first great empiricists were Heraclitus and Protagoras. Heraclitus handled the metaphysics, and Protagoras the epistemology. Metaphysics and epistemology go together like Scarlatti and the harpsichord. Where you find the one, you immediately think of the other.

The first problem of metaphysics is answering the question, 'What is the nature of reality?' To this Heraclitus gave the answer, 'becoming,' for, looking out of his window he saw

---

6. Phelan, *St. Thomas and Analogy*, p. 20.

rivers flowing, trees growing, and babies crawling. If nature is reality, then reality is becoming, for all of nature is in flux.

"All things are exchanged for fire and fire for all things, just as wares are exchanged for gold and gold for wares. All things flow; nothing abides. One cannot step twice into the same river."[7]

The first problem of epistemology is answering the question, 'How can reality be known?' Now it is evident that if reality is nature, the world of change, then the *only* way to know it is through the sense perception. If one expects to know what a pear tastes like, he must open his mouth and try it. Mathematics will not help him here. For Protagoras, then, knowledge *is* sensation.

B. *Critique*

Let us lump together these two empiricists and show how they failed to solve man's predicament because they came too close to the flux. What we advance against this early form of empiricism applies equally to all forms of consistent empiricism. Most of the criticisms were set down by Plato in his remarkable dialogue, *Theaetetus.*

1. *Empiricism makes man the author of reality.* If knowledge is sensation, then qualities are created by the mind, for the perception of qualities depends upon the physiological state of the observer, as in color blindness. The person who sees red and the person who sees green are equally qualified to report on what the color in *rerum natura* is. The real color is both, for knowledge is a report of the real and sensation is knowledge. This is metaphysical skepticism.

2. *All judgments are true.* If all sensations are knowledge, all are true. Then he who thinks that Protagoras is wrong, is making a true judgment. Being wrong, we may dismiss the claims of Protagoras to truth.

---

7. Bakewell, *Source Book in Ancient Philosophy,* p. 33. Heraclitus taught the existence of the *logos,* too, but only by a happy inconsistency in his empirical epistemology.

3. *All judgments are false.* Since true and false are correlatives, that is, each depends upon the other for its meaning, it follows that all being true, there is no true. If there is no true, then all is just as false as it is true. Once again Protagoras' philosophy is false.

4. *Changeless criteria are impossible.* If all is in flux, then even the proposition, 'all is in flux,' is in flux, and nothing has meaning. "Inasmuch as truth is the same today, tomorrow, and forever, there can be no certain and final knowledge if everything perceived by the senses constantly changes."[8] Without changeless criteria, all meaning is destroyed.

5. *Society is impossible.* "Epicharmos already made fun of it by putting it as an argument into the mouth of a debtor who did not wish to pay. How could he be liable, seeing he is not the same man that contracted the debt?"[9]

6. *Significant speech is impossible.* No word can adequately describe reality, since before the word can be gotten out of the mouth, reality has changed. *Panta rei!* If words cannot be chosen because they fit the facts, then, they must be chosen for aesthetic reasons. But further, "all answers . . . to any question are equally correct. But all are inexact, for the very words used, even the words 'this' and 'thus,' imply some sort of stability and definiteness which the theory rules out."[10]

7. *Involves subjectivism.* Unless truth is changeless, there is no use arguing about anything, for one can never rise above opinion. When we speak of truth, goodness, and beauty, we are just describing how we feel.

> For, if subjectivism is true, the arguments will not succeed in making any pronouncement on the subject to which they purport to relate; they will only succeed in telling us something about the opinions of subjectivists who use them.

---

8. Weber, *History of Philosophy,* p. 35.
9. Burnet, *Greek Philosophy,* Part I, p. 63.
10. Martin *et al., History of Philosophy,* p. 96.

> Thus, if the conclusions which subjectivism asserts are correct, there can be no arguments for them, since the truth both of the argument and of their conclusion must be subjective. Hence, to affirm that subjectivism is true will mean merely that it suits some people, those, namely, who maintain subjectivist views, to believe in it.[11]

When subjective, truth exists *for us*. This is skepticism. "Truth is a relative thing, a matter of taste, temperament, and education. Metaphysical controversies are therefore utterly vain."[12]

III. The Problem of the One

So much for the fate of those who come too close to the universe. Let us now trace briefly the lot of those who withdraw from the universe.

A. Example of Withdrawing Too Far from the Universe

Parmenides and Gorgias decided that the world of flux was illusory. Turning, therefore, from the spectral character of the phenomenal, they looked to logic and conceivableness to tell them what reality was. As with Hegel, the real is the rational and the rational is the real. The mobs and the *hoi polloi* might trust sensation, but not the philosopher. The tumultuous rabble think that the real is *panem et circenses,* 'bread and circuses.' In contemporary terms this would be 'a full dinner pail and a weekly movie.' For the rationalist, the real is the eternal and changeless realm of coherent truth.

The reason why Parmenides and Gorgias rejected the world of sensation was that the senses seemed to say motion was possible, while reason says that it is not. Zeno had proved that motion is impossible. The most popular argument of Zeno is the puzzle of Achilles and the tortoise. "Achilles must first reach the place from which the tortoise started. By that time the tortoise will have got on a little way. Achilles must then traverse that, and still the tortoise will be ahead.

---

11. Joad, *God and Evil,* p. 186.
12. Weber, *op. cit.,* p. 61.

He is always coming nearer, but he never makes up to it."[13] Change presumably destroys the law of excluded middle by asserting that A is either B or non-B. In change, A is neither B nor non-B. It is *becoming.* This is illogical.

Thus there is "one path only: That Being doth be;"[14] thought Parmenides. Gorgias took this thought of Being over and vaporized it out of existence.

> And Being does not exist. For, if it did, it would be either eternal or generated . . . Now, if it is eternal, for we must begin here, it has no source. Everything generated has some source, but the eternal, because it stands ungenerated, has no source, and, not having a source, it is infinite. If, however, it is infinite, it is nowhere. For, if it were somewhere, something else would exist in which it would be, and so Being, enclosed by something, would no longer be infinite, since that which encloses is greater than the thing enclosed, whereas nothing is greater than the infinite, and so the infinite is nowhere.[15]

By this sort of dialectic the Being of Gorgias was worn so thin that "it resembles the garment of the king, the fine texture of which everybody pretended to admire, until, at last, a little child exclaimed, in the simplicity of its heart: 'Why, the king is naked!' "[16]

B. Critique

Save for the bad use of logic which Parmenides and Gorgias made, the Christian objection to the employment of dialectic as a sole means to know reality is that it leads inevitably to a neglect of the world of blood and sweat and tears, the world in which the human drama is transpiring. There *is* a changing world here which must be explained. Until it is, man cannot find happiness.

The courage of the rationalist to think that the real and the rational are the same grows out of an erroneous notion of the connection between the many. His hope is that all

13. Bakewell, *op. cit.*, p. 24.
14. *Ibid.*, p. 15.
15. Quoted in Martin *et al.*, *op. cit.*, p. 82.
16. Weber, *op. cit.*, p. 32.

connections are logically necessary, *i.e.* deductive. He believes that to know one blade of grass thoroughly would be to give one enough information to deduce necessarily the totality of reality. The Christian rejects this on the ground that the relation between the number of blades of grass in Bolivia and king pythons in Africa is *teleological,* not necessary. By knowing a tree one cannot by logical deduction determine where Napoleon fought his battles. For the Christian the source of unity is the mind of Christ, a source which unifies the particulars in the time-space universe according to teleology. "From him and through him and to him are all things. To him be glory forever."[17] For the Christian, God, not logic, is the ultimate reason for things, for God is the author of logic itself. The reason for this will appear subsequently.

IV. The Persistent Philosophical Danger

A. The Contemporary Problem

We are still tempted to make an either/or affair of what must be a both/and. We cannot choose between logic and experience. Without logic our experience cannot be normative; without experience our logic cannot be relevant to the human situation. This problem, like the poor, is always with us.

> Either one describes the universe—the spiritual as well as the physical—in terms of material existence and of objectivity, and then one has to go as far as to 'epiphenomenalism' and consent never to meet anything that might resemble what we call consciousness, idea, finality, will. Or else one agrees to place oneself at a given moment into the very center of consciousness and to start from the *cogito*; in this latter case one will meet above the Heraclitean becoming the Platonic world of essences, and at the same time the inevitable problems of idealism and realism, of the subjective and the objective, of being and thought. Such is the alternative which, even after the admirable attempt made by Mr. Dewey, seems to us still to confront human reflection.[18]

---

17. Romans 11:36.
18. *The Philosophy of John Dewey* (Schilpp, ed.), *The Library of Living Philosophers,* Volume 1, p. 242.

B. The Christian's Attitude

Both levels of reality are admitted by the Christian, the normative (the one) and the contingent (the many).

1. *The world of the many.* Paul sets the mood of the Christian as he pleads for the empirical proofs for Christ's death and resurrection, confessing, "I am persuaded that none of these things has escaped his notice, *for this was not done in a corner.*"[19] The maid may sweep the dirt in the corner to hide it, but Christ was raised openly before men. As a verification of the Christian faith, then, the Christian shall plead the veracity of the Biblical interpretation of the many. Christianity is a philosophy which meets the real world.

2. *The world of the one.* Christ is the principle of the one and the author of the many, for "in him all things were created . . . through him and for him. He is before all things, and *in him all things hold together.*"[20] Christ is the I AM. Possession of the knowledge of Christ, thus, is possession of the highest form of reality. For this reason the Christian admonishes men that there is a difference in value between the two levels of being. God is necessary being, while His creation is contingent being. Being contingent upon God's will, it is this will, and not an antecedent system of logic, which gives meaning to the movement of the time-space world. The many are teleologically related to each other according as God has decreed the end (*telos*) of things.

For this reason the church universal preaches that the chief end of man is to love God and to enjoy Him forever. The possession of God is likened in Holy Writ to the ownership of a treasure hid in a field. So valuable is the treasure, that a wise man is willing to sell all that he has for it. Again, it is likened to a great pearl, of more worth than all pearls. For the possession of this pearl, a prudent man will do likewise. It is in this context of the problem of the one within the many and

19. Acts 26:26.
20. Colossians 1:16-17.

the orders of being that the Parable of the Rich Fool is to be interpreted. The man who prefers barns and wealth to the Author of barns and wealth is a fool,[21] even as it is the fool who says in his heart there is no God.[22] The fool is he who, having failed to solve the one within the many on its highest level, misses the point in life, and chooses to follow a way which seems right to him but the end thereof are the ways of death.[23]

---

21. Luke 12:16-21.

22. Psalm 14:1. The perfect pattern for the solution to the relation between unity and diversity is found in what Van Til calls "the eternal one and many." By this is meant that "Unity in God is no more fundamental than diversity and diversity in God is no more fundamental than unity. The persons of the Trinity are mutually exhaustive of one another." *Christian Apologetics,* p. 14. When referring to God in this volume, therefore, we mean — unless otherwise indicated — God *essentially,* not *personally. Qua* essence God is Deity; *qua* person God is Father, Son, and Holy Spirit. The essence of Deity — the One — is equally exhausted in the Persons — the Many.

23. Proverbs 14:12. The theoretical, like the practical human predicament, is a problem only because of the antecedent existence of *the predicament of sin.* The intellect of man is involved in the effects of the fall of man just as surely as are the rest of the faculties of man's heart. Man must look through a glass dimly. He must walk by faith, i.e. he must learn by the painful process of discursiveness. Adam enjoyed a perfect creaturely intuition of God's will. All of Adam's offspring have been blinded because of sin. Cf. Romans 1-3. Man is totally depraved on the side of his ability to be pleasing to God. Man is not totally depraved, however, on the side of his ability negatively to know that he is unhappy. If man did not see that he is unhappy, the promises of happiness in the gospel would be completely foolish and no point of appeal would exist. But Christ did appeal to men that were heavy laden to come to him for rest. The value of proceeding through the theoretical predicament of man to his sinful predicament is twofold. First, the former, which is known to man, can be used as a fulcrum for moving man into an appreciation of the latter, which is unknown. To start an apology for conservative Christianity by appealing to that of which the natural man is ignorant is to cast pearls before swine. Secondly, not only does the natural man not believe he is a sinner, but he is actively in rebellion against all who teach that he is. It is pedagogically wiser, therefore, to have man admit his unhappiness before showing him the deeper reason why this unhappiness exists. This preparatory work will not remove man's blindness to the fact that God is needed for full peace and tranquility of heart, but it may serve to prepare the way for the display of those objective evidences for Christianity through which the Holy Spirit may be pleased to effect regeneration. Faith is a gift of God. Christian values are refractory to man's unregenerate heart.

Part II

THE RISE OF THE CHRISTIAN WORLD-VIEW

Chapter III

The Problem of Truth

I am the truth. — Jesus Christ

WE have learned thus far that man is a creature in time and space who is primarily interested in happiness. Yet, before this desired state of well-being can become real, three definite conditions must be met. First, the hope for immortality must be secured, because without this hope man is harassed and vexed by the fear of death. Secondly, a rational view of the universe must be plotted, for the fear of death cannot be dissipated simply by rubbing some wonderful lamp of Aladdin. It can be disposed of only when man succeeds in learning that death is not his final judge. Thirdly, man must know what truth is that he may have a norm by which a true solution to the problem of the one within the many may be recognized when it comes along. We have already given what we think are the basic hints in the Christian solution of the one within the many. The next problem which we must face is that of the nature and test of truth.

I. The Nature of Truth

The simplest way to break into the question of the nature of truth is to show by concrete illustrations exactly what is meant by saying that a judgment is true. The true is a quality of that judgment or proposition which, when followed out into the total witness of facts in our experience, does not disappoint our expectations. Thus, if I am told that under a large white basswood tree in the city square, there is now buried a lost treasure; and if, after dodging the watchful eyes of the town fathers, I uproot the tree in question, but locate no treasure, I may conclude that my benefactor has lied. His judgment, 'There is now treasure under the white basswood tree in the city square,' is false because it fails to sustain me in the aggregate of my experience. Again, when little Johnny says that there are fifty steps leading up to the spring in the park, and actual scientific count reveals that there are just that number, then we say that he speaks, or has, the truth. He has made a good judgment. If, however, the number exceeds or falls short of the designated fifty, then we properly say that he speaks falsely. He has made a bad judgment; he has not the truth.

Truth, then, in its simplest dimension, is a judgment which corresponds to things as they actually are. If I say it is raining outside and experience shows that it is so, I am speaking the truth. But if experience fails to sustain my expectations, and reveals that there is no rain, I am speaking error. In the former case my judgment is true because it represents the meaning of things as these things actually are in reality, while in the latter case my judgment is false because it fails to represent the meaning of things as these things actually are in reality.

This definition of truth, however, is deficient from the Christian point of view, for it does not link truth with the mind of God sharply enough. For the Christian, God is truth because He is the Author of all facts and all meaning. There is no reality apart from the eternal nature of God Himself and the universe which He has created to display His glory. All meaning, then, flows from the mind of God, for that mind was the blueprint according to which the contingent universe was formed. God called the world into being *ex nihilo* according to the pattern of things which He preserved in the whole counsel of His will.

> He has made the earth by his power,
> He has established the world by his wisdom;
> And by his understanding has he
> Stretched out the heavens.[1]

1. Jeremiah 10:12.

Since the mind of God perfectly knows reality, truth is a property of that judgment which coincides with the mind of God. If man, thus, fails to say about reality what God says about it, he has made an error: for God, the source and power of all proper meaning and fact, cannot err in His judgment. Truth for the Christian, then, is defined as *correspondence with the mind of God.* On any level of judgment, therefore, man has truth only as long as he says about facts what God says about these facts. If man says that his chief end is to eat, drink, and be merry, he tells the truth only if that is what God says is man's chief end, too.

II. The Test for Truth

With this observation, however, a new difficulty arises. It is this. How do we know when our judgments *do* correspond to the mind of God? This is the problem of error. We need a test for truth to aid us in determining when our thoughts are the same as God's thoughts. Although many tests for truth are proposed at sundry times by various thinkers, we shall limit our enquiry to a typical list of ten.[2] We include these tests here, not because they are equal in proof-power, but rather for two reasons. First, they may serve as pedagogical devices through the use of which the philosophically untutored may be guided in his grasp of epistemology. Secondly, since the man on the street is led by false criteria most of the time, he will not be guided in the way of truth until he is instructed properly.

A. Instinct

Instinct is that natural aptitude of the species which leads to the fulfillment of some unpremeditated action, as when the pigeon returns to the loft, the bird builds its nest, and the mother protects her child. But, though instincts may provide sentient beings with certain motives for action, they cannot

2. This list comes *en bloc* from Brightman's *An Introduction to Philosophy,* pp. 35-66. The reader is advised to read Professor Brightman's fuller account of these criteria.

be the test for truth, since they cannot distinguish between what is legitimately natural to the species and what is acquired. Only the mind can do that.

B. Custom

Custom is any habit or practice which has come to be associated with the uniform actions or beliefs of a given individual or group by reason of its long continuance or uniformity, as saluting the flag or following certain rules of etiquette while in Rome. But customs can be good or bad, true or false. Something beyond and outside of custom, therefore, must test the validity of customs themselves.

C. Tradition

Tradition is the more normative body of customs. It is the corpus of criteria and standards which has been handed down in a group from early times. The *prima facie* argument for tradition is that so many people could not be deceived for so long a time. Though it is a favorite argument of the impressively huge Roman Catholic Church, the bubble of tradition can be easily pricked by pointing out that there are in existence so many traditions, so conflicting in essentials, that only in a madhouse could they all be justified. Since there are admittedly true and false traditions, as Christ pointed out,[3] truth must establish tradition and not tradition truth.

D. Consensus Gentium

By this is meant the consent of the nations. What is believed by all, everywhere, always, seems to be a foolproof standard for truth. If we cannot trust the corporate judgment of men, how can we rely upon the individual? This sounds more impressive than it actually is.

> Not many generations ago, in the Western world, it was a practically universal belief that the earth is the astronomical center of the universe, that heavy bodies fall with greater

---

3. "So, for the sake of your tradition, you have made void the law of God. You hypocrites!" Matthew 15:6-7.

> acceleration than light ones, that night air is apt to cause malaria, that people who doubt orthodox religious ideas are immoral, that old women who act queerly are probably trafficking with the devil.[4]

A proposition must be true to be worthy of the belief of all, but it does not follow that what is believed by all is true.

E. *Feeling*

Feeling is that apperceptive faculty of the soul by means of which one has an inward impression of the state of some object, person, or relation, as when one has a feeling that he is being followed, or a conviction that certain signs of the zodiac portend things to come. Hunches, inspirations, and feelings, however, are little more than subjective suggestions of the soul; they must be screened from without for their truth or error qualities. Some men feel they are Napoleon himself. Others vow that God has told them to chop their right arm off or fast to death. Still others feel certain that when the crow tips his wing at a ninety degree angle, there will be a large crop of toddy-producing coconuts in Madagascar. Without reason to guide it, feeling is irresponsible—a woman's intuition notwithstanding.

F. *Sense Perception*

Sensation—seeing, tasting, feeling, smelling, and hearing—provides us with what is sometimes called 'knowledge by acquaintance,' as opposed to 'knowledge by inference or reflection.' A look at the evening sunset provides us with more of an immediate awareness of God's wonders to the sons of men than can the precision of five erudite volumes on color refraction. True as this may be, however, sense perception is but a source for truth, not its definition or test. Our senses often deceive us. We have already refuted the notion that sense-perception is knowledge, so we need not here carry that argument on.

---

4. Burtt, *Right Thinking*, p. 46.

G. Intuition

Favorite stamping ground of the mystics, intuition is that eye of the soul which sees with immediacy. By intuition one knows first postulates and axioms. One sees immediately that the whole is equal to the sum of its parts or that a straight line is the shortest distance between two points. But here, as elsewhere, since intuitions cannot detect false intuitions (and they are many), we must say that intuitions are a source of, and not a test for, truth. We shall have more to say about the fallacy of mysticism in due time.

H. Correspondence

The devotees of correspondence[5] claim that an idea is true when it corresponds to reality. The idea 'piano' is true when it meets successfully with the piano out there in nature. The fallacy of this position has been pointed out too many times to labor over it here. If reality is extra-ideational, then how can we compare our ideas of the mind with it? How can the piano be brought into the mind to see if our idea is like it? The mind can only compare ideas together; these and nothing else.

I. Pragmatism

Pragmatism is essentially an American philosophy. Conceived by Charles S. Peirce through the help of certain Kantian concepts (*praktish* and *pragmatisch*), and popularized by William James and John Dewey, pragmatism marks a reaction from rationalism and idealism to that theory of epistemology which holds that truth is discovered, not by rational coherence, but through successful empirical action, conduct, adaptation to environment, and practical satisfaction of human needs. Peirce maintained that until a proposition can be carried into an actual empirical experiment in the laboratory of life, it is not said to be properly verified, inasmuch as the rational purport of every proposition lies exclusively in its ability to bear

---

5. Not to be confused with the Scholastic notion of correspondence.

upon conduct in life. William James called this the 'cash value' of truth, pleading that the true "is only the expedient in the way of our thinking, just as 'the right' is only the expedient in the way of our behaving."[6] Truth is not simply *found* in experience; it *is* the experience. "Truth *happens* to an idea. It *becomes* true, is *made* true by events. Its verity *is* in fact an event, a process: the process namely of its verifying itself, its veri-*fication*. Its validity is the process of its valid-*ation*."[7] Any idea which does not entangle our anticipations in frustrations, that succeeds in fitting and adapting our life to reality's full setting, fulfills the pragmatic definition of truth. Coherence has but an oracular solution to the problem of truth, not a real one.

Let us illustrate this by an example which James proposes. Some men say, 'The highest ultimate is matter,' others, 'The highest ultimate is spirit.' "What do we *mean* by matter? What practical difference can it make *now* that the world should be run by matter or by spirit?" asks James.[8] The pragmatist says that there is no difference between these two theories. If everything came from matter or from God, the same stuff is here and the world continues as it did of old. Experientially both theories are saying the same thing in different words. The materialist regards his matter with awe and the theist regards God with awe. "The pragmatist must consequently say that the two theories, in spite of their different-sounding names, mean exactly the same thing, and that the dispute is purely verbal."[9] God and matter *mean* the same thing: a power to make the world. Matter, functionally considered, is just as divine an entity as God, and it has the advantage of being free from churchy, clerical connotations. Matter can do everything that God can, so why quibble over terms?

---

6. James, *Pragmatism*, p. 222.
7. *Ibid.*, p. 201.
8. *Ibid.*, p. 96.
9. *Ibid.*, p. 97.

As the papists continually link pragmatism with the mood of Protestantism, we ought to consider any energy put forth in refuting the movement as well spent. However, it is impossible in this type of book to do more than show the inability of the pragmatist to solve the problem of the one within the many. The real refutation of this theory of knowledge was given by Brand Blanshard in his voluminous classic, *The Nature of Thought,* Volume One, Chapter Ten. The reader must pursue the work itself to appreciate its level of criticism. To try to copy Blanshard's arguments here would be like attempting to copy a Rembrandt—the finished product would have all of the characteristic earmarks of a forgery.

Pragmatism is admittedly an alluring field of operation; workability *is* evidently a *pro tanto* sign of truth's presence. But the very limitation of the method makes it an impossible way to solve the problem of the one within the many and give man a reason for living. The pragmatist divides knowledge into the two species, 'virtual' and 'terminated,' the former being anticipated experience and the latter present verified experience. The proposition 'There are four peaches on the table' is but virtual knowledge until the concept in the mind terminates upon a percept in experience, in which case the virtual knowledge becomes terminated.[10] Virtual knowledge is potential truth, a substitute for expectations of immediacy. Concepts derive their power in their ability to suggest avenues of experience. Virtual knowing passes into terminated knowing when you experience a fulfillment of the conditions determined by your concepts and you are able to say, 'This is exactly what I expected,' or 'This is not what I looked for,' depending on whether your virtual knowledge passes into terminated knowledge or into error. "Thus a concept of tree, or method of dealing with tree, is conclusively verified only when terminated."[11] When the idea of tree is verified in experience, the experience adds no knowledge, but only gives man the theoretic right to affirm the idea as it stands. "Reality,

10. *Cf.*, James, *Radical Empiricism*, p. 68.
11. Perry, *In the Spirit of William James*, p. 69.

taken as the counterpart of the culminating knowledge, is *as experience perceives and not as ideas conceive.*"[12]

What we have here to point out is that, if concepts are but substitutes for immediacy and extract their strength from their power to suggest experience, then it follows that we must already possess a faith that the universe is of such a character that it can meaningfully be anticipated. We *expect* the great block of virtual knowledge which fills our thousands of libraries *to pass* into terminated knowledge whenever we elect to test it in our experience. Let us take the proposition, 'Helium is lighter than air.' This is but virtual knowledge; yet we fully and confidently expect it to lead us without frustration into our experience tomorrow. It is *because* we believe that the universe is regular, that we trust in that virtual knowledge which is before us. The pragmatist *expects* the train he rides on to take him to New York City and not to turn into green lizards or peach peacock feathers in five seconds. He *expects* the world to hold still long enough for him to speak about nature with confident anticipation. What the Christian wants to know is, where has this assurance come from? How can the pragmatist establish a connection between his theory of knowledge and his daily actions?

The Christian can plan on tomorrow's regularity, because God has sworn to keep the seasons regular and never again to inundate the world with a flood; but in the virtue of whose decree can the pragmatist so trust? The proposition, 'The universe is regular,' is *itself* but virtual knowledge until it terminates upon experience. This means that the regularity of the universe is contingent upon a moment-by-moment experience of man. The universe, therefore, is open, for both regularity and irregularity are possibilities which the pragmatist must entertain every moment. But, if the universe is open, *anything* can happen, for there is no antecedent necessity upon the part of anything to be itself for another moment; there is, in other words, no providence of God for the prag-

12. *Ibid.*, p. 61.

matist. God gives order to the seasons and limit to the electrons. But the pragmatist, if consistent, has no God. By the very limitation of his epistemology he could never have terminated knowledge of God, for God has no body; He is without parts and passions, and thus not subject to empirical experience in the strict sense of the term. God can be conceived, not felt, tasted, or touched. But this keeps God in the category of virtual knowledge; thus we can never *know* Him in that sense which is necessary for us to trust Him to govern and guide the universe providentially.

With no sovereign God to set the course of reality and to give promises of hope to man, there is a 50/50 chance of anything happening. In five minutes, not only may elephants fly and roots grow up, but doors may have only one side, spinach may grow in patches of square circles, the sun may turn to silk, the moon to mink, up may be down, right may be left, and good may be bad. On the pragmatist's premises, one cannot meaningfully talk about virtual knowledge at all, for there is equal probability of the veracity of any given proposition and its contradiction, since in an open universe *anything* can happen. The pragmatist, by cutting himself loose from God, has left himself in a shoreless, bottomless ocean in a compassless, rudderless boat.[13]

The rebuttal to this argument is based upon the conviction that we have a right to argue to future regularity upon the basis of *past* regularity. The sun has always risen; therefore, it is folly to propose that the probability of the sun's rising

---

13. Clark expresses our sentiments perfectly. "One may wonder whether some brash student ever asked James why he should not enter the fray on the side of evil. The outcome is uncertain, and sometimes it would seem that the forces of evil have the better chance of winning. And since in the pragmatic theory truth is what works and success is the ultimate test, it follows that if we can contribute to the success of evil, we have at least fought in the cause of truth. In any case it is difficult to see why one should engage in a dangerous fight for the purpose of making cockroaches happy." *A Christian Philosophy of Education,* pp. 55-56. Is the proposition, 'An atomic war is a bad thing,' more than but 'virtual' knowing on the scheme of the pragmatist? To make this 'terminated' knowledge may be equivalent to the destruction of civilization itself. But even if the pragmatist succeeds in showing that atom warfare is bad today, he cannot deny that it *might* be good tomorrow.

tomorrow is 50/50. To this we reply that it will not help to argue from the past regularity of the universe to its future regularity unless we have assurance on other grounds that there is a rational connection between the past and the future of things. But how can this connection be established? There are but two ways. Either we have a revelation of God, the Author of the universe, Who tells us that we may expect the seasons in their order, or we must find our principles of cohesion within here-and-now experience. The pragmatist must elect the latter alternative since he has rejected the former. He can never have 'terminated' knowledge of God, since God's infinity can never be encompassed within any crucial time-space experiment. All the pragmatist can do, if he is consistent, is to wait and see what nature is going to do tomorrow. And if the pragmatist persists in his conviction that the past and the future are organically connected, it seems that his conviction is based more upon a fixation which has resulted from observing past regularities than upon a logically consistent insight into the problem.

Pragmatism is barking up the wrong tree to catch that fox which is causing human sorrow. Linked with a humanistic social program, pragmatism is devoted to the assuagement of human misery and maladjustment on the level of historical contingencies. Now, though this social work is proper and in order, it fails to penetrate into the fundamental source of human sorrow: the fear of death. Man indeed wants his societal relations to be tranquilized, for maladjustments of this sort or that are a real source of soul-sorrow. But what man really craves for is life. If pragmatism is to be of real service to man in his quest for happiness, it must expose the relation which exists between man's life and the problem of death. But within the frame of these demands, where can the pragmatist stand? How is it possible to have 'terminated' knowledge of either the proposition, 'Death does end all,' or 'Death does not end all,' until one dies and looks around to see what the situation is like, in which case the knowledge is proffered too late to placate the heart of man now. But it is at present that the question of the meaning of things must be determined.

J. Systematic Consistency

The Christian believes that a judgment is true when it corresponds to the mind of God, since God is the Author of all facts and their meaning. The test to which he proposes to subject his propositions, to know when he does correspond to God's mind, is, as another thinker has phrased it, 'systematic consistency.' A judgment is true and may be trusted when it sticks together with all of the facts of our experience, while a judgment is false when it cannot. When one says, for instance, that Gustav Ratzenhofer was an Austrian general, philosopher, and sociologist of the nineteenth and early twentieth centuries, who published, in 1898, a three-volume work entitled *Die Soziologische Erkenntnis,* what he means, if he claims to speak the truth, is that if one will carefully examine all of the data of history, he will find that the above judgment is one which he must assent to if he expects to make a smooth, systematically consistent picture out of his whole experience. By 'experience' we mean that total breadth of human consciousness which embraces the entire rational, volitional, and emotional life of man, both within and without. So, whether a man tastes pomegranates, dreams of rowing a dinghy, struggles to carry out the value of *pi* beyond the conventional 3.14159265, or meditates upon the problem of cosmology, he *is* experiencing. It is this breadth of definition which saves the Christian from the narrowness of either Spinozistic rationalism on the one hand, or Humean empiricism on the other.

There are two separate parts to this test for truth. First, there is consistency. Secondly, there is the thought that this consistency must be systematic. Let us examine in detail these two components as they relate to the generic question of truth.

1. By *consistency* we mean obedience to the law of contradiction. In any judgment a term must mean one thing at a

time if it is to convey truth. The formal statement of the law of contradiction is as follows: A is not non-A. Plato said that the "same thing clearly cannot act or be acted upon in the same part or in relation to the same thing at the same time,"[14] while Aristotle sharpened the law by stating that "the same attribute cannot at the same time belong and not belong to the same subject and in the same respect."[15] Without consistency in our meaning, we cannot tell the lunatic from the expert. The former is known by his frequent violation of the law of contradiction. He says one thing one minute and the exact opposite the next. The latter, however, is as consistent in his judgment as one can be while working under the limitations of discursive reasoning.

Consistency is our surest test for the absence of truth. It is the test of consistency that the jury applies to the evidence during the trial. It is consistency that we apply in daily contact one with another. If one says that he was in New York City yesterday, only to follow it by an admission that he was in Bermuda on a fishing trip at the same time, we suspect that one statement, or possibly both, is in error. One cannot both be and not be in Bermuda at the same time in the same sense with the same attributes. Finally, it is consistency that provides critics with an argument against the church. When people complain about hypocrites, what they mean is that certain people say that they love Christ on the one hand, and then live like the evil one on the other. They break the law of contradiction, in other words.

The law of contradiction is so basic to meaningful thought and, consequently, to truth [for truth is concerned only with meaning] that it cannot be demonstrated. The only proof for the law is that nothing is meaningful without the law's validity being presupposed.

---

14. *Republic,* 436b.
15. *Metaphysics* IV (1005b).

> The word *lamp* must signify a single thing both in the real world and in consciousness. If it signify a definite number of things, such as a piece of furniture, an ornament, and a paper weight, a special name may be given to each signification so that each name would signify one thing. But, if the significations be infinite, as those who deny this axiom must hold, then this lamp is also *not-lamp,* and, since it is not a lamp, it is both a calendar and not a calendar, as well as a book and not a book. That is to say, since the word *lamp* designates nothing . . . speech and philosophy have become impossible. The result is that all judgments become purely subjective and man is the measure of all things.[16]

If a word does not mean one thing at a time in a given universe of discourse or inferential whole, rationality is impossible. Even Lewis Carroll, the composer of the delightful tale of the land wherein the law of contradiction is played with fast and loose, *Alice's Adventures in Wonderland,* was under obligation to take the law seriously to succeed in meaningfully communicating meaninglessness. The surest way to destroy all hope of knowing truth, therefore, is to deny that we must construe our concepts according to the demands of the law of contradiction. To say that a rational man may assent simultaneously to contradictory propositions, such as 'There is no water in the cistern before me,' and 'There is water in the cistern before me,' is to take from the word *rational* all meaning. Without consistency, we have absolutely no way of telling the voice of the fool from the voice of the expert. The first element in any system of truth, therefore, is consistency. Wherever we find contradictions, we can be sure that truth is conspicuous by its absence.[17]

2. Sheer consistency in the use of our terms, however, is not a proof that we have truth. It only means negatively that where we are not consistent, there we are involved in error.

---

16. Martin *et al*, *A History of Philosophy,* pp. 166-7. *Cf.* Aristotle, *Metaphysics,* IV (1006a) for a full discussion of the reduction to absurdity of a denial of the validity of the law of contradiction.

17. The Christian will maintain that the revelation of God in word and in fact does not commit error because it construes its major postulates consistently. This will be dealt with in Chapter VI.

Consistency "tells us in general that all things must stand together; it does not tell us specifically how, or where, or why they are to stand."[18] An example of consistency which does not tell the truth is the following syllogism: All turtles are apes; all philosophy professors are turtles; therefore all philosophy professors are apes. This syllogism is formally valid, because it does not violate any of the eight rules for the syllogism. It has the right number and kind of terms and premises, and it adheres to the various canons of distribution. But, fortunately for philosophy professors, the syllogism is materially false, since it starts off with false premises. As a matter of fact turtles are not apes and philosophy professors are not turtles.

This observation forces us to distinguish between formal and material truth. The former is concerned only with validity or consistency. Such truth, as exemplified in mathematics and logic, need not pass into systematic consistency. Sheer consistency is enough. The latter, however, is concerned not only with formal validity, but with the relation between terms and the real course of history. Material truth, the truth which we seek in Christianity, pertains always to the totality of what is real. The real is whatever is, that is, whatever may be brought into our experience. This, as can readily be seen, not only includes the consistency of formal logic and mathematics, but also goes on to embrace chairs, planets, eels, and the like.

Systematic consistency is the combination of formal and material truth. It is a *consistency* because it is based upon a rigid application of the law of contradiction, and it is a *systematic* consistency because the data which are formed into this consistent system are taken from the totality of our experience, within and without. Validity without real facts is, in Kant's terms, empty (save in mathematics and logic), and the facts of experience without the formal direction of the law of contradiction are blind. If we reject the law of contra-

18. Brightman, *An Introduction to Philosophy,* p. 60.

diction, we have nothing to talk about because nothing means anything if the canon be not true; and if we reject the facts of experience, we have nothing in history to talk about because there is no reality beyond us as a point of reference to give content to our words. Facts without logic have no direction and logic without facts has but formal validity and cannot terminate upon the time-space universe.

Systematic consistency, then, is fortified by a double approach. Consistency is its negative characteristic and being systematic is its affirmative. Let us examine these briefly.

Negatively, systematic consistency is true because it does not violate the law of contradiction. It construes its terms meaningfully by refusing to say that A can be both A and non-A at the same time in the same sense. To admit that something is both itself and not itself is nonsense; under such conditions meaningful speaking is destroyed. The *sine qua non* for any system of truth, then, is consistency. Without consistency, there is no truth. Truth is always chaperoned by consistency. It is in the light of this observation that one facet of Christianity's claim to truth is to be evaluated. God "never lies" (Titus 1:2). He is "the Father of lights with whom there is no variation or shadow due to change" (James 1:17). "The Strength of Israel will not lie nor repent; for he is not a man, that he should repent" (I Samuel 15:29). God is absolute consistency. He never affirms and denies the same thing at the same time. Negatively, then, God does not break the law of contradiction and involve Himself in error.[19] The Christian, therefore, is not afraid to apply the law of contradiction to God's revelation in word and fact. He will

---

19. Since God is the definition of consistency, for consistency is what He does, it is well to point out that the law of contradiction has final meaning only in relation to God. God is above the law of contradiction in the sense that God is consistent by nature. Man must learn to be consistent.

not always see the consistency in God's thoughts, but he is convinced that there is a consistency.[20]

Affirmatively, systematic consistency is marked by a devotion to all of the facts of experience, for it is they that make up the content of our knowledge. The real is whatever we experience. We may not be able to explain such things as motion and change, but it is not a solution to suppose, with Parmenides and Zeno, that motion and change are therefore not real. The law of contradiction forbids our affirming what is real in experience while denying it in our logic. Truth is a systematic account of reality. We do not wait until we can see rational connections in reality before we affirm such reality. The reason for this is twofold. First, if we waited until we saw the rational connection between things, we would not know anything in nature. There is no demonstrable reason why one atom of oxygen and two atoms of hydrogen should logically form that colorless fluid called water. Science describes nature by showing us that this combination always produces water, but there is no law of logic which says that it must. Secondly, and here we presuppose the Christian major premise, the discrete facts of the empirical universe are related to each other, not by demonstrable necessity, but by teleology. The world is knit together according to the plan which existed in the mind of the Creator. The relation, therefore, between the number of goats in Albania and the weight of the nearest star, or the relation between the depth of the Atlantic Ocean in its center to the death of Christ on the cross, is teleological. God freely elected to create the world. There was no antecedent compulsion, either from within or from without, which determined that God should make this world rather than another. God freely elected to display His glory in this world, and the motive behind the choice was that it pleased God, this and none other. The present world is a consistent world and it is

---

20. It is evident that we are here appealing to special revelation, when we have not as yet established our right to do so. The justification for this is that we do establish the prerogative later. The present appeal, therefore, is not gratuitous. It is based upon systematically consistent reasons which will appear *infra,* Chapters IX-X.

the best world, because God made it; for God is consistency and goodness.

III. Recapitulation

In short, perfect systematic consistency is a perfect correspondence with the mind of God. With this thought we are ready to conclude our study of truth.

A. God and Truth

Words are but arbitrary signs of the meaning which we intend to convey when we speak or write. When we wish to describe what we mean by a thing, we give it a name, as 'dog,' 'birch tree,' or 'egg.' The sole worth of a name is its ability to communicate meaning. If the term 'Stop!' does not convey the concept 'Bring your vehicle to a standstill!' to those who approach a dangerous intersection, it is useless as a sign and might just as well be a word written in a foreign tongue. Agreement of words, therefore, is by no means a certain sign that there is agreement of meaning. The modernist, for instance, uses the term 'Christ' and means by it those ideals which he considers most God-like. The conservative uses the same term and means by it the second Person of the ontological Trinity. The meaning of terms is discovered by definition.

Definition sets the limits to what we mean by terms. It is the medium that we must employ if we wish to let others know what is behind the words that we are using. We cannot know what a man's judgment is until we know how he is using his terms. It is the meaning of the words, therefore, and not the words themselves which are capable of being true or false. But meaning is a property of mind.

We say that the more perfect a mind is, the more perfect is the meaning that that mind has in any act of judgment. The mother is more perfect than the child, and the expert is more perfect than the mother (unless the mother is an expert, too). When we carry this through, what mind is the most perfect receptacle of all meaning? There is no alternative. It is God's mind, for such a mind is His than which no greater may be conceived. He, then, is truth, for, being perfect, He cannot err. The meaning He gives to things is absolute, for He is the

Author of things. Truth, therefore, is correspondence with the mind of God. The test for truth is systematic consistency, for God is consistent and the world that He teleologically orders gives system to this consistency. As we unite validity with experience, we have a perfect test for truth.

B. *The Bible and Truth*

God not only reveals His systematic consistency in fact, but He also has committed to writing that portion of the meaning of reality which man must have if he is to adjust himself to God harmoniously and to enjoy eternal life. The Bible was given as a cure for soul-sorrow. It tells us how man may be reconciled with God. The Bible was written "that you may believe that Jesus is the Christ, the Son of God, and that believing you may have life in his name" (John 20:31). Therefore, contrary to the hypothesis of some, the Bible is not an account of the religious experiences of men in given ages. Rather, it is "the revelation of the mystery which was kept secret for long ages but is now disclosed and through the prophetic writings is made known to all nations, according to the command of the eternal God, to bring about obedience to the faith" (Romans 16:25-26). The Bible, since it contains a system of meaning which is systematically consistent, is a reflection of the mind of Christ. Knowing this corpus of revelation, through the witness of the Spirit in our hearts, we can say with Paul, "we have the mind of Christ" (I Corinthians 2:16). The mind of Christ is truth; we see it in God's revelation of word and fact. Soul-sorrow is cured by our seeing and embracing this truth. "If you continue in my word, you are my disciples, and you will know the truth, and the truth will make you free" (John 8:32).

C. *Creatures and Truth*

Because Christ is truth (John 14:6), He is the source of all rationality. He is the "true light that enlightens (gives a rational nature to) every man" (John 1:9). The ability to think God's thoughts after Him is what provides the univocal point of meeting between God and man.

It is the ministry of the Spirit, the third person of the Trinity, to apply the truth to our hearts. As Christ spoke only the things of the Father, so the Spirit speaks to us only the things of the Son (John 16:13). As we are brought into systematic consistency, we are being led by the Spirit of God, for God is truth. This admission that no man can know God apart from the work of the Spirit does not involve us in mysticism, however, for the work of the Spirit is carried on in conjunction with the revelation of God in word and in fact. "The word is the instrument, by which the Lord dispenses to believers the illumination of his Spirit,"[21] even as the facts of nature are the instrument, by which the Lord dispenses to men an illumination of God's glory and the meaning of history. The Spirit's work is to insure a proper response to evidence, not to create evidence.

D. Conclusion

Before leaving the problem of truth, let us make reference to a prerogative which adoption of systematic consistency gives us. A proposition is true when it can be systematically related to all of our experience. This breadth of implication relieves the Christian of the skepticism of positivism, in which

> . . . a very large part of philosophy, religion, and science would be instantly dropped as meaningless, since such concepts as that of God in the traditional sense, of reality as opposed to appearance, of an ultimate good, of the other side of the moon, of electrons and protons, of the physical universe generally outside the range of the 200-inch telescope, unquestionably claim a reference beyond the bounds of my own experience, either present or future.[22]

The Christian, by systematic consistency, will be privileged to speak not only of the other side of the moon and of an absolute good, but also of creation, the flood, angels, heaven, and hell. The significance of this will appear shortly.

---

21. Calvin, *Institutes,* I, 9, 3.

22. Blanshard, *The Nature of Thought,* I, p. 375. For a very good refutation of the limitations of positivism as a theory of knowledge, see Hall's chapter on metaphysics in *Twentieth Century Philosophy* (Runes, ed.), pp. 145-194.

Chapter IV

What Is Faith?

Without faith it is impossible to please Him.
—Book of Hebrews

IT is necessary at this point in the defense of conservative Christianity to give a statement of our philosophy of faith. The reason for this is that the modern man says he wants to live by *knowledge and truth* while "the righteous shall live by his *faith*" (Habakkuk 2:4). The purpose of this chapter is to point out that the division between faith and the apprehension of truth is false. It is contrary to Christian theology. ". . . faith is limited by knowledge. We can believe only what we know, *i. e.,* what we intelligently apprehend. If a proposition be announced to us in an unknown language, we can affirm nothing about it. We can neither believe nor disbelieve it."[1]

Too often faith is used as an epistemological device to avoid the hard labor of straight thinking. How simple, and yet disgusting, it is for one to say when pressed to give an account for his hope, 'I need give no intelligent account, for my hope is grounded in faith.' Under such a philosophy there is little wonder that the modern university student looks upon faith as a synonym for ignorance and devotion to religious ideals as a phenomenon that falls under the general head of abnormal psychology. Surely, if faith is not related to knowledge and truth, it is meaningless. It is more ouija-board than science. The Christian religion is indeed based upon the act of faith, but faith that is not grounded in knowledge is but respectable (?) superstition.

---

1. Hodge, *Systematic Theology,* Volume III, p. 84.

I. The Nature and Test of Faith Distinguished

We face a problem here which is quite parallel to that with which we dealt in the preceding chapter. As we had to distinguish between the *definition* of truth and the *test* of truth, even so now we must make a careful distinction between the *nature* of faith and the *test* for faith. Just as there was right and wrong knowledge, so also there is right and wrong faith. When we know what the test for faith is, we will be in a position to separate false faith from true faith, even as when we have a criterion of truth we can separate error from truth.

A. The Nature of Faith

When the Christian talks of faith, he means a very simple thing by it. Faith is but a whole-soul trust in God's word as true. When God says something, it is true, for God cannot lie; and when man reposes in God's word, he has faith. If he fails to rest in it as truth, we call him an infidel, *i. e.,* he is not one of the faithful. The power by which the heart is enabled to see that the word of God is true is the Holy Spirit. The word of God is thus self-authenticating. It bears its own testimony to truth; it seals its own validity. If the word required something more certain than itself to give it validity, it would no longer be *God's* word. If God, by definition, is that than which no greater may be conceived, then His word is that than which no truer may be conceived. It would be a derogation to the efficiency of revelation to suppose that any more than God's Spirit is needed to seal the word to the hearts of believers. "When, therefore, it is said that faith is founded on testimony, it is meant that it is not founded on sense, reason, or feeling, but on the authority of him by whom it is authenticated."[2]

Psychologically, the assurance of faith precedes the test for faith in the same way that the assurance of truth precedes the test for truth. We believe, for example, that the earth has a center long before we have thought of a way to prove the same. In like manner we repose in God's revelation in word and fact

---

2. Hodge, *op. cit.*, p. 63.

long before we are able to give a rational vindication of the act. So, just as the ignorant are able to adjust themselves to the complexities of social life without having the slightest idea of how they might rationally account for their actions, so also the poor and the ignorant can see and receive the complex riches of salvation in God's word by faith and yet be quite unable to construct a worthy test for their faith.

B. The Test for Faith

This state of ignorance cannot be our final resting point, however, for we have yet to face the problem of a test for faith. Though the ignorant may not concern themselves with a test for their faith, the wise cannot dodge the issue. Faith may be trust in God's word, even as truth may be correspondence to His mind, but the question is, how do we know here that it is God's and not the devil's word that we actually trust? Even as our former problem was how do we know that the ideas which we entertain actually correspond to the mind of God and not to the mind of the devil? The problems are obviously parallel. It is the question of how to detect error.

The question is made more urgent in the study of faith, however, for there are hundreds of conflicting faiths in the world, many, if not all, of which claim to be based upon some manifestation of the witness of God's Spirit to our hearts. These claims cannot all be true, for they are inconsistent, and consistency is the first property of truth. One faith, for instance, says that Jesus was raised from the dead according to the Scriptures, while another denies it. They cannot both be right at the same time in a rational universe. It cannot simultaneously be true that Christ was and was not raised from the dead according to the Scriptures. Only one may be right, though both may be wrong. Unless, therefore, we are to throw our apologetics to the wind at this point, a test for faith must be devised. The Christian is a lover of light; he wants to bring his faith to the test of light so that his deeds of faith may be approved. The test which the Christian proposes has two facets to it. There is the internal test, and there is the external test. Let us consider them in this order.

1. *The internal test.* The surest proof one can have that his faith in God's word is valid is the internal witness of the Spirit of God in his heart. The Spirit may convict men upon the occasion of rational debate and diatribe, but it is the Spirit, not the latter, which assures them of the truth. The false claims of other religions do not necessarily mean that the Christian claim to an inward witness of the Spirit is likewise erroneous. "But the Counselor, the Holy Spirit, whom the Father will send in my name, he will teach you all things, and bring to your remembrance all that I have said to you" (John 14:26). There is no substitute for the Spirit's internal witness.

An illustration of this inward assurance is found in Luke 24. Christ overtook two men who were on their way to a village called Emmaus and spoke to them words of truth. "And beginning with Moses and all the prophets, he interpreted to them in all the scriptures the things concerning himself" (verse 27). When the Spirit sealed to their hearts the truth of Scripture, they said, "Did not our hearts burn within us while he talked to us on the road, while he opened to us the scriptures?" (verse 32). This *burning* is what the Christian means when he says that "as God alone is a sufficient witness of himself in his own word, so also the word will never gain credit in the hearts of men, till it be confirmed by the internal testimony of the Spirit."[3]

2. *The external test.* Although the Christian does not question the sufficiency of the Spirit's internal testimony in his heart to seal to his soul the truth of God's word, yet, when he is called upon by unbelievers to "give an account for the hope" that is in him, he is assured that there is yet a fuller activity of the Spirit to which he may appeal to buttress the validity of the inward witness. The Spirit witnesses to our hearts not only immediately, as traced above, but also mediately through the

3. Calvin, *Institutes,* I, vii, 4.

heart's apprehension of truth on every level of life. The Spirit of God is active in sealing God's revelation in word and fact whenever and wherever man sees and appropriates the truth. Whether a man assents to the proposition that in right-angled triangles the square on the hypotenuse equals the sum of the squares on the other sides, or to the proposition that Victor Hugo was born in the year 1802, that man, if these propositions be true, *is* being led by the Spirit of God. He acts wisely here, for his mind rests in the sufficiency of the evidence. Because there is this relation between the apprehension of truth and the leading of the Spirit of God, the Christian is able to construct an apologetic for his Biblical faith. "If the contents of the Bible did not correspond with the truths which God has revealed in his external world and the constitution of our nature, it could not be received as coming from Him, for God cannot contradict himself."[4] In short, the Christian can say that where there is inconsistency, *i. e.,* where the law of contradiction is broken, there the spirit of the evil one is leading; God is the source of consistency. He cannot contradict Himself. Faith, then, is, as Augustine put it, "reason with assent."[5] "Faith is not a blind, irrational conviction. In order to believe, we must know what we believe, and the grounds on which our faith rests."[6] By uniting proper faith with systematic consistency, the Christian can always plead that "there is no legitimate religion unconnected with truth."[7]

To recapitulate, Christian faith is based upon the soul's assurance of truth. This truth is sealed to the hearts of men by the Spirit of God in two ways. First, there is the inward testimony, by which the Spirit opens up the heart of the believer to see God's truth in the Bible. Secondly, there is the mediate testimony, by which the Spirit opens up our hearts to see the truth which God has revealed through nature in general revelation. The former requires special grace and the

---

4. Hodge, *op cit.,* p. 83.
5. *Cum assensione cogitare. De Praed. Sanct.,* 5.
6. Hodge, *ibid.*
7. Calvin, *op. cit.,* I, 6, 3.

latter common grace. All men by nature are qualified to see certain thresholds of truth as they are revealed by God in the facts of nature, but it takes a special gift from God to have faith in the Bible as truth. Yet, when the Christian, to whom this gift is given, is called upon to give an account of his faith, and when he is warned, "Beloved, do not believe every spirit, but test the spirits to see whether they are of God; for many false prophets have gone out into the world" (I John 4:1), he is not lost for a test by which to learn whether his faith is properly grounded or not. This test is systematic consistency. If what is being believed makes peace with the law of contradiction and the facts of experience, it is a faith which is prompted by the Spirit of God. If what is being believed fails to correspond with the mind of God, *i. e.,* is not systematically consistent, such a faith is prompted by other than the Spirit of God. The Spirit can speak only the truth; it can witness only to the mind of God.

It is this union of faith and truth that makes it possible to construct a Christian apologetics. But apologetics can only prepare the heart for faith, for faith is a gift from God. Logic can be the means by which the Spirit leads a man into faith, but it is the Spirit, not logic, which finally seals the faith to the heart.

Having completed our point, we may assume that there are some objections to this construction of faith. But, with the permission of the reader, we shall save them until we have set down the other two alternative bases: authoritative decrees and subjective immediacy. With these behind us we shall have a perspective with which to judge the merits of the conservative structure.

II. Faith Based on Authoritative Decrees

If faith is not a resting of the soul in the sufficiency of the evidence, then it is either a resting of the soul in the brute authority of another or in the testimony of the heart. Let us check on the former alternative first.

The success of totalitarian movements is contingent on the ability of the leader to extract implicit faith from his followers. This was true of the Nazi regime under Hitler even as it is now politically true in Russia under Stalin and theologically true throughout the whole Catholic world under the pope. The church of Rome officially decrees that her children need not see the coherence of everything she teaches. Rome is quick to point out that the ignorant masses lack the critical apparatus requisite to canvass the rational evidence for a theological system of truth. A learned caste of priests and bishops, therefore, must carry the weight of working out the truth; then the ignorant multitude is to follow implicitly what this body of doctors concurrently decides is the truth. When the pope speaks *ex cathedra,* he claims to speak, as does any dictator, with authority which may not be questioned. *Ipse dixit* is the only evidence that a totalitarian system need advance to substantiate its system of teachings. When the church speaks, debate is then out of order.

Rome next appeals to an analogy to help her case. In society it appears that we submit to the doctor's prescription, the judge's verdict, and the mathematician's deductions without facetiously pretending to have canvassed all of their evidences. How many have checked on Einstein? And yet all men believe he approaches the truth in his basic convictions of the relation between mass and energy. The atom bomb is a proof of his formula. If society is run by a system of authority, shall we expect God to operate differently in matters of religion?

Let us be clear what the issue is. The conservative ardently defends a system of authority. It was the conviction of the coherence of Scripture's authority which touched off the Reformation. What the conservative does reject, and what is here being analysed, is the notion that authoritative decree *per se,* unaccompanied by rational evidences of its authority, can be a basis for faith.

A. Affirmative Considerations

1. Stressing implicit rather than explicit faith has the pragmatic benefit of making allegiance to Rome a relatively simple matter to achieve. Compare Francis Xavier who baptized thousands of Orientals, with the evangelical missionary who labors fifty years at times before one convert can be called truly possessed with saving faith. It is always more difficult to persuade people of the truth than to instruct in them what they *must* believe.

2. Absolute dogmatic law has the inspiring effect of putting truths out of range of the relativisms of time and space, lending an air of eternity to the system. Thus the Roman Church boasts a timelessness in time. No other institution is comparable to her at this point. This permanence and stability gives men spiritual peace and releases them from the task of constructing doctrine, allowing them to engage in the peaceful act of spiritual meditation. Observe the tranquility of the monk in his garden as he recites the canonical hours in peaceful meditation over against the evangelical seminarian who spends his time frantically scouring for secondhand theology books and vehemently arguing the pros and cons of election and predestination.

B. Negative Considerations

1. Without reason to canvass the evidence of a given authority, how can one segregate a right authority from a wrong one? Shall we count the number of words used, to distinguish between the worth of the Vedas, the Shastras, the writings of Confucius, the Koran, the Book of Mormon, the works of Mary Baker Eddy, the Scriptures, and the *ex cathedra* pronouncements of the popes? Without systematic consistency to aid us, it appears that all we can do is to draw straws, count noses, or flip coins to choose an authority. Once we *do* apply the law of contradiction, we are no longer appealing to *ipse dixit* authority, but to coherent truth. "A right faith is always a reasonable faith; that is to say, it is accorded only to an

authority which commends itself to reason as a sound authority, which it would be unreasonable not to trust."[8]

2. The analogy from society is false. A normal person does not submit his life to an authority until, guided by reason, he is fully assured in his mind that the authority in question is trustworthy. One trusts his family doctor because he knows that the doctor is ethically committed to the Hippocratic oath. No sane citizen will give his body to a doctor who, in fact, is reported to have a questionable practice in medicine. This is also true in the home and in the state. Though the child is bound by the parents, the child is free to report the parents to the proper authorities when the parents leave those bounds of decency which are set down by the laws of God. In like manner, though we are governed by the authority of the state, that authority holds good only as long as the state conducts itself within the ethical framework of God's revelation. When a government leaves the truth of God for a lie, Christians are obliged to follow God rather than man. Thus, one is bound by the external authority of the church *only* in so far as the church teaches what is compatible with the eternal law of God. This law is found in Holy Writ.

The Reformation stemmed from a sanctified application of systematic consistency to the teachings of the Roman Catholic Church. The Reformers, one and all, saw that the Bible teaches we are saved *solely* by grace through faith, while the Romish Church says we are saved by grace *plus* the merit which accrues by our own good works. In a rational universe these two propositions cannot simultaneously be true. If the problem of dogmatic authority is pressed it either descends to irrationalism, or it leaves its claims to primacy and pleads the primacy of truth. The Scriptures tell us to *test* the spirits (I John 4:1). This can be done only by applying the canons of truth. God cannot lie. His authority, therefore, and coherent truth are coincident at every point. Truth, not blind authority, saves us from being blind followers of the blind.

---

8. Warfield, *Studies in Tertullian and Augustine,* pp. 154-155.

III. Faith Based on Subjective Immediacy

If rational truth cannot sustain our faith, and if we reject *ipse dixit* authority, then there is but one major source of assurance left. This way of faith is through the heart; it yields a subjective or religious intuition which neither an application of systematic consistency nor external authority can provide.

There are an endless number of ways to state this position. The voluntarists claim that the will knows reality immediately. Trueblood argues for the validity of the religious experience as a way of getting at ultimate reality. Barth talks of the 'crisis.' Brunner speaks of the 'divine-human encounter.' The mystics speak of 'inward illumination.' Reinhold Niebuhr defends the notion of 'religious faith.' But, rather than attempt a treatment of each position separately, let us here deal with the general statement of the over-all conviction that God can be known through the heart with an assurance secure enough to provide a firm foundation for faith.

Classically, the argument from religious experience has come through Schleiermacher, Ritschl, and succeeding modernists. The foundation-conviction of this movement is that, since God cannot be known through the understanding, as Kant showed in his first *Critique,* He can be known only through feeling or religious insight. It is the *heart* which detects God's being. As Pascal phrased it, "the heart has its reasons which reason does not know."

A. Affirmative Considerations

1. Feeling in the heart seems to be a strong force in man. A Gothic cathedral brings the feeling of reverence, while the peals of a mighty organ can bring tears. If the beauty of the lily can be known through an immediate whole-soul experience, *a fortiori* how much more may God be known in this way? God is the loveliest of fragrant flowers. "I myself believe that the evidence for God lies primarily in inner personal experi-

ences," testifies the famous philosopher, William James.[9] The proof for God's existence through feeling is impressive. I feel the presence of God's loving care in my heart. He walks with me and talks with me, giving me daily courage and peace. The only hypothesis I can advance to cover this vivid inwardness of peace is that God, the Author of my feelings, exists. "What can we say in the face of testimonies so tremendous, testimonies repeated in so many generations? Drugs and delusions may sustain men for a time, but here is something which wears out all opposition. It makes weak men bold and proud men humble. Words seem impertinent and silence the only adequate response. If that which sustains men and makes them praise God in both bright and dark hours be not reality, where is reality to be found?"[10] This datum is considered as solid as the evidence for symmetry and loveliness when one hears the strains of Bach's *Jesu, Joy of Man's Desiring,* or the evidence for kindness when one views the *Mona Lisa* of Leonardo da Vinci, or the evidence for beauty when one stands knee-deep in a field of gorgeous flowers. Is not God perfect beauty, perfect symmetry, perfect kindness, and perfect art, passing the finite expressions of these realities as night is surpassed by day in brightness? Is it not likely that the mysterious power that leads birds home to the nest and foxes to their dens, should also lead man back to the Maker from Whom he has come?

2. Coupled with this is the great block of empirical evidence which stems from the testimonies of men in all ages that they have known God. The number of reporters is immense. From all parts of the world they come. The quality of the reporters is uniform: God has been known by the heart. He sustains; He gives courage; He sets the moral standards of the heart. The peculiar part of this mass of testimony is the fact that the intrusion of God into the heart was completed contrary to the expectations and the wills of the experiencers. "When they

---

9. *Pragmatism,* p. 109.
10. Trueblood, *The Logic of Belief,* p. 213.

came, I was living the fullest, strongest, sanest, deepest life. I was not seeking them. What I was seeking, with resolute determination, was to live more intensely my own life, as against what I knew would be the adverse judgment of the world. It was in the most real seasons that the Real Presence came, and I was aware that I was immersed in the infinite ocean of God."[11] What can be said in the face of such overwhelming testimony?

B. Negative Considerations

1. Classic mysticism renders the object of faith meaningless as something to be talked about. William James correctly names 'ineffability' as one of the four marks of the inward experience. This means that the 'Reality' which is 'felt in the heart' cannot be significantly talked about. But, until the mystic succeeds in communicating his experience in such a way that the terms he employs properly stand for the 'Reality' being experienced, we have no way of knowing what he has reference to. "No adequate report of its contents can be given in words. . . . No one can make clear to another who has never had a certain feeling, in what the quality or worth of it consists."[12] Being ineffable, the object of the mystic experience can neither be established nor refuted.

2. In the more irrational forms of religious intuition, as in Barth and Brunner, not only is the object of faith meaningless, but it also makes for a permanent split between theology and science. This is a fatal gesture.

> The difficulty with a faith of this kind is that it runs out into a nebulosity approximating absolute zero. There is nothing in particular that it enjoins us to be, do, feel, or believe. It has refined itself out of existence. On the other hand, it may insist on a content of its own that is aggressively and defiantly irrational. In that case its position is worse. It has

---

11. Quoted in James, *Varieties of Religious Experience*, p. 389.
12. James, *op. cit.*, p. 371.

> thrown down the gauge to reason by insisting that the incoherent may still be real. And so far as it takes that line, as some Barthians are apparently ready to do, theology is declaring war on philosophy and science. I think I know how such a war is bound to end. It will end in the annihilation of theology, as much by internal paralysis as by external attack. I will not argue this matter beyond quoting Dr. McTaggart to the effect that no one ever tried to break logic but what logic broke him.[13]

3. Again, with respect to the feeling theology of the classic mystics and the modern neo-supernaturalists, Barth and Brunner, since the object of faith is irrational and since faith and actions go together, our actions may be irritational, too.* If a man by an inward 'crisis' experience thinks that he is called to rule the world, as did Hitler, then the validity of his act is just as secure as the validity of his original heart-vision. The object of the vision is above and beyond the check of the law of contradiction, for the very reason that it is either ineffable or irrational. If the 'crisis' can be followed, then irrational actions may be tolerated for the same reason. But this would involve a complete breakdown of the entire ethical system which binds rational men together, since *meaningful* conduct must stem from *meaningful* standards. But where the law of contradiction is excluded, there *is* no meaning! The meaningful is the rational, that and nothing more. On Barth's position of religious immediacy, however, the fratricide and the kleptomaniac cannot be consistently thought of as guilty of any crime if they plead that their acts stemmed from a 'crisis' experience. God is best experienced by these men during the acts of crime. The only way Barth can detect a false 'crisis' is by an appeal to philosophic propositions; but this method he has rejected. Contemporary existentialists and neo-realists may not care for this twist to their theology, but personal disgruntlement cannot pass for good argument. Any theology

---

13. Blanshard, "The Inner Light," *The Harvard Divinity School Bulletin*, Volume XLIII, March 10, 1946, p. 62.

* See note 23, page 88 in this connection.

which rejects Aristotle's fourth book of the *Metaphysics* is big with the elements of its own destruction.[14]

4. Theology is no longer a science, and it has lost its glory. If subjective experience replaces objectively verifiable, propositional revelation, then agreement among competent investigators is impossible, for how can feelings agree when the object of feeling is a directly intuited 'Reality'? By feeling alone one cannot even be sure that another is seeing the same beauty in the sunset as he is, let alone being certain that what another means by 'God' is what he means by the 'divine undergirding' of the universe. How *can* one experience be checked with another? If one says that he has experienced something, there is no higher court of appeal than the testimony of the one having the experience. The laboratory sciences have sense perception as a check, and Christianity has propositional revelation, but what has the feeling theologian? If feelings are a proper source to knowing reality, in and by themselves, then we must drop the 'ology' of theology, for it is now every man for himself.

5. Feeling theology limits the perception of God to those of a certain physiological construction. Legion are the scientists whose work is careful and honest in the laboratory, who testify to no such experience of an inward feeling of God, even though they have professed willingness to submit to an experi-

---

14. "The trouble with the doctrine, however, is not merely that the Divinity in us is made to put its superscription on what turns out to be untrue, but also that, once the check of common reason is taken away, it may counsel sheer fanaticism. This danger could be exemplified many times over from the early passages of Quaker history. A zealous young preacher named Farnsworth proposed a preaching tour on a diet of nothing but spring water and Scripture. Richard Sale, a constable, felt moved to go through Chester barefoot and bare-legged, in sackcloth and ashes, flowers in his right hand and 'stinking weeds' in his left; this was supposed to be a sign. He felt moved also to walk through Eastgate Street, London, carrying a lighted candle as a testimony against worship by candlelight. A Quakeress named Susanna Pearson was convinced she could bring back to life a young man who had drowned himself; so she had his corpse unearthed, lay on it, and prayed; unfortunately it had to be reinterred." Blanshard, *Harvard Divinity School Bulletin, op. cit.*, p. 57. To this might be added the observation that feeling theology is generally associated with the quacks and the cults, not with the precisely conceived systematic theologies.

ment on the subject. It appears, therefore, that one's glands must be arranged in a certain way before he can participate in a feeling for God. This unfortunate shutting out of the kingdom to many can be eliminated only when a rationally perceived proposition is made the standard for knowledge of God, for all men are made in the image of God.[15]

6. Against all forms of argument from religious experience we pit the argument that feelings are not qualified to criticise themselves. If feeling rather than intellect is the most qualified organ of man to know God, it follows that all of the feelings must be normative witnesses. Schleiermacher preferred the feeling of personal piety, but his selection does not exhaust the possibilities. There is also anger, jealousy, laughter, spite, love, and the like. Which of these feelings is the best channel through which to approach the Divine? We can decide this matter neither by feelings nor by the intellect. Feelings are not critical and the intellect is ruled out because of its impotency to know God through propositions. It must be, then, as Clark has tersely put it, "The emotion which emotes most emotionally is on its own authority best and most valuable."[16] How shall I express my religious emotions? Any way I elect! Jerking, rolling, screaming, weeping, trembling, or frothing. No higher court of appeal can be brought into the picture than my own feelings. This is not to be construed as ridicule or sarcasm. It is but a realistic attempt to expose the distasteful elements in a theology unfortified by rational coherence.

7. Next, feeling theology involves polytheism. By propositional revelation the conservative can defend monotheism. "Hear, O Israel: Jehovah our God is one Jehovah" (Deuteronomy 6:4) But this is because the Christian clings to the doctrine that the reason is the most qualified faculty by which

---

15. Obviously here we exclude both from the side of the opponent and from our own, all abnormal people such as idiots, etc.; we here speak of all *normal* men. Idiots are made in the image of God, but they have lost control of their rationality.

16. *A Christian Philosophy of Education*, p. 176.

to detect coherent meaning. When feeling is made the test for God's existence, then there are as many gods as there are different feelings, inasmuch as God's nature is defined in terms of the particular type of feeling which is employed by the zealot at the time of his discovering 'Reality.' As the character of God is determined by the nature of the feeling which discovers it, Schleiermacher, believing that the feeling of piety indicates the way to know God, defined the God which he felt as that being which gives rise to the feeling of piety. In like manner the aesthetic feeling has as its concomitant a cosmic poet; the dynamic feeling yields a great source of cosmic power; the bellicose feeling conveniently produces a God of Mars (much to the delight of Adolph Hitler); the feeling of pessimism grinds out a finite being harrassed by some evil in reality against which he struggles; the feeling which comes from smelling pine knots manages to give conviction to the idea that there is a great woodsman; and the thud of hoofs furnishes the American Indian with a conviction that there is a Big Chief who is preparing a happy hunting ground for the braves and their squaws.

It might be objected that we have here refuted a straw man and not the real thing. Even as a diamond has many facets to it, so also these so-called different gods are but various ways of looking at the one God. One may observe a diamond from many different angles. The number of perspectives only enhance the beauty of the gem. If this is true of a piece of stone, why is it not true also of the Author of that stone, God? May He not be viewed from an indefinite number of angles?

But this reply assumes the very point at issue. Certainly *if* God is infinite, He *may* be viewed from various perspectives; but what we here are struggling with is the question whether there is a God or not. If one tries to prove God through feeling, he discovers that the method is such a wonderful proof, that many gods can be proved. If he abandons his feeling theology at this point and turns to reason, he is to be charged with a shift in position. *The first rule of a coherent system is that all of its parts be ordered and related according to principles which are considered basic to the system in question.* Follow feeling and you are led to polytheism; follow reason and you have appealed to an unwarranted criterion.

8. Finally, and philosophically most serious, feeling theologians have ruined the love of wisdom by defending an unknown God. To know something is to perceive it with the understanding, *i. e.,* to have an intellectual awareness of coherence in the light of the law of contradiction. But when the theologian of feeling contends that God cannot be made subject to the limitations of the reason of man, he says in effect that God is unknowable; to know Him would be equivalent to limiting Him, since He would be subject to the law of contradiction at that point. But if *this* unknowable can be tolerated by philosophy, then there is no presently conceivable way to check other unknowables from being hypostatized, as snarks, boojums, splinth, and gobble-de-gook. With the sluice gate opened to unknowables, the whole philosophic discipline is thrown into confusion, and precision is impossible.

Some people rejoice that Kant showed in his first *Critique* that God's existence, since it cannot be known, cannot be disproved by science, not realizing that not only is God's *existence* safe under these conditions, but so is His *nonexistence.* The work of Kant has been a detriment to theology, not a benefit. Kant so nicely removed God from being an object of the understanding, that he left the propositions, 'God exists,' and 'God does not exist' equally possible alternatives. One can choose between them for aesthetic reasons if he wants, but this is hardly to be construed as a meaningful basis for faith.

Let us close our critique of the theology of feeling by giving a quotation from that great Christian apologist, James Orr. "A religion based on mere feeling is the vaguest, most unreliable, most unstable of all things. A strong, stable, religious life can be built up on no other ground than that of intelligent conviction."[17]

---

17. *The Christian View of God and the World,* p. 20.

I ask no dream, no prophet-ecstasies,
No sudden rending of the veil of clay,
No angel-visitant, no opening skies;
But take the dimness of my soul away.

In sum, as Professor Brightman has put it, religious emotions, if worthy, must conform to truth and not truth to religious emotions.[18]

IV. Objections to the Christian View of Faith

A. Faith is Childlike, not a Mature Rational Gesture

Machen has already answered this objection. First, when we say that faith is a resting of the soul in the sufficiency of the evidence, it does not commit us to the position that reason is temporally prior to faith. When a man has faith, the *whole soul* cooperates. We may know and love a person at the same instant. "But what we do maintain is that at no point is faith independent of the knowledge upon which it is logically based."[19] Secondly, a child does not act without knowledge. Though his knowledge is immature or innocent, it is knowledge nonetheless. The child can tell his parent from a gorilla. Faith can, indeed, be childlike. Thirdly, when Christ bade the children to come to Him as a paradigm of perfect faith, it was to illustrate the alacrity and simplicity with which the kingdom of God ought to be received, not to show how people may be ignorant and yet believe. Adults would have served as examples for that just as well. The child exhibits a self-abandonment in what he does. "The more we know of God, the more unreservedly we trust Him; the greater be our progress in theology, the simpler and more childlike will be our faith."[20]

---

18. Perhaps the most serious objection to the theology of feeling has not even been touched upon in our discussion, and this is that neglect of the Bible which inevitably results when one has a private voice of guidance within him. When the Bible is neglected, Christianity is lost; with Christianity lost, one cannot solve the problem of the one within the many to give man happiness. Feeling takes its rise by being a proposed supplementary aid to the Bible; but soon it becomes a coequal voice; only to end up by replacing special revelation completely.

19. Machen, *What is Faith?* p. 94.

20. *Ibid.*, p. 96.

B. Contrary to Hebrews 11:1

The first reading of Hebrews 11:1, "Now faith is the assurance of things hoped for, the conviction of things not seen," seems to be a definition of faith which does not begin to resemble the notion that faith is a resting of the heart in the sufficiency of the evidence.

In answer let us point out that this is not, strictly speaking, a philosophic definition. The "word 'describes' is perhaps more strictly correct than 'defines:' for the words which follow are not a definition of that in which faith consists, but of that which faith serves as and secures to us."[21] A familiar illustration will serve to show what we mean. In archaeological circles the story is told of the discovery of the bones of a man who had evidently been a messenger for some woman who, in an effort to ground her claims for a certain property, had given a message into the hands of this servant with the command to speed to the prefect of Egypt therewith. Still discernible upon the face of the scroll were these words, "In order that my lord, the praefect, may know that my claims are just, I enclose herewith my *hypostasis*." When they opened the contents further they discovered that the *hypostasis* was simply the title deed to her property. In like manner, the text says that faith is our *hypostasis,* our title deed, of things to come. Faith is the title deed of things hoped for, the conviction of things not seen. Look within! Do you have faith? That faith has been given to you as your deed of assurance that the promises of the gospel are yours. The apprehension of truth—the resting of the heart in the sufficiency of the evidence—*is* your title deed.

C. Makes the Church Creedal

The word 'creedal' has two meanings. First, it may mean that the church, on our view of faith, will be guided by creeds as compendious statements of the meaning of Scripture. In this sense the church not only may be creedal, it *must* be.

---

21. Alford, *Greek Testament,* Vol. IV.

Without creeds to determine what the meaning of the Bible is, when the law of contradiction is applied to it, there will be as many interpretations of the Scriptures as there are persons. The church, like any organization, must have laws and statutes to run it. Laws are the creeds of the state, useful for the praise of the good and the punishment of the evil. Church creeds preserve the church from unbridled anarchy.

But there is a second meaning of 'creedal,' and it surely is this which the objector has in mind. It is 'dead orthodoxy' or a preserving of the 'letter of the law' as opposed to the spirit. But this need not follow from our view of faith. Paul tells us that there is a perfect relation between the head and the heart when the whole soul is engaged in faith. "I will pray with the *spirit* and I will pray with the *mind* also: I will sing with the *spirit* and I will sing with the *mind* also." (I Corinthians 14:15). It is the truth of God's word which gives the spirit of man its power, for it is this truth that the spirit of God uses in assuring our spirits that we are the children of God. (Romans 8:16). In fact, it is only within systematic consistency that 'dead orthodoxy' can be attacked. It is guilty of incoherence, since it is part of the meaning of Scripture that the precepts of Christ should be applied to the whole mind, the whole will, and the whole emotions. It is truth which gives us happiness by assuring us that our sins are forgiven and that we are on the way to heaven. But this truth cannot be communicated without the precision of creeds. "It is a strange idea of many who urge this objection in the interests of what they conceive to be a more spiritual form of Christianity, that 'spirituality' in a religion is somehow synonymous with vagueness and indefiniteness; that the more perfectly they can vaporize or volatilize Christianity into a nebulous haze, in which nothing can be perceived distinctly, the nearer they bring it to the ideal of a spiritual religion."[22] *Our personal happiness is only as secure as the precision of our system of truth.*

---

22. Orr, *op. cit.*, pp. 21-22.

D. Engenders Controversy

Quite so. Truth is worth defending. Moses defended it, as did the prophets and apostles after him. Christ disputed with the doctors in the temple over the law of Moses. Tolerance of everything is a mark of an empty head, not a mark of *agape* love. Theological pacificism is the death of theology. It is neither Scriptural nor logical to refrain from intelligent controversy. The perfect pattern of argumentation is set in I Peter 3:15. *The preparation*: "In your hearts reverence Christ as Lord." *The assignment*: "Always be prepared to make a defense to any one who calls you to account for the hope that is in you. *The mood*: "Yet do it with gentleness and reverence." Nor are we much impressed by those who think that defenders of a system are on the 'defensive' and are fearful that they are wrong. Rather, it is the firm conviction that Christianity *is* true which goads men on to propagate it with aggressive arguments.

E. Contrary to Paul

Paul teaches that the gospel is foolish, not logical, so how can we rest in it by an application of systematic consistency? "Greeks seek wisdom, but we preach Christ crucified, a stumbling-block to Jews and folly to Gentiles . . . For the foolishness of God is wiser than men, and the weakness of God is stronger than men" (I Corinthians 1:22-25). No few thinkers have tried to make out from this passage that the gospel can be irrational when tested by the conventional laws of logic, but their position is weak. The gospel is foolish to the natural man because he faultily applies systematic consistency, not because he is so logical that Christianity is foolish in relation to him. The foolishness is what some *think* the gospel is, not what it *actually is*. Christ is the wisdom of God, the coherence of meaning. If Paul were teaching that the crucified Christ were objectively foolish, in the sense that He cannot be rationally categorized, then he would have pointed to the insane and the demented as incarnations of truth.

Paul again teaches that "the written code kills, but the Spirit gives life" (II Corinthians 3:6). Is this not contrary to the doctrine of him who follows propositional revelation? We need not spend time with this. The context clearly indicates that the contrast in Paul's mind is not between the intellect and the emotions, but rather between the law of God which condemns to death and the Spirit of Jesus Christ which brings life.

F. Inhibits Progress

With the canon of propositional revelation closed, we can make no progress. Our theology becomes frozen. On the contrary, if there are no fixed points to serve as goals, there is nothing to recede from and nothing to progress to. Sheer movement is not progress. The fixed goal in Christ makes progress possible rather than inhibiting it.

G. Deifies Reason

If we rest only in the reasonable, reason replaces God. Not so. Reason is the test for truth. It detects truth; it does not manufacture it. Truth is always superior to the logic which establishes it.

H. The Devils Believe

As for the devils believing and trembling, the Bible says that they did (James 2:19). It does not belittle their believing; it only belittles those who do not go further in their trust than the demons. Demon-faith does not fructify in whole-soul love for God. The demons know that the judgment of God awaits them; they know no remedy for their condition because of their evil natures.

V. Ensuing Practical Benefits

By defending the primacy of coherently apprehended propositional revelation as the proper basis for faith, the Christian enjoys the fruit of certain practical benefits.

A. Educated Ministry

Convinced that faith has for its first step the acquisition of that system of truth which is outlined in Holy Writ, holy men will gravitate in the general direction of holy scholarship. The more faithfully one studies the Word, the more he is illumined and led by the Spirit of the Living God. The original Hebrew and Greek languages will be mastered; publications will flood our presses in delineation of the faith; and great and accurate hymns of praise will be written.

B. Humility

When a man comes to the realization that the strength of his faith is conditioned to the accuracy of his knowledge, he will constantly perceive how little he actually knows and thus be humbled before God. When feelings are displaced by the law of contradiction in interpreting the authoritative word of God, much of the conceit of private judgment is expelled from the heart in favor of a contrite and broken spirit before God. Ignorance is the spark which fires blind dogma and intolerance.

C. Church Unity

"Behold, how good and how pleasant it is for brethren to dwell together in unity!" (Psalm 133:1) With objective knowledge rather than subjective feeling as the basis for determining sound doctrine, a vast step will be taken toward unifying the now scandalously disorganized church of Jesus Christ. One can only guess how many denominations would cease their peculiar stresses and join with the main trunk of the church, were systematic consistency, not emotions, given its rightful place. Without a criterion to determine where truth leaves off and heresy begins, no unity can be had. But without the guidance of reason, we have no criterion to tell what the truth is.

D. Proper Place For Feeling

Instead of being the fruit of some stirring in the spleen, Christian feeling is based upon the solid rock of objective truth. Apprehension of the truth of the gospel secures proper emotions and causes the Christian to shout with joy, "Oh happy day! when Jesus washed my sins away!" Feelings are only as secure as the system of truth which fortifies them.

> Discouraged by the work of life,
> Disheartened by its load,
> Shamed by its failures or its fears,
> I sink beside the road.
> But let me only think of Thee,
> And then new heart springs up in me.

Nehemiah, chapter eight, gives an example of the concomitance of faith and feeling in Christianity. When Ezra opened the law of Moses, the people heard the reading of the word and understood it with their minds. Being convinced in the whole soul that it was the truth, the people wept for their sins. This was contrition. Then they celebrated with eating and drinking and made great mirth, *"because they had understood the words that were declared unto them"* (Verse 12). This was emotional joy. Here, in perfection, we see the Christian doctrine of the primacy of truth and the ability of that truth to assuage the whole man. Proper feeling, like proper mysticism, follows upon the establishment of the truth of the law of God. Truth establishes feelings; feelings do not establish truth.[23]

---

23. An ambiguity in language threatens to betray us into a serious misunderstanding. *All* of the followers of neo-orthodoxy, and Barth and Brunner in particular, stand opposed to mysticism. How, then, can we charge the school with the errors of mysticism? The answer is that mysticism comes in at least two different forms. First, there is metaphysical mysticism, where an ontological continuity of man and God is defended, as in all forms of pantheism. God and man are contiguous in being. *It is against this form of mysticism that Barth and Brunner are arguing.* Holding to a dialectical relation between time and eternity, they reject all forms of immanence. Immanence is the optimism that man, using resident abilities, can discover God.

Secondly, there is epistemological mysticism, that view which denies the power of logic to interpret ultimate reality, such reality being *personal* and not factual. *It is this form of mysticism which the text has in mind.* As a result of their revolt from philosophic foundations, Barth and Brunner have driven a wedge between personal, or encounter truth (*Du Wahrheit*) and philosophic truth (*Es Wahrheit*). This is bad subjectivism.

Chapter V

The Christian Hypothesis

Lord, to whom shall we go? You have the words of eternal life; and we have believed, and have come to know, that you are the Holy One of God.

—Simon Peter

THE time has now come for us to face a serious objection to our structure. The objection grows out of the anti-metaphysical mood of modern empiricism and takes on the form of a challenge of our right even to consider the possibility of supernatural revelation as a solution to the problem of the one within the many. But just now, let us review our findings. Three problems wait for the philosopher's solution. First, truth must be located. Secondly, a rational universe must be plotted. Finally, these two must be so united that they will provide a basis for trust in personal immortality. These three problems, when bundled together, make up one difficulty, the problem of locating a consistent world-view; since, when we properly pass judgment upon the general character of the totality of reality, we *have* come to grips with the problems of truth, rationality, and personal happiness. A world-view is but a series of logically knit hypotheses, on the order of scientific hypotheses, which the mind advances as a coherent meaning-pattern to explain the origin of, the present purpose of, and the final end of the aggregate of all reality. The purpose of any hypothesis is to exhibit relations and connections between observable and cognizable facts.

Based upon the ultimate postulate, the existence of the God Who has revealed Himself in Scripture, Christianity claims to be a world-view which *is* qualified to solve these basic problems of epistemology and metaphysics, and to outline the nature and destiny of man. In briefest compass, the Christian solution to the problems of personal happiness, the rationality in the universe, and coherent truth, is as follows.

First, happiness is secured for man by Jesus Christ, Who, being true God, consubstantial with the Father and the Holy Spirit, having left heaven, took on the form of a servant, fulfilled the covenant of grace by obeying the law of God perfectly, died an expiatory death on the cross as a full atonement for the sins of many, and now lives eternally as the God-Man making intercession for the righteous. "Man or angel would have been too low in respect of God: and an unveiled God would have been too high, in respect of sinful men, unable to bear intercourse with such heavenly Majesty. Wherefore the Son of God, that he might be fit to mediate, as he, being God equal with the Father, was high enough in respect of the party offended; so he consented to become low enough in respect of the party offending, by his becoming man."[1] Because of His saving mission, Christ could say, "He who hears my word and believes him who sent me, has eternal life; he does not come into judgment, but has passed from death to life" (John 5:24). In Christ, man possesses all things, "For all things are yours, whether . . . life or death or the present or the future, all are yours; and you are Christ's; and Christ is God's" (I Corinthians 3:21-22).

Not all the blood of beasts
  On Jewish altars slain,
Could give the guilty conscience peace,
  Or wash away the stain.

But Christ, the heavenly Lamb,
  Takes all our sins away,
A sacrifice of nobler name,
  And richer blood than they.

Secondly, a rational universe is established by God's being the Author of the movement of history. "Jehovah by wisdom

1. Boston, *A View of the Covenant of Grace*, p. 71.

founded the earth; by understanding he established the heavens" (Proverbs 3:19). History is the plan which was conceived in the mind of God from eternity to be the medium through which His glory would be displayed to all, and by means of which many sons should be brought to glory.

Finally, truth is established because God is the repository of wisdom. In the act of creation, God endowed both the world and man with rationality. Because of God, therefore, the world bears meaning, and this meaning, when systematically ordered, is truth. If there were not this antecedent meaning in history, we could not have a world-view. "In thy light shall we see light" (Psalm 36:9).

Let us now face the prejudice. The critic views the above structure as he would a piece of poetry. It sounds nice, and it would be nice in reality, *if* it only were true. But a rational man can no longer believe in a supernaturally ordered world, for Kant has demonstrated in his *Critique of Pure Reason* that in matters that pertain to metaphysics, such as God, heaven, and the angels, the understanding is impotent. And if a man cannot understand God, what virtue is there in talking about Him?

I. The Nature of Assumptions

We feel that the objection to the Christian's appeal to the Bible in solving philosophic problems is a prejudice because of the very nature of assumptions themselves. What the Christian does when he assumes that the Bible is a meaning-situation which must be reckoned with before reality can properly be known, is no more pretentious than the non-Christian's faith that the Bible is not a meaning-situation which must be reckoned with before reality properly can be known. Each is an assumption.

It may be asked why we make assumptions at all. Why not stay with the facts? The answer to this is *very easy* indeed! We make assumptions because we must make assumptions to think at all. All knowledge is inferential and all inferences are assumptions. Knowledge is the mind's construction of *mean-*

ing, and properly construed meaning is truth. It is therefore useless to say, 'Stay with the facts,' unless we mean, 'Keep your hypotheses in conformity to facts.' Facts just *are.* Knowledge is inference drawn from facts. A fact is any unit of being which is capable of bearing meaning, but it is the meaning, not the fact, which is the knowledge. "Knowledge of objects, then, knowledge of the real, involves always two elements, the element of given and ineffable presentation, and the element of conceptual interpretation which represents the mind's response. We might say that the conceptual is the formal element, of order or relation, and the given is the material or content element."[2] An expert in geology can see meaning in rocks. This is because of his fertile, highly trained mind, not because the rocks have tags on them telling what they mean. When interpreting the strata, the geologist is appealing to assumptions. He is saying, in effect, 'Grant me the assumption of the Pleistocene epoch, and I can make a more coherent picture out of your experience.' But let us not forget that this 'Pleistocene epoch' business is a pure hypothesis, a pure assumption. The same is true for all knowledge. Whether we explain a broken window or conjecture whether God exists or no, our answers are meaning-plans (hypotheses) which we entertain in the mind to cover coherently what we consider the meaning of the real world to be.

A. Assumptions in Daily Life

We are bombarded with facts all of the time: lost shoes, sour orange juice, dead batteries, soiled clothing, broken glass, smell of gas, and the like. Each of these fact-situations must be explained; our explanation is an hypothesis. When we smell smoke, we think of a number of possible explanations. That one which leads us coherently into all of our experience is the true one. Every Monday morning the laundress must make that all-important decision whether to hang out the clothing or not. She listens to weather reports, notes the density of the clouds, and then acts upon the strength of whatever hypothesis

2. Lewis, *Mind and the World-Order,* p. 143.

she decides. If, after hanging the clothing out, the rain comes, she can be assured that she rested in a faultily construed assumption.

B. Assumptions in Science

The scientist's procedure is the same as the housewife's, save that it is conducted on a little more refined scale. The flash-insights of the scientist, out of which come hypotheses, can be tested by complicated apparatus which is not at hand for the laundress. Let us show that scientific conclusions are just as truly assumptions as are the opinions of the average citizen.

Archimedes, if we may trust tradition, figured out the law of water displacement when he stepped into a tub full of water and observed the liquid run over from the act. A nice piece of imagination. Kepler's first law of motion—that planetary orbits are ellipses with the sun as their common focus—was not found by direct observation, for that simply indicates the varying direction of the line which joins our planet, the earth, with the planet under investigation. Kepler assumed the hypothesis that planets follow elliptical rather than circular orbits because with it he could make a smoother picture out of the heavens than without it. Watt, we are told, conceived his idea of the engine by watching the escape of steam from a teakettle. Another nice piece of imagination. Galileo, while watching the rhythmical motion of a swinging chandelier, lighted upon the principle which is now known in physics as isochronism in pendulums. We are not here suggesting that the hypotheses of the scientist are just pulled out of thin air; rather they were advanced by disciplined minds which had soaked long in relevant facts. Our point is that all hypotheses are but patterns of meaning which are thought out by the mind of the investigator to explain the configuration of data which it faces. The hypotheses that work well are called 'theories,' and theories that stick are called 'laws.' But let us not forget that these laws are but good hypotheses. We shall capitalize upon this observation when we discuss the possibility of miracles.

C. World-View Assumptions

The mistake of the modern man is that he pronounces the benediction when the scientist has spoken, not realizing that there are yet super-hypotheses which must be made before even the subordinate laws of science are significant. As we shall discuss this matter more fully in a subsequent chapter, let us here but briefly point out what some of these world-view assumptions are which the scientist must presuppose.

1. *Epistemology.* If a law is to be meaningful, it must be true. Every successful scientist, then, must assume that knowledge is possible. But establishing the possibility of knowledge is a job for philosophy, for there is no crucial empirical experiment which can settle problems of epistemology.

2. *Metaphysics.* Science assumes that the universe is regular, but how can that hypothesis be made significant without a world-view which allows for regularity? Without metaphysics we can have no confidence for tomorow. "Physics points back to and is founded in metaphysics."[3]

3. *Ethics.* All scientists know that a man must be honest before his conclusions can be trusted, but how can the empiricist show, by a laboratory experiment, that honesty is a normative affair? Science can only describe.

The enigmatic situation in the modern world is that the scientist rejects the Christian world-view because it involves certain nonempirical, metaphysical hypotheses, while assuming for himself a truckload, each of which goes as much beyond sensory observation as does the Christian's postulate of the God Who has revealed Himself in Scripture. The Christian questions the sport of this game. Fair rules in the contest of hypothesis-making ought to dictate that the winner be he who can produce the best set of assumptions to account for the totality of reality. If the Christian is disqualified from the

3. Bavinck, *The Philosophy of Revelation*, p. 88.

arena by rules which his opponent makes, it is evident that the game has been 'fixed.' Good sportsmanship, to say nothing of common sense, requires that in a contest, all participants be given the same advantages as well as the same handicaps. Without these conditions, there is no sport.

II. Philosophy and Assumptions

Let us pursue this matter further. In daily life we give meaning to smoke, bottles, tooth brushes, and lamps. In science we give meaning to molecules, planets, and lizards. But in philosophy we give meaning to everything. "Everything in the universe, which in any way enters into human experience, or affects, or is known by human beings, is of interest to philosophy."[4] Coherence cannot stop with a segment of our experience; it must go on to embrace it all. Then it becomes philosophy.

Let us point out quickly that being a philosopher is not a task that we can elect *ad lib.* We *must* pass judgment upon the whole of reality; it is not optional. We are in the process of history, and what we think of reality will govern our actions in history. One cannot open his eyes without beholding vast spaces of the universe, a universe which must be accounted for just as truly as a dead battery in a stalled automobile or the recurrence of earthquakes in Japan. It is impossible for a man not to think of the universe in a certain way. Even if he says that the universe's character cannot be known, he is saying that the universe is a never-can-be-known affair, which itself is a bold negative assumption of no mean dimensions.

A. Examples of Philosophic Assumptions

1. Plato, to account for epistemology and metaphysics, assumed the existence of the Good, God, the world of Ideas, the demiurge, and the time-space receptacle, and in so doing could solve the problems of "How can one thing be another? How can many things be one? How can permanence be harmonized

4. Brightman, *An Introduction to Philosophy*, p. 4.

with flux? How can one know anything? What is the object of knowledge?"[5] The validity of one's assumptions is determined by the ability of those hypotheses to make sense out of life by answering problems. "The theory of ideas, then, is not *a priori;* its validity rests upon its power to explain the phenomena."[6]

2. Aristotle thought he could improve upon Plato by bringing in the notions of the Unmoved Mover, the intelligences, form, matter, and entelechy. We shall not take time to give our reasons here, but we fail to see where he solved more problems than Plato did. His empiricism led to skepticism in Hume.

3. Kant, to solve the problem of knowledge, proposed the existence of the forms of time and space and the categories of the understanding. But Kant never smelled or tasted a category. He conceived of them as part of an hypothesis to account for the possibility of knowledge. The skepticism of modern positivism may be a clue to our determining whether Kant succeeded in his theory of knowledge or not.

4. Christianity assumes the existence of the God Who has revealed Himself in Scripture to solve both metaphysical and epistemological problems. With this postulate he can explain, not deny, experience. His major premise is no more ostentatious than that of those who deny the existence of God as a condition *sine qua non* for interpreting reality.

It might be profitable to point out once again that a man cannot be neutral with the question of God's existence. One believes either that he will fall into God's judgment or that he will not. An agnostic may protest this observation, but his effort is in vain.

> If his protestation were sincere, however, he would have to admit that there was one chance in two that divine judgment would overtake him. If he knows nothing, and if there must be either a judgment or not a judgment, then so far as he knows the chances are even that there will be a judgment.

5. Martin *et al.*, *History of Philosophy,* p. 106.
6. Demos, *The Philosophy of Plato,* p. 176.

> And if a man really believed in the possibility, not to say the probability, of a judgment of God's wrath on sin, he would not adopt the attitude of indifference characteristic of self-styled agnostics. Their indifference is clear evidence that they believe that they are safe, that no judgment awaits them. Their life and actions show what they believe. Actions speak louder than words. Hence, whether one wish it or no, one is forced to adopt this or that theory.[7]

All men *must* decide what the over-all nature of reality is, and when they do this they are philosophers. Good philosophers are those who can construct systematically consistent systems of meaning, while poor ones are those who cannot. This conclusion establishes the *possibility* of Christianity as an answer to life's dilemma. Careful investigation of it as a system might establish its *actuality*.

B. The Bilateral Character of Philosophic Hypotheses

When the Christian claims that in bringing the Bible into the philosophic picture, he is able to make more sense out of life than without it, the strength of that assertion is contingent upon two factors.

1. *The positive side.* The positive strength of an hypothesis is its ability to make good what it claims. When Plato says, "Grant me this, and I hope to be able to show you the nature of the cause, and to prove the immortality of the soul,"[8] the positive test of this claim is to see if it fulfills what it sets out to establish. So, in Christianity, its first test is to see if it can live up to its lofty claims by giving a basis of personal hope in immortality, a rational view of the universe, and a solution to the problem of truth.

2. *The negative side.* By this we mean a consideration of what one is left with if he gives up a given hypothesis. This is the fundamental strength of the Christian-theistic theory of knowledge, for all its rival alternatives lead to skepticism. In considering Christianity, then, one must pay attention not only

---

7. Clark, *A Christian Philosophy of Education,* pp. 42-43.
8. *Phaedo,* 100b.

to the implications which flow from it as a given hypothesis, *but also those which flow from its denial.* One may not personally care for the Christian world-view, but before his protestations can be seriously heeded by the Christian, the former must produce a world-view which is simpler and more coherent than that which he is rejecting. A rational man will accept that system which is attended by the *fewest* difficulties.

C. Dangers in Making Assumptions in Philosophy

In constructing philosophic assumptions, two extremes must be avoided. The first is the fear of making hypotheses at all, and the second is the complete lack of fear. These are the Scylla and Charybdis in right thinking.

1. The former phobia is part of the conviction of those unadventurously conditioned individuals who shy away from passing judgment on things because they might 'go beyond the facts.' To these we say, with Huxley, that he who does not go beyond the facts will seldom get as far as the facts. One *must* go beyond the facts if he is ever conceptually to know anything, for knowledge is the meaning of facts, not the facts themselves. When the imagination is throttled, freedom to construct meaningful, dynamic interconnections between the facts of the universe is impossible.

2. The other danger attends those hypothesis-happy souls, who, having a minimum of patience with the facts and a maximum of free imagination, grind out hypotheses faster than competent examining committees can manage to canvass their validity. This fallacy of Procrusteanizing and geometrizing reality is commonly committed by rationalists and idealists. These philosophers forget that the imagination must be *relevant* as well as free. The followers of Hegel are an example of this practice. "Baur, on the basis of his Hegelian philosophy, with its 'thesis, antithesis, and synthesis,' expected to find a conflict in the apostolic age with a gradual compromise and settlement. And so he found that phenomenon surely enough—in defiance of the facts, but in agreement with his philosophy."[9]

---

9. Machen, *What Is Faith?* p. 63.

This is known as the 'fallacy of special pleading,' as the landlord who proves that he is providing enough heat for an apartment by putting the thermometer on the radiator instead of on the wall over a window.

A perfect hypothesis is one which is free enough to *explain* the facts and yet restricted enough to explain the *facts*. Too much stress upon explanation leads one upon the high and dry *a priori* road of rationalism and idealism, while too little interest in it drives one into the slough of positivism. The rationalistic solution is heroic and free, but it is not relevant to the human situation; while the positivistic solution is relevant, but is not a solution.

D. *The Problem of Selecting Hypotheses*

Inasmuch as there is a vast variety of possible world views, which shall one choose? The answer is, plainly, the 'simplest.' Three rules are suggested to help one recognize simplicity when he sees it.

1. Coherence. "Since an explanatory hypothesis is a possible patterning of facts which purports to explain them by arranging them in a more intelligible sort of order, we should expect it to be self-consistent, or free from internal contradictions."[10] In choosing between the system of Kant and the system of Christ, see, first of all, which makes better peace with the law of contradiction.

2. An hypothesis is simpler than another if it resorts to fewer ultimate principles to explain things. "One hypothesis is said to be simpler than another if the number of independent types of elements in the first is smaller than in the second."[11] Thus Christianity is simpler than Zoroastrianism, for the latter requires two ultimates—light and darkness—while the former requires only one—Light. Plato needed three or four principles, while the Christian needs only God.

---

10. Larrabee, *Reliable Knowledge*, p. 202.

11. Cohen and Nagel, *An Introduction to Logic and Scientific Method*, p. 213.

3. An hypothesis is simpler if it uses fewer *ad hoc* assumptions than another. This is the fundamental sense in which Christianity is simple. All things are teleologically related to the mind of God.

> Two hypotheses may be both capable of introducing order into a certain domain. But one theory may be able to show that various facts in the domain are related on the basis of the *systematic implications of its assumptions.* The second theory, however, may be able to formulate an order only on the basis of special assumptions formulated *ad hoc* which are unconnected in any systematic fashion. The first theory is then said to be simpler than the second. Simplicity in this sense is the *simplicity of system* . . . One theory will therefore be said to be more simple or general than another if the first can, while the second cannot, exhibit the connections it is investigating as *special instances* of the relations it takes as fundamental.[12]

Under one assumption the Christian succeeds in unfolding the implications of his theory of immortality, rational universe, and truth. Science cannot do this. Therefore the scientific method is less simple than Christianity.

The modernist believes that his system is simpler than the conservative's, for all he defends is the Fatherhood of God and the brotherhood of man, while the latter has to handle the unwieldy sixty-six books of covenantal theology in canonical Scripture. The modernist has misinterpreted the nature of simplicity, however. The mathematics of Einstein is technically more difficult than that of Newton, but it is simpler because under one assumption it can account for more of reality than the mathematics of Newton can. Complexity in a system is not what makes for lack of simplicity by any means. Simplicity of system pertains to the number of special assumptions which must be brought in that cannot be systematically related to the fundamentals of the system. Christianity may seem more cumbersome than modernism, but it succeeds in explaining all reality with fewer ultimate postulates than does mod-

12. *Ibid.*, p. 214. Newton is more simple than Ptolemy because he requires fewer special assumptions to work out his heliocentric theory of astronomy.

ernism. Thus, it is simpler. We shall not pause to establish that here. Modernism is in such a state of decay today that only the wholly benighted can fail to see the handwriting on the wall.

In this same manner conservatives can better explain things than Thomists, for the latter must introduce the *two* epistemological ultimates, faith and reason, before they can complete things; while the former, following Augustine, need only introduce faith. The Thomist, when his reason is depleted, must change horses epistemologically in the middle of the stream, and turn to faith. This is a lack of simplicity.

III. Objections to the Christian Hypothesis

A. Double Assumption

The Christian assumes both God and the Scriptures. May we not apply Occam's razor and assume just a good God? In answer, the Christian points out that his assumption is really but one. God is the *ratio essendi* (the ground for the Scriptures) while the Scriptures are the *ratio cognoscendi* (that through which God is apprehended). God is the Christian's only major premise, but this God is known through the Scriptures. The ontological and epistemological presuppositions go together. God apart from His self-revelation would be unknown, while revelation without God's authority behind it would be useless. But we would add also, that in explaining the world, one must beware of committing the fallacy of over-simplification. The world is complicated, and if ten assumptions are required to solve its problems, then one is not consistent to use only nine. The Christian makes but one assumption—the God Who has revealed Himself in Scripture—but if he did have more, and if with these he succeeded in making a coherent picture out of reality, he could not be censored.

B. Petitio Principii

The Christian begs the question by assuming the truth of God's existence to establish that very existence. Indeed! This is true for establishing the validity of any ultimate. The truth of the law of contradiction must be assumed to prove the validity of that axiom. Nature must be assumed to prove nature. Strict demonstration of a first postulate is impossible, as Aristotle pointed out, for it leads either to infinite regress or to circular reasoning.

C. Christianity Anticipates Nature

The Christian finds his system in the Bible and then makes nature fit it. There are two answers to this. First, the Christian finds his system of philosophy in the Bible, to be sure, but he accepts this, not simply because it is in the Bible, but because, when tested, it makes better sense out of life than other systems of philosophy make. Secondly, even if Christianity does anticipate nature, there is no inherent wrongness here, provided, of course, that it succeeds in solving problems in so doing. The test of a system is its ability to make difficulties plain. If nature must be anticipated to accomplish this, there can be no objection. In the game of locating truth, the winner is he who establishes coherence. The method he elects to follow is an irrelevant issue.

Chapter VI

The Criteria of Verification

Test everything; hold fast what is good.—Paul

IF religion is man's whole-soul attitude toward what he conceives to be the highest unit of reality, one can easily detect that the basic problem of religion is *verification;* since it is always theoretically possible that what has been conceived to be God, the solution to the problem of the one within the many, is in reality nothing but the fruit of an auto-projection.[1] Critics since the days of Xenophanes have declared that most forms of religion are nothing but the imagination or the glands of man working overtime. This charge might not bother some religions, but Christianity is different. It is built upon a structure of theology which denies the distinction between having faith and assenting to truth. This means that it must prove that the Red Sea actually parted, that Lazarus actually rose from the grave, and that there is a heaven and a hell toward which the righteous and the unrighteous are gravitating. However, it is always a salutary gesture in any discussion to insist upon a clarification of the terms used. Proof has been called for, but do we know what the nature of proof is?

I. The Nature of Proof

A. Demonstrative Proof

When one demonstrates a proposition, he shows that it is the necessary conclusion of a premise which is already known

---

1. Favorite illustration is the little boy who, having no playmates, projects one for himself, and then proceeds to make mud pies as if his friend actually existed. In like manner, lonely man projects a cosmic Friend and denominates him 'God.' But the latter entity, as the former, has no existential status. The only existence that each has lies in the mind of the individual.

to be true, as all A is P and all S is A, therefore, all S is P. The conclusion follows from the premises necessarily because all S is included in P. This is direct demonstration. Indirect demonstration establishes a proposition "by disproving its contradictory, or showing that the conclusion cannot be supposed untrue."[2] Moot-Smith gives a stock example of indirect demonstration.[3]

> *Problem*: In a faraway land there dwelt two races. The Ananias were inveterate liars, while the Diogenes were unfailingly veracious. Once upon a time a stranger visited the land, and on meeting a party of three inhabitants inquired to what race they belonged. The first murmured something that the stranger did not catch. The second remarked, 'He said he was an Anania.' The third said to the second, 'You're a liar!' Now the question is, of what race was this third man? *Solution*: Every inhabitant was bound to say that he was a Diogene — the Diogenes because they were truthful and the Ananias because they were liars. Hence the second man's assertion must have been false, and since the third spoke truly he was a Diogene.

One can easily detect that pure demonstration is operative only within a system of formal symbols, as in logic and mathematics. But its importance cannot be minimized, for by location of absurdities and contradictions in a system of thought, philosophers are able to segregate the true from the false. As Russell points out, "absurdities are the experiments of the logician."[4] Demonstrative proof, seen in its best form in dialectics and formal logic, is a perfect application of the law of contradiction. If a man admits that all men are mortals, and that Socrates is a man, he breaks the law of contradiction not to admit that Socrates is also a mortal; for the validity of the conclusion has already been admitted in the major and minor premises. It is evident, however, that perfect proof cannot begin to cover all avenues of learning. Pure demonstration is but formal. Kant saw this clearly.

---

2. Jevons, *Elementary Lessons in Logic*, p. 335.
3. *Mathematical Puzzles for Beginners and Enthusiasts*, pp. 13 and 146.
4. *Twentieth Century Philosophy* (Runes, ed.), p. 244.

> We can say beforehand that the proposition 'circles are square' is a false proposition since it runs counter to the *form* of logical, and therefore of true, thinking. At the same time . . . the formal structure of thought does not forbid apples from being blue as it forbids circles from being square . . . if we try to convert the *formal* truth of our proposition into *material* truth by arguing that since the proposition is valid in logic it must also hold true of experience, we fall into error.[5]

Reality cannot be connected by formal logic alone, because historical facts are united teleologically, not by logical implication. Logical truth cannot pass into material truth until the facts of life are introduced into the picture. This leads us to the second type of proof.

B. *Inductive Proof*

When one moves from formal demonstration into concrete history, he is conscious of a loss of demonstrative certainty. Compare, for example, the precision of the Pythagorean theorem with the estimation of the weight of the Egyptian pyramids or the distance between the earth and the nearest star. Here one cannot rise above probability. The computation of the weight of the pyramids may be off thousands of tons and the distance from earth to the nearest star may be miscalculated by several light years. This is due to both the complexity of the data and to the fact that "no human observer is infallible . . . and no human being's knowledge of all the relevant facts about anything, let alone a command of all their imaginable patternings, is demonstrably complete."[6] Some years back there was an attack of nausea in New York City, the cause of which was traced to bacteria in the water which the people were using. When the people left off drinking that water, the illness disappeared, leaving the health authorities with the firm conviction that they had *proved* the cause of the sickness. And, indeed, they had, within a threshold of probability. But the induction did not involve a perfect demonstration, because

---

5. Fuller, *History of Philosophy* (Modern), p. 269.
6. Larrabee, *Reliable Knowledge*. p. 318.

the possibility that the cause of the illness was due to a change in the moon's surface or to a series of earthquakes on the far side of China always remained. A premise is demonstrated only when it is the necessary implication of a self-evident premise or when its contradiction is shown to be false. Probability, as Butler established, is the guide of life.[7]

C. Proof by Systematic Consistency

Since all we can find in history is *probability,* and since all we can find in logic and mathematics is *formal* validity, we can not have complete truth until we unite them. Truth is the properly construed meaning of *all* experience. Perfect coherence always involves two elements: the law of contradiction to give formal validity, and concrete facts of history to give material validity. Without formal validity we have no universality and necessity in truth, and without material validity we have no relevance to the world in which we live. This is proof by coherence, characterized by what we have earlier called the 'sticking-togetherness' of our propositions. C. I. Lewis states this proof very accurately.[8]

> It is of the essence of the dialectical or reflective method that we should recognize that proof, in philosophy, can be nothing more at bottom than persuasion. It makes no difference what the manner of presentation should be, whether deductive from initial assumptions, or inductive from example, or merely following the order dictated by clarity of exposition. If it be deductive, then the initial assumptions cannot coerce the mind. There are no propositions which are self-evident in isolation . . . If the method be inductive from example, then the principles to be proved are implicit in the assumption that cited examples are veridical and typical and genuinely fall under the category to be investigated. There can be no Archimedian point for the philosopher. Proof, he can offer only in the sense of so connecting his theses as to exhibit their mutual support, and only through appeal to other

---

7. "The conclusion is that demonstration is an ideal which is only rarely attained. For the most part we have to content ourselves with probability, and this can seldom be accurately determined." Bowne, *Theory of Thought and Knowledge,* p. 191.

8. *Mind and the World-Order,* p. 23.

> minds to reflect upon their experience and their own attitudes and perceive that he correctly portrays them.

An example of proof by coherence from ancient philosophy is seen in the way Anaximander refuted Thales. Thales said that water was the 'material cause' of all things. Anaximander pointed out that, if all was of water, there would be no fire, for water is the extinguisher of, not the creator of, fire. Thales, in other words, was incoherent. He was not construing his propositions systematically, since he admitted simultaneously that all is from water and yet that fire exists. Observe, however, that neither empirical nor demonstrative proof was offered by Anaximander; there was no empirical experiment which could prove that all did not come from water, nor was there any necessarily evident deduction by which it could be shown. The only possible proof that Anaximander could resort to was coherence, showing that his propositions stuck together better than those of Thales.

We have earlier pointed out that every man is a philosopher of a sort, and must pass judgment upon the whole course of reality. But the only proof he can offer, both for his system of philosophy and for the actions which flow from it, is *systematic coherence*. Here, our theories of truth as coherence, faith as trust in coherence, and proof as founded in coherence, meet. The better our propositions stick together, the more truth we have; the more truth we have, the more faith we have; the more faith we have, the more coherence we have. It is in this framework that the Christian offers proof for his system: it sticks together. It can solve the problems of personal happiness, present a rational view of the universe, and give a basis for truth. In one hypothesis—the existence of God Who has revealed Himself in Scripture—the Christian can correlate time and eternity in one meaningful picture. This is what we mean by proof from coherence. An idiot is the least coherent of rational beings. A child is more coherent. An adult still more. The trained expert is most coherent. God is absolute consistency. And the will of God has been revealed in Holy Writ.

II. The Criteria of Verification in Christianity

Christians are deeply system-conscious. Within the pattern of meaning found in revealed religion, John the Baptist challenged the moral life of Herod, Christ heaped invectives upon the Pharisees, and Paul scathingly denounced the Judaizers in Galatia. Believing that God is rational and that by being rational one comes closest to God's mind (and we mean by 'rational' the state of coherence), the Christian is jealous to apply the canons of systematic consistency to all of living. God is truth, and that system of meaning in the Bible which flows from Him "has a character, coherence, and unity of its own, and stands in sharp contrast with counter theories and speculations, and . . . has the stamp of reason and reality upon itself, and can amply justify itself at the bar both of history and of experience."[9]

A. Horizontal Self-Consistency

The first criterion of a philosophy of life is that all of the major assumptions be so related together that they placate the rules of formal logic, chief of which is the law of contradiction. If one refuses to construe his propositions according to the axiom of contradiction, all one can do is to check him off his calling list. There is no longer anything to talk about.

The Christian looks with suspicion upon all who pride themselves in their rejection of the law of contradiction as but a 'negative check on truth,' or as an 'insufficient lead into the richness of reality.' These thinkers remove the only test we have for detecting the consistency of any meaning-patterns. All theologies and philosophies which boast their lack of rationality (as in French existentialism, philosophically, and neo-orthodoxy, theologically) simply peacock their deficiency in objective truth.

> Start with the assumption that what God says must at least make human sense, and we know what to think when some dervish from the desert or from Berchtesgaden raises his

9. Orr, *The Christian View of God and the World,* p. 16.

> voice to claim guidance from above. Start from the assumption of Kierkegaard, Barth, and Brunner, that revelation must needs be an offence to our understanding, and what is to prevent us also from becoming blind followers of the blind?[10]

The first test for validity is an application of the law of contradiction. This is what we shall mean here, and elsewhere, by 'horizontal self-consistency.'

B. Vertical Fitting of the Facts

Self-consistency, though it is a formal condition *sine qua non* for truth, does not in and of itself tell the whole story of truth. Without it, truth is absent, but with it, truth may be truncated. Plenary truth must embrace a solution to the problem of the one within the many. This means that coherence involves an interpretation of the real concrete facts of human history—rocks, bones, and planets. Without a union of both facts and meaning, perfect coherence is impossible.

When the Christian applies to the course of history that horizontally self-consistent structure of philosophy which he finds in Scripture, he is pleasantly surprised to discover the jot-and-tittle correspondence of the Bible to the facts. To exhibit fully this correspondence would lead us into the special studies, a task which is pointless in a book which has as its theme the solution to the basic practical and theoretical dilemmas of man. The books on evidences are open for public inspection. The following, however, will briefly indicate those lines of evidence which the Christian pleads when defending his case. By *fitting the facts* we mean *being true to nature.*

1. *External Experience*

a. *History as fact.* Christianity vertically fits the facts of history, both ancient and recent. One need only check the quantity of archaeology volumes which have been published in the past century to appreciate the accuracy of the Bible nar-

---

10. Blanshard, *Harvard Divinity School Bulletin,* Volume XLIII, March 10, 1946, p. 63.

ratives. It is not enough simply to say that the canonical Scriptures are but the expression of the religious development of man and make no claim to historical accuracy. The writers of the Bible spoke under divine afflatus both in their spiritual prophecies and in their historical judgments. Review the findings of the archaeologist to learn of the Bible's precision with respect to the walls of Jericho, Shechem, the high place at Gezer, Solomon's stables, Jeroboam's seal, David's wall, Hezekiah's tunnel, Sargon's inscriptions, Sennacherib's exploits, Nineveh, and the hundreds of other historical points of tangency. We do not say that there are not problems remaining, for there are; the spade has much more dirt to turn over. We only say that archaeology is remarkably confirmatory of the Bible accounts, not hit or miss; this is what we should expect if Scripture has been inerrantly preserved by God.

The other main feature of Christianity as it relates to far history is its interpretation of the historical Christ. Only upon the assumption of the God Who has revealed Himself in Scripture can one explain the historical Jesus. When one leaves the documents of the Bible, which portray Christ as God, there is no consistent stopping point short of agnosticism over Who this One could possibly be that lived but thirty-three years and yet in that time set the basic pattern for Western culture. Our moral standards stem out of the Hebrew-Christian tradition as found in the Bible and delineated by Jesus Christ. If Christ is not God, He is an inexplicable madman, for He went to great length to make it clear that He was equal with the Father.[11] But He cannot be a madman, for the sublimity of His ethical teachings is incontestably secure. Then is He just giving pious advice in His Gospel? Pious advice could not have started the Christian church with its thousands of martyrs. For almost twenty centuries millions in every age

---

11. So thoroughly had Christ convinced the Jews that He really claimed to be the Son of God, that they used that point as a basis for His conviction. "This is why the Jews sought all the more to kill him, because he not only broke the sabbath but also called God his Father, making himself equal with God," John 5:18.

have testified to the veracity of Christ's word. If His word be not truth—the mind of God—what then is it?[12]

Christianity not only fits the facts of ancient history, it also does justice to recent history. It explains the nature of man, the frailty of his body, the sin in his heart, and his quest for life and peace. Christianity can account for our three social institutions, the state, the church, and the family, for it orders their founding and directs their purpose and prerogatives. Christianity embraces explicit or implicit solutions to every conceivable social problem: labor and race relations, divorce and infidelity, equity in business, standards of jurisprudence. It explains the universality of religion and the bloody sacrifice. It accounts for the actions of both those who commit war atrocities and live in debauchery and drunkenness, and those who wait in fear and trembling for the judgment of God.

The only fundamental, historical problem which Christianity still struggles with is the relation between the age of man that science gives and that of the Bible traced through the genealogies. In this regard, let us point out that the dates which appear in the margin of the King James Bible are not part of the inspired text but are rather a hypothetical structure proposed by James Ussher. Careful exegetes today point out that there are vast stretches of time in the Biblical genealogies which we had not heretofore reckoned with. But we frankly admit that there is yet much thought to be expended before we can say that science's age of man and the Bible's are perfectly coincident. It would be philosophically stupid, however, to jettison Christianity because of this difficulty. A rational man settles for that position which is attended by the fewest difficulties, not one which is unattended by any. We shall have more comments to make upon this matter when we discuss the problem of Biblical criticism.

---

12. We do not state this position dogmatically, for the proof has been completed by Orr, in *The Christian View of God and the World,* Lecture II. By an appeal to history he has shown the irresistibility of skepticism when one leaves the doctrine that Christ is God for a mediating position.

b. *History as process.* Christianity, with one major premise, nicely explains the beginning of the universe, its present purpose, and its final disposition. We shall go into these matters when we come to the Christian philosophy of history. Here, observe that Christianity claims coherently to envelop the whole gamut of the movement of history. The regularity of the universe is explained, plus its mixed character of good and evil. The sovereignty of the God Who has revealed Himself in Scripture is the key to the meaning of history as process.

Christianity's problem at this point is organic evolution, for the Bible cannot sustain the view that man is genetically related to the lower animals. Only he who plays fast and loose with the rights of language can deny that Moses taught that man came from the dust, by a special act of God, not through an organic development from a lower animal. When we come to discussion of Christianity and the scientific method, we shall set down our observations on this problem. We feel that men have been rather hasty in their judgment that structural similarity means genetic relationship.

2. *Internal Experience*

The Bible accurately describes man—body and spirit—as a unit endowed with rationality, a moral nature, and an insatiable desire for self-preservation. Christianity accounts for the universality of the fear of God and of the knowledge of right and wrong. Christianity explains why men tremble and fear before they go to the gallows: they know God's judgment awaits them, their conscience bearing witness. Christianity explains man's quest for hope; and it meets this hope by providing personal salvation and immortality. Little wonder that Christ's accurate commentary upon our hearts has caused men in all ages to say, when accosted by the words of Jesus, "No man ever spoke like this man!" (John 7:46). How can another compete with Christ, when He (if Christianity is true) is the eternal Logos, the meaning of history, the wisdom of God, and the Savior of the world? He Who fully saw

Nathanael when the latter was hidden under the fig tree (John 1:48) can also read the intentions of the hearts of all men with infallible precision.

But let us leave the question of the evidences for Christianity, for our work is apologetic, not historical and exegetical, and press on to a new problem which grows out of what we have committed ourselves to in this chapter. Having agreed that rational probability is the guide of life, some may say that we cannot declare with Paul, "I am not ashamed, for I *know* whom I have believed and I am *sure* that he is able to guard until that Day what has been entrusted to me" (II Timothy 1:12). Perhaps nothing keeps Fundamentalists from logically defending their faith more than a fear of losing their soul-peace. We contend that this attitude is unfounded. If Christianity is true, the heart has nothing to fear. If it is not true, the heart ought to rest its hope somewhere else. The increase of truth should mean the increase of subjective peace, not *vice versa.* Let us devote some thought to this problem.

III. Probability and the Problem of Moral Certainty

First, let us establish securely the fact that proof for the Christian faith, as proof for any world-view that is worth talking about, cannot rise above rational probability. Probability is that state of coherence in which more evidences can be corralled for a given hypothesis than can be amassed against it. The more the evidences increase, the more the strength of probability increases.

A. Christianity and Probability

Since Christianity is a way of life, and not an unabridged edition of the Pythagorean theorem, it cannot enjoy the demonstrative certainty of the latter. There are two fundamental reasons for this.

1. *Historical facts.* The first reason why Christianity cannot—and does not want to—rise to demonstration is that it is founded on historical facts, which, by their very nature, cannot

be demonstrated with geometric certainty. All judgments of historical particulars are at the mercy of the complexity of the time-space universe. *"All interpretation of particulars and all knowledge of objects is probable only,* however high the degree of its probability."[13] If the scientist cannot rise above rational probability in his empirical investigation, why should the Christian claim more?

The rock-bottom fact upon which Christianity rests is the Person, death, and resurrection of Jesus Christ. "The great weapon with which the disciples of Jesus set out to conquer the world was not a mere comprehension of eternal principles; it was an historical message, an acount of something that had recently happened, it was the message, 'He is risen.' "[14] When proof for a given historical event is demanded, it does little good to appeal to the laws of logic or the axioms of mathematics alone, for these, by themselves, cannot clinch the issue. By no presently known manipulation of symbols can one demonstrate either that Christ did rise from the grave or that He did not. Systematic consistency is our only means for proving or disproving either theory of the resurrection. We must set up that hypothesis which is based upon a careful sifting and screening of the relevant data. When one shows that Julius Caesar was born 100 B. C., he does not take down a volume of higher calculus and pore over it; he goes to the painful work of evaluating the actual evidence of what happened in history. A coherent hypothesis, let us recall, is one which can smoothly lead us into the totality of our experience, inside and outside.

This admission that Christianity's proof for the resurrection of Christ cannot rise above probability is not a form of weakness; it is rather an indication that the Christian is in possession of a world-view which is making a sincere effort to come to grips with actual history. Christianity is not a deductively necessary system of thought which has been spun out of a philosopher's head, wholly indifferent to the march of human

---

13. Lewis, *Mind and the World-Order,* p. 281.
14. Machen, *Christianity and Liberalism,* pp. 28-29.

history below it; rather it is a plan of salvation, a coherent solution to the persistent problem of man, What must I do to be saved?[15]

2. *Moral values.* The second reason why Christianity cannot formally demonstrate its truth is that it is based upon moral values. A man may be told that he ought to have his decayed teeth taken care of at once, and yet not do anything about the matter, simply because he does not have an appreciation of a value-situation. In like manner, unless one sees that he ought to accept Christ's mercies for salvation, *i. e.*, unless he perceives the value of Christ, trust in Christ will not follow. Value is a point of personal interest and appreciation beyond which there is no further ground of appeal; logic is only as strong as the human equation in all matters pertaining to personal value. A medico *qua* medico can show me how to get well, but he can not show me that I *should* get well without stirring in me a sense of values. If I do not care to live, that is all there is to it.

Christianity is a system of values built around the question, "What will it profit a man, if he gains the whole world and forfeits his life? Or what shall a man give in return for his life?" (Matthew 16:26). If a man, who is a sinner and under the condemnation of God, does not realize his condition and will not submit to the yoke of Christ for mercy, no mathematical demonstration can force him to see it. As you can lead a horse to water but you cannot make him drink, so you can lead a man to Christ but you cannot make him trust in Him. Trust is the result of a *cordial* spirit in the heart. The mother may try to persuade her son not to drink strong liquor, but only persuasion, not geometry can succeed, for a son convinced against his will is of the same opinion still. This is the second reason why Christianity cannot rise above probability. It is a system of moral values as well as a judgment

15. For those who are still disappointed by the admission of probability in Christianity, let them take courage by remembering that if our analysis is correct, then the system of Christianity can be refuted only by probability. Perhaps our loss is gain?

upon particular events in history. The Christian is no greater than his Master. "O Jerusalem, Jerusalem, killing the prophets and stoning those who are sent to you! How often would I have gathered your children together as a hen gathers her brood under her wings, and you would not!" (Matthew 23:37).

At this point we may profitably interject the observation that, though the way of life found in Christianity is accepted by few because it is narrow and hard, it does not follow from this that it is not a true way. Other reasons may enter into the picture to spoil a man's acceptance of this system of truth, the basis of which is personal sin. Sin vitiates the soul's seeing light in Christ, as a disease in the eye impairs clear vision of physical light. Man is, by nature, a sinner. "The fact that modern man has been able to preserve such a good opinion of himself, despite all the obvious refutations of his optimism, particularly in his own history," observes Niebuhr, "leads to the conclusion that there is a very stubborn source of resistance in man to the acceptance of the most obvious and irrefutable evidence about his moral qualities."[16] The impotency of the Christian to prove his system is thus not due *necessarily* to the fact that the system cannot make peace with the law of contradiction and the facts of history; but rather it *may* be that the heart of the natural man is adverse to what Christianity teaches. Moral values cannot be demonstrated; a moral value is either seen by a man or it is not. If a man believes that a new automobile is worth more than salvation in Christ, he has a false standard of values and ought to be prayed for earnestly. Some day, when he is overtaken by death, he may repent with tears.

B. *Christianity and Moral Certainty*

For some reason, not all theologians have seen that rational probability and perfect moral, or subjective, assurance are quite compatible. The Ritschlians went headfirst into feeling theology, believing that "the characteristic certitude of the

---

16. *Human Nature*, p. 121.

religious believer tends to be impaired, at least temporarily, when the doctrines of the faith upon which he has been building his life and his hopes for the future are treated as mere metaphysical theories, to be tested by their rationality and their agreement with empirical fact."[17] This divorce of faith and rationality has given the *coup de grâce* to modernism, for faith without objectively verifiable truth is comparable to the sort of certainty which goes along with snake-handlers, sun-adorers, and esoteric faith-healing cults of sundry species. That private insight which exclaims, 'I have it but I cannot express it,' is not the type of coherence which is necessary for science. Faith must be founded in objectively verifiable metaphysical theories even if they fail to provide perfect demonstration. Apart from this, theology *has* no logic.

Let us now show that there is no concomitant relation between the strength of a rationally construed proposition and the moral or subjective assurance which flows from it. Moral assurance grows out of a conviction that a proposition is coherent, not that it may be geometrically demonstrated. By 'moral assurance' we mean that apprehended strength of evidence which causes us to be convinced of the truth of a given meaning-pattern, and to act upon its strength.

Perfect coherence is that state in which symbols are so related one to another, that failure of acceptance involves one in self-contradiction, as in mathematics, geometry, and formal logic. In this case we have complete rational certainty. Imperfect coherence is that state of probability which need not be affirmed without involving one in self-contradiction, as in the inductive inference that Goethe died in the year 1832. Observe, however, that whether the rational certainty be perfect or imperfect, wherever the mind detects a state of coherence, complete moral or subjective certainty follows. One is morally no less sure that Goethe died in 1832 than that two times two is four, though the rational certainty of the former is less than that of the latter. Whenever a man says, 'I believe this is

17. *Twentieth Century Philosophy* (Runes, ed.), p. 206.

true," he *has* complete moral assurance; in other words, he is acting on the strength of the evidence.

It is of the very nature of hypotheses that they need not bear complete rational certainty to be embraced by the soul. Plato was well aware of that. He contended that, since we cannot have perfection in life, we may as well settle for a 'second best.' "As is familiar to all students, Plato has the category of the second best, which he uses in all kinds of circumstance. Failing the best, we should avail ourselves of the second best . . . In fact, it is an inevitable compromise so long as the soul is in the body."[18] It is impossible rationally to demonstrate that there was a Second World War, but that fact does not result in a lessening of moral assurance that there was this international conflict. Rational probability and complete or perfect moral assurance are by no means incompatible. We are morally assured that there was a man called George Washington, though the rational evidence for his existence is only probable. All the mind need be convinced of is coherence to be morally assured. Not to act upon the strength of coherence, or to attempt to do so, is to flee in the face of what the intellect reports to be true, in which case the act is immoral. Thus, the arguments for Christianity—though but probable in rational strength—move the Christian to act upon the supposition of the truth of the Christian faith. The evidences for the Way—their nature, extent, and interlocking—create in the Christian a powerful impulse in the direction of Christianity's truth. Once again we have complete moral certainty from a system which is but rationally probable. The Christian *can* say with Paul, I *know* whom I have believed.

IV. Objections to Probability

A. History is Ineffective as a Foundation for Faith

Not all theologians are assured that faith can rest upon those historical acts of Christ which were not done in a corner.

---

18. Demos, *The Philosophy of Plato*, pp. 26-27.

"The reason that historical truths," says Nygren, "are insufficient as a foundation for faith is their relative degree of certainty. Even the facts most definitely ascertained possess but relative certainty, while the very nature of faith requires absolute certainty for its foundation."[19] We can dispose of this objection easily, for it confounds rational with moral certainty. First, why should faith be exempted from the general rule that all belief is subjected to the law of contradiction in the light of the facts of history? What higher floor in the building of knowledge is there than coherence? Secondly, on this basis Christianity cannot be defended and the problem of the one within the many remains unsolved, for Christianity *is* an historical religion. "That which was from the beginning, which we have *heard,* which we have *seen with our eyes,* which we have *looked upon and touched with our hands,* concerning the word of life" (I John 1:1). Christianity's coherence is its power to explain history as well as its ability to maintain logical self-consistency. When we reject history, we either fall back on formal logic and mathematics, which cannot draw near to the real world, or we fall back upon some mystical, ineffable, esoteric, subjective, faith-leap, in which case the voice of God cannot be distinguished from the voice of the devil. The Christian would prefer to be erroneously labeled a 'rationalist' rather than give up his faith in a rational God, who made a rational universe with rational minds in it, in favor of a religious immediacy where all universality and necessity is lost.

B. Makes God a Matter of Probability

It seems that if Christianity is but probable, we pray to a God who but *probably* exists. The fallacy of this is the same. The mystic who shuns evidence which is external and the Christian who basks in it, are both convinced that God exists; the former through some 'inner light,' or private persuasion, and the latter through a rational appraisal of the evi-

19. Quoted in Ferré, *Swedish Contributions to Theology,* p. 55.

dences of logic and history. The mystic prays to the God that he is fully convinced exists and the Christian does likewise. Between the two there is no difference as far as the strength of the moral certainty is concerned—both are persuaded, mystic and Christian. The difference between them is marked, however, when we compare their rational merits. The Christian has moral certainty plus a rationally conceived system of thought, while the mystic has moral certainty without a rational basis. We may answer our question now by pointing out that just as George Washington's existence is sure, though it can be established only by rational probability, so also God's existence is sure, though the strength of our apprehending it is but probable. One may be morally certain that God exists, and pray with full assurance, though the objective evidence is but rationally probable.

C. Makes Christianity Tentative

If Christianity is but probable, it seems to be tentative and uncertain, and, like natural law, subject to change without notice. This is not enough for faith. First, the Christian admits that Christianity is true only as long as it is horizontally self-consistent and it vertically fits the facts. Not to say this would be to betray all we have said so far. To hold to Christianity after it had been shown to be incoherent would be to remove our only basis for telling the word of God from the suggestions of the devil. Secondly, let us distinguish between the system of Christianity and the rational proof that sustains it. The system is final, though proof for it is but probable. Christianity claims to be based upon a supernatural revelation from God. This distinguishes it from the laws of science; the latter are subject to change because they are made by man, but the former (if true) has been sent by God. True revelation is as immutable as its Giver. Establishing the fact that it *is* a valid revelation may not soar above probability, but that does not jeopardize the finality of the system *qua* system.[20]

Let us sum up our analysis of the criteria of verification and proceed to a new topic. Having no perfect system of thought while we walk by faith and not by sight, the Christian suggests that a rational man settle for that system which is attended by the fewest difficulties. The worth of a system of thought is conditioned to its ability significantly to answer those basic questions of life which all men must face. In the light of these observations the Christian throws forth his major premise—the existence of God Who has revealed Himself in Scripture—as a foundation for rational coherence.[21]

---

20. Machen rightly challenges the duplicity of those modernists who reject the absoluteness of Christianity and yet continue to call themselves Christians. "At the foundation of the life of every corporation is the incorporation paper, in which the objects of the corporation are set forth. Other objects may be vastly more desirable than those objects, but if the directors use the name and the resources of the corporation to pursue the other objects they are acting *ultra vires* of the corporation. So it is with Christianity . . . the question what Christianity is can be determined only by an examination of the beginnings of Christianity." Machen, *Christianity and Liberalism*, p. 20. Is one still an Aristotelian who follows Bergson? Can one be a Christian who rejects the validity of the documents which support Christianity?

21. It may seem that we have by-passed the Roman Catholic objection to our structure to the effect that Protestants are impotent to apply their criteria of horizontal self-consistency and vertical fitting of the facts. Lippmann sums up the problem in his *A Preface to Morals*, p. 34. "Complete as was Dr. Machen's victory over the Protestant liberals, he did not long remain in possession of the field. There is a deeper fundamentalism than his, and it is based on a longer continuous experience. This is the teaching of the Roman Catholic Church. From a priest of that church, Father Riggs, has come the most searching criticism of Dr. Machen's case. Writing in the *Commonweal* Fr. Riggs points out that 'the fundamentalists are well-nigh powerless. They are estopped, so to speak, from stemming the ravening waters of agnosticism because they cannot, while remaining loyal to the (Protestant) reformers . . . set limits to destructive criticism of the Bible without making an un-Protestant appeal to tradition.' Father Riggs, in other words, is asking the Protestant fundamentalists, like Dr. Machen, how they can be certain that they know these *facts* upon which they assert that the Christian religion is founded." The answer to this is easy. The Christian knows the facts upon which he bases his system by the grammatico-historical method. How does the Roman Catholic scholar know? By tradition? How does he know the tradition? By another tradition? He must stop somewhere, and when he does, he will either advance the criteria that we have suggested, or he will retreat to a religious immediacy and mysticism. If he elects the former, he has no case against Machen; and if he chooses the latter, he cannot verify his tradition.

Chapter VII

Starting Point: Nature

As for the word that you have spoken unto us in the name of Jehovah, we will not hearken unto you. But we will certainly perform every word that is gone forth out of our mouth, to burn incense unto the queen of heaven, and to pour out drink-offerings unto her, as we have done, we and our fathers . . . for then we had plenty of victuals, and were well, and saw no evil. But since we left off burning incense to the queen of heaven, and pouring out drink-offerings unto her, we have wanted all things, and have been consumed by the sword and by the famine.—Book of Jeremiah.

INASMUCH as one is inside a system of philosophy before he knows the details of just how he arrived there, probably no more difficult question can be faced in setting up a world-view than that of starting point. This is especially true of Christianity, for most of its followers have either been reared in its precepts or have been converted into it as a system of theology *en bloc*. But personal satisfaction within a system of thought is not enough to win others to it. To a person outside of the Christian fold, Christianity, rather than being coherent, seems a least likely candidate for truth. It is thus very necessary that we detail with care that crucial step which one must take to work his way into an appreciation of a given movement of thought.

Two schools of thought vie for recognition on the issue of starting point and its importance. The one claims that a starting point determines the system,[1] while the other thinks it a

---

1. Lewis, *Mind and the World-Order,* p. 1. "The general character of any philosophy is likely to be determined by its initial assumptions and its method."

matter of indifference.[2] The latter position seems to be the more cogent, as it appears to be of little consequence where one begins an investigation, as long as he is true to all of his experience before he is through. If a coin is lost on a plot of grass, obviously one can start here or there without jeopardizing his chances of finally finding the piece of money, providing, of course, that he has enough time to cover the entire area before he turns away. The same seems to be so in philosophy; but in reality the cases are not parallel, and this for at least two reasons. First, a philosopher has but threescore years and ten, and thus cannot cover all relevant experience possible. To overcome this deficiency man compensates by becoming set in his way and thinking that he *has* covered all of the germane experience. Once an empiricist, always an empiricist. The exception only serves to establish the cogency of the rule. Secondly, when one begins his philosophy apart from the assumption of the existence of a rational God, he has thrown himself into a sea of objectively unrelated facts. Even in infinity a finite man could not succeed in uniting the endless facts which are sired out of the womb of chance. And even if he did. his interpretation would be subject to change without notice, for the flux of reality might shift at any moment.

The Christian believes that starting point controls both method and conclusion. Philosophy is like a railway without switches—once a man is committed to a given direction, he is determined in his outcome. Should he change his mind about the wisdom of his course, his only recourse is to go back and start on another track. A change from idealism to pragmatism involves a change in starting point, method, and conclusion.

I. The Nature of Starting Point

Broadly speaking, *experience* is the only possible starting point for any philosophy, for thought does not operate in a vacuum; a man must be alive to think, and to think is to have

2. Brightman, *A Philosophy of Religion,* p. 343. "In any event, one's starting point is not decisive in a philosophical investigation. The main thing is to include the whole range of relevant experience before we are through."

experience. But in saying this we have said very little, for the fact that we begin thinking with experience does not constitute a point of dispute among philosophers. The skeptic as well as the absolute idealist begins with experience. Let us therefore break up the question into more precise dimensions. Three general starting points are discernible—temporal, logical, and synoptic. Our terms are wholly arbitrary, but they represent three genuine approaches to a philosophic system.

A. Temporal Starting Point

By this we mean that natural conditioning which one receives as he passes from adolescence to adulthood, when prejudices, proclivities, and presuppositions become a real part of the philosopher's equipment.[3] We may pass over this level, however, for it is common to all men and therefore cancels out.

B. Logical Starting Point

The logical starting point is the coordinating ultimate which gives being and meaning to the many of the time-space universe. For Thales it was water; for Anaximines it was air. For Plato it was the Good; and for the Christian it is the Trinity. The logical starting point is the highest principle which one introduces to give unity and order to his interpretation of reality. This is why it is the *logical* starting point—it is what one logically conceives as the over-all synthesizing element which unites the particulars.

C. Synoptic Starting Point

All logical ultimates must be tested, however, and the only way to do this is to work out a still more primitive starting procedure. The synoptic starting point is the servant of the logical starting point. It is the answer to the question, How

---

3. Typical is Kant. "His mother was a Pietist . . . Our philosopher was so immersed in religion from morning to night that on the one hand he experienced a reaction which led him to stay away from church all through his adult life; and on the other hand he kept to the end the sombre stamp of the German Puritan, and felt, as he grew old, a great longing to preserve for himself and the world the essentials, at least, of the faith so deeply inculcated in him by his mother." Durant, *The Story of Philosophy,* p. 285.

do you prove the logical starting point? A man will synoptically start his textbook in philosophy at that point which, when carried out to the end, will establish the grounds for what the system requires as its logical starting point. The worth of a synoptic starting point is conditioned to its ability to make good the case for the logical starting point. For a man to say that he begins his system with God is not to say anything significant, until it is pointed out when and how this starting point can be enjoyed.

Since the divergence between philosophies grows out of variously conceived synoptic starting points, it is most important that we be precise at this juncture in our study. As we conceive it, there are three synoptic starting points: internal ineffable experience, internal effable experience, and external effable experience. Let us expatiate a bit on these.

1. *Internal ineffable experience.* This is that activity of consciousness which brings an immediate assurance to the soul of reality that is overwhelming and ineffable, as the mystic experience of being swallowed up in God. We must pass over this for reasons stated earlier. Truth is systematic consistency and must be expressed in communicable propositions. But this is impossible in mysticism.

2. *Internal effable experience.* Not all experience in the soul is incapable of being expressed in words. As the history of rationalism proves, myriad are those keen minds which have been convinced that through a search of the soul's resident abilities universal and necessary principles, which are independent of sense perception, can be located and plotted. This is the course which the Christian will follow, so let us by-pass it for the time being to return to it later. The security of this position is not to be confused with mysticism's ineffable subjectivism, however, for by the method of effable internal experience "a truth is seen in its relations to other knowledge, and so with something of the certainty that goes with demonstration," but it is "no unique and mystical warrant that guarantees it, but mere coherence."[4]

---

4. Blanshard, *The Nature of Truth,* II, p. 224.

3. *Effable external experience.* Disappointed with the little which can be found by searching the soul, men have turned to the sense perception as the vehicle of the data out of which knowledge is built. Started classically by Aristotle and Aquinas, this method, known as empiricism, has enjoyed tremendous attention. We shall reject it, however, because of its inability to provide immutable truth. Truth, like water, rises no higher than its source.

II. A Critique of Natural Theology

As theology is the 'science of God,' natural theology is that method of epistemology which one follows when he seeks to establish the existence of God from an examination of the content of sense perception. Thomas Aquinas defended natural theology in classic dimensions. "The only road which can lead us to a knowledge of the Creator must be cut through the things of sense."[5] "Faith presupposes natural knowledge, even as grace presupposes nature and perfection the perfectible."[6] This means that Thomas is closed up to all of the difficulties of a *tabula rasa* epistemology.

> Sense impressions are the only primary source of knowledge. *Nihil est in intellectu nisi prius fuerit in sensu.* There are no 'inborn ideas'; nor are there any notions, within the natural range of experience, infused into the mind by a Divine influence. Before the intellect has received the impressions of sense, it is *tabula rasa,* a tablet — the comparison is taken from tablets covered with wax for making notes — without any sign engraved on it. Stimulation of the senses by some object existing outside of the organism is the necessary condition for the start of mental life. If a sense is lacking, no corresponding ideas can be formed by the mind.[7]

Following Hugo of St. Victor, Thomas said that reason deals with what can be demonstrated, while faith deals with what is taken on authority. Reason can demonstrate the existence of God without the aid of revelation; it works only with data

---

5. Gilson, *The Philosophy of St. Thomas Aquinas,* p. 64.
6. Aquinas, *Summa,* I. Q. 2, A. 2.
7. *Essays in Thomism* (Brennan, O.P., ed), p. 41.

abstracted from the world of sensation. Thomas wavers in this *tabula rasa* epistemology, however, when he confesses that "to know God exists in a general and confused way is implanted in us by nature,"[8] for, if the knowledge of God is not innate, how then can it be 'implanted' in us by nature?

Let us examine the theistic proofs which Thomas uses to demonstrate the existence of God from sense experience. If Thomas can succeed in this imposing demonstration, surely the gesture will dwarf anything which centuries of careful application of the scientific method has begun to enjoy.[9]

A. Empirical Proofs for God's Existence

1. *From motion.* Motion is the change which a thing undergoes when it goes from potency to act, as the boy, who may grow, grows. Unless one can trust his senses that motion is real, life is an illusion and nothing has meaning. But for an object to go from potency to act, it must be acted on by another, even as the growing boy is acted upon by the nutrients in the body. If this were not so, everything would simultaneously be in act and in potency, a state of affairs repugnant to reason. Every act is the result of act. But we cannot go to infinity, for then there would be no first act and, hence, no subsequent motion. But there *is* subsequent motion. Therefore, a Prime Mover exists, and this we know to be God.[10]

2. *From efficient cause.* Sense perceptions inform us that there are effects which follow from efficient causes. But an efficient cause cannot be the cause of itself, for then it would be anterior to itself, which is contradictory. This series cannot go to infinity, for then there would be no first efficient cause and no intermediate causes and effects. But experience abun-

---

8. *Summa,* I. Q. 2, A. 1.

9. Let us be careful to point out that Thomas is referring to deductive *demonstration,* not probable induction, in his proof for God. "We can *demonstrate* the existence of God from His effects." *Summa,* I, Q. 2, A. 2. This means that the proof must bear the same compulsion as a mathematical equation or a case of the syllogism.

10. "We say therefore that God is a living being, eternal, most good, so that life and duration continuous and eternally belong to God; for this *is* God." Aristotle, *Metaphysics,* XII (1072b).

dantly testifies to the existence of intermediate causes. Therefore, God, the first efficient Cause, exists.

3. *From contingency.* Experience teaches us that all things are dependent for their being upon another, since they are capable of either being or not being. But, if everything can not-be, then, in infinite time everything would not-be, since in infinity all possible combinations are consummated. But from nothing, nothing can come; therefore, nothing presently exists. But this is ridiculous. Therefore, we must postulate a necessary Being, and this all people call God. In short, if all is contingent, *i. e.,* if all depends for its existence on another, then God must exist as the Sustainer of contingency. Did not Kant even suggest that if *something* exists, something *necessarily* exists?

4. *From grades of perfection.* The arguments from motion and efficient cause account for the existence, not the perfection, of God. In the universe we see effects which are in the positive and comparative states—good, better, noble, nobler, etc. But these rest for their meaning upon their superlatives, for, without these superlatives, the comparatives are unintelligible. A thing is better only in relation to that which is best. But, as Thomas presupposes, no perfections can exist in the effect in a comparative degree which did not first exist in the cause as a superlative. The best is the exemplary cause of the better, and this exemplary cause is God.

5. *From government and teleology.* Experience tells us that nature is wisely managed, since bodies act for specific ends. But such action is the result of purpose, for teleology can stem only from a planning mind. Some cosmic mind must exist, then, to direct the acorn into the oak and the child into the man. Natural selection or mechanism are inadequate to account for the present order of perfection. The Being whose mind controls nature, all come to know as God.[11]

---

11. The full text of these proofs is located in the second question of the first part of the *Summa.* For reasons of economy we have not quoted them here.

B. General Objections to the Empirical Proofs

1. *Empiricism ends in skepticism.* Hume took Thomas' dictum, *nihil est in intellectu nisi prius fuerit in sensu,*[12] seriously and showed that by it nothing normative can be found. If all the mind has to work with are sense perceptions as reports to the mind of what is going on in the external world, knowledge can never rise to the universal and the necessary, for from flux only flux can come. One can never ascend to a demonstration of the immutable from evidence which the senses report, since they witness only to a succession of impressions. Augustine points out that immutable truth does not and cannot exist in mortal beings. "For, whatever exists in some thing cannot endure unless that endures in which it exists. But we have just granted that truth endures even when true things pass away. Therefore, truth does not have its existence in mortal things."[13] The skepticism of Hume results when one builds his epistemology upon the witness of sense experience. All one can do upon this basis is describe a series of disjointed impressions. To take immutability from the mutable would out-Houdini Houdini.

2. *Principle of economy eliminates the Christian God.* Hume has set the pace for all empiricists by dictating that the cause be proportionate to the effect, meaning that one may inductively introduce no more to explain an effect than a cause great enough to account for the effect, but not greater. Indeed if this rule were not rigidly enforced, one could demonstrate from the watch the age of the watchmaker, the color of his hair, the frequency of his shaving, and whether or not he takes Sunday afternoon walks by the lagoon. Is it not amazing, in the light of this rule of economy, that Thomas could *demonstrate* the unity, infinity, holiness, goodness, and eternity of God from the quivering of a single, finite blade of grass?

---

12. "There is nothing in the intellect which was not first in the senses." Famous Thomistic dictum. *Summa,* I, Q. 84, A. 6; Q. 85, A. 1. *De Veritate,* Q. 10, A. 6.

13. *Soliloquia,* I. 15.

The Trinity is infinite; therefore it is eliminated as that Being which may be proved by empiricism. The reason for this is that the world is finite—so say our senses—and to account for a finite effect one need introduce but a cause equivalent to produce the known effect.

> When we infer any particular cause from an effect, we must proportion the one to the other, and can never be allowed to ascribe to the cause any qualities, but what are exactly sufficient to produce the effect. A body of ten ounces raised in any scale may serve as a proof, that the counterbalancing weight exceeds ten ounces; but can never afford a reason that it exceeds a hundred. If the cause, assigned for any effect, be not sufficient to produce it, we must either reject that cause, or add to it such qualities as will give it a just proportion to the effect. But if we ascribe to it further qualities, or affirm it capable of producing other effects, we can only indulge the license of conjecture, and arbitrarily suppose the existence of qualities and energies without reason or authority.[14]

This conclusion of Hume is too evident to labor over. The Christian God is infinite; while all one needs to explain a finite universe is a finite god. Therefore one cannot *empirically* introduce the Christian God as that cause which demonstrably follows from an examination of a flow of sensory impressions. Empirically something *less* than God is required to account for things. We stress this here for two reasons. First, Thomas meant empirically to demonstrate an infinite God. He failed. Secondly, without the Trinity the problem of the one within the many cannot be solved. With this loss goes the loss of truth, a rational view of the universe, and personal hope in immortality. The loss is not to be minimized.

3. *The fallacy of impartation.* Thomas retorts that he is freed from the pincers of the economy rule by appealing to the dictum of impartation, viz., that the Cause of the world did not exhaust His attributes in giving being to the world, but merely imparted some of them, a proportionate amount. The artist who molds the clay is a cause which possesses all of the

---

14. Hume, *Inquiry,* Section XI.

perfection found in the effect, "and it may possess more."[15] Thus, we *can* defend the Trinity, for a cause may have more perfections than are imparted to the effect.

Granted that a cause *may* have more perfections than are seen in the effect—as the watchmaker *may* possess more attributes than are seen displayed in the work of any one watch—yet, there is no *empirical* way of determining whether or not the added perfections presumed present in the cause are actually there—as one cannot demonstrate from the watch that the watchmaker *could* have made a better watch: he *may* have expended all of his ability on *this* watch. The principle of economy is iron clad. From the proposition, 'All A is B,' by simple conversion one can only demonstrate the proposition, 'Some B is A,' although, to be sure, 'All B *might* be A.' The proposition informs us simply that B is at least as extensive as A; whether B is more extensive than, or is coextensive with, A, no hints are given in the problem itself. One can please himself and speculate, but in so doing he has left the realm of strict demonstration. In like manner, the finite universe does not *require* for its explanation the existence of an infinite cause. One might know on other grounds that God has more perfections than the universe displays—a method which we shall very shortly follow—but this method is not a demonstration. It is an inductive hypothesis based upon a careful analysis of the evidence. Demonstration is present only when a conclusion is shown to follow necessarily from a self-evident premise or when the contradictory of the proposition is shown to be false.

4. *Fallacy of the one God.* Empirically Thomas has tried to reason to the existence of *one* God by five different proofs. Why does this follow? We need a further empirical proof to show that one, not five different gods, is being demonstrated. How can we be assured that the God who is proved in the first argument is the same Deity who is the moral Governor of the world? Since none need to be infinite, for the effect is finite, there is room for not just five, but thousands of gods.

---

15. Burtt, *Types of Religious Philosophy*, p. 100.

5. *Fallacy of anticipation.* "Thomas and others, coming to the universe on revelational assumptions, could find God written in every area of it; there is more significance than usually thought in the statement that only a Christian could have framed the 'five-fold proof.' "[16] The Germans call this procedure *Tendenz*—that strong inclination which bends the investigator to a given conclusion before the data are examined.

Although Aristotle never dreamed of demonstrating a personal, creating, sustaining, God, the Deity which Thomas purported to arrive at was all of this and more. Aristotle's Unmoved Mover was ignorant of nature's present structure. It created nothing; it offered no self-revelation; and it maintained no providence over the universe. So un-Christian was Aristotle's principle of physics to account for motion, that men like Alexander of Aphrodisias (200 A. D.) interpreted Aristotle *naturalistically and behavioristically,* thus relieving the Stagirite of all theistic connotations.

Yet against all of this Thomas sets out to Christianize Aristotle's God. Why? Because he had a greater insight into the nature of empiricism than the Philosopher? Hardly, for he had access to no more data than did Aristotle before him. Rather, having learned to know and love God through His revelation, he then turned back to nature, pleading pure empiricism. Armed with the conviction that the Trinity is the true God, Thomas had no difficulty reintroducing into the system of Aristotle such notions as divine creation, exemplarism, and providence. The very eagerness which Thomas evinced to renovate Aristotle is glaring proof that he anticipated nature with a God that he found by other than empirical means. William Adams Brown sums up this fallacy well.[17]

> The professed purpose of the argument is to discover a cause adequate to account for the world we see, but the implied assumption is that this cause must at the same time be such as to satisfy the religious longings and needs of man. But this result is possible only as we read into the evidence data

---

16. Henry, *Remaking the Modern Mind,* p. 225.
17. *Pathways to Certainty,* p. 160.

> which our religious intuitions supply; in other words, as we introduce into our procedure judgments of value of a kind which ordinary scientific reasoning excludes.

This observation applies to Thomas and not to the conservative because the former, unlike the latter, is appealing to empirical demonstration as a basis for knowledge of God. Aristotle demonstrated a principle of physics; Thomas used exactly the same arguments and came out with a personal God. Was this not because Thomas *already* had heart-experience of the true God? Now, "if God were a personality, manifesting Himself in the values, but transcending them, it was impossible any longer to conceive him on Aristotle's model, for a personality is interested and active."[18]

6. *Predicament of commitment.* When one starts off his philosophy in a given way, he is committed to its implications to the bitter end. By following empiricism, one proves (if the arguments are valid) not the Christian God, but the God of Aristotle. Now, once we are committed to this position, how can we show that what we have demonstrated is the Father of Jesus Christ? Another demonstration is in order to show this transition. Some try to avoid the difficulty by saying there is no problem at all. "What Catholic theology does maintain is that reason by itself can discover *a* God, and that this God which it discovers is already the true God, precisely because there is no other, and that whatever truth we know about God can consequently apply to Him alone."[19] This argument does not succeed, however, for it assumes the very point in question —namely, that the Christian God *is* the true God. That has by no means been demonstrated yet. The data of nature are satisfied by Aristotle's idea of highest form, so why move on to the more complex principle, the Trinity? Furthermore, why is the Unmoved Mover to be identified with the Trinity? Why not one of the gods of the heathen? A good empiricist ought to come forth with another demonstration to help us out

---

18. Joad, *God and Evil,* p. 224.
19. Gilson, *Christianity and Philosophy,* p. 38.

here. The inability of the God of Aristotle to be converted into the Christian Trinity by empirical demonstration is a warning to the Christian, not to Christianize Aristotle, but, rather, to reject the empiricism upon which the proof for this God is based.

7. *Nonempirical presuppositions.* To prove God's existence from the flux of nature requires concepts which cannot be found in nature itself. To know motion, one must first know its correlative, the unmoved; to know the caused one must first know the uncaused; even as to know the contingent one must know the noncontingent, imperfect the perfect, and relative the absolute. Thus, the empirical arguments for God are successful only by beginning with concepts which are significant when God is already known, for He alone is the unmoved, uncaused, noncontingent, perfect, and absolute. Nothing in the *panta rei* of history can give us a sensory impression of these concepts. All experience can offer is a series of pointer-readings; the flux of experience can be manipulated, but not known.

C. *Specific Objections to the Empirical Proofs*

1. *Argument from motion.* Although clearest to the mind of Thomas, this argument has lost its force today. The universe of the modern man is dynamic; it *is* in motion. Newton's first law of motion teaches that every moving body continues to move in the same direction and with the same velocity until inhibited by an external force. *Direction of motion,* therefore. not motion, is all that one need empirically explain. But change of motion can nicely be accounted for within the course of experience itself and any recourse to the postulate of an Unmoved Mover is rendered superfluous.

Next, since sense experience can tell us only that all things are in flux, we cannot appeal to the Aristotelian potency-act doctrine, the basis for the argument, in which case the validity of the structure collapses. According to Hume, the norm of empiricists, the mind has simply a flow of impressions. This observation eliminates the motions of act and potency, for all impressions are homogeneous. In experience alone we can discern no *connection* between impressions, thus there is no potency and act.

> As early as the eighteenth century, Hume had shown that there was no possibility of demonstrating either productive capacity or compulsion. There was, he pointed out, every reason for supposing that cause and effect were related *as if* the cause produced and necessarily produced the effect, but no ground for supposing that it actually did so. There were various answers to Hume, but none were convincing, except perhaps such as outflanked the problem by denying the existence of a world of physical events altogether.[20]

The intellect cannot be resorted to as a basis for the potency-act structure, for that is ruled out on a *tabula rasa* epistemology. Reason can only work with impressions and there is no impression of act or potency. Impressions just are.

Finally, motion, instead of being the most evident thing to the senses, is, in reality, a most wretched, complex affair. Empirically we can *describe* impressions, but we have no notion of what the essence of phenomena are. The electron, presumably the center of motion, is a mystery to the scientist. How, then, can motion be empirically appealed to as a proof for God? The unknown is generally known through the known, not through another unknown. The empiricist can not know the essence of motion from experience, for the impression of motion is not observed to carry along with it its own explanation. One does not solve an already difficult problem by introducing a more difficult one.

2. *Argument from efficient cause.* We may argue the same here. Hume carefully showed that what we think is a connection between cause and effect is but a fixation of the mind and does not represent a valid inference from sense perception. Cause and effect are but habits or conventions of the intellect which express invariably related impressions that have taken rise from one's viewing the concourse of flux. Causation "implies no more than this, that like objects have always been

---

20. Joad, *op. cit.*, p. 119.

placed in like relations of contingency and succession."[21] This removes the support of the argument.

Again, what the empiricist wants to know is why the universe need have an efficient cause at all. If no reason need be given for God's uncaused state, why not shift that prerogative to the universe? "By supposing it to contain the principle of its order within itself, we really assert it to be God; and the sooner we arrive at that Divine Being, so much the better. When you go one step beyond the mundane system, you only excite an inquisitive humor which it is impossible ever to satisfy."[22] Again,

> For ought we can know *a priori,* matter may contain the source or spring of order originally within itself as well as mind does; and there is no more difficulty in conceiving, that the several elements, from an internal unknown cause, may fall into the most exquisite arrangement, than to conceive that their ideas, in the great universal mind, from a like internal unknown cause, fall into that arrangement.[23]

3. *Argument from contingency.* If the universe is contingent throughout, of course, it must have a cause. That follows from the definition of contingent. But is there any empirical evidence that the *whole* universe is contingent? Hardly. We have not begun to explore all of this world. The most optimistic approach one can take is to say that *to date* all observable facts are contingent. But can "a conclusion, with any propriety, be transferred from parts to the whole? Does not the great disproportion bar all comparison and inference? From observing the growth of a hair, can we learn anything concerning the generation of a man? Would the manner of a leaf's blowing, even though perfectly known, afford us any instruction concerning the vegetation of a tree?"[24] When Thomas reasons from contingency to the existence of God,

---

21. Hume, *Treatise,* Book I, Part III. It will do no good to reply that Hume leads to skepticism, for that simply makes the predicament of Thomas all the worse, for he, no less than Hume, is an empiricist.
22. Hume, *Dialogues,* Part IV.
23. *Ibid,* Part II.
24. *Ibid.*

he has ceased playing the role of an empiricist. One ought at least wait until he has looked the other side of the moon over before he is so sure that all is contingent. Perhaps there is some noncontingency there that will satisfy our need.

4. *Grades of perfection.* Empirically this is very weak, for from sensation alone one can draw no distinction between good and bad, perfect and imperfect. An empiricist can only describe what happens in the world of change, for beyond bare description he is no longer an empiricist. *Tabula rasa,* it is meaningless to speak of a four-legged calf as being *better* than a five-legged one. The latter, no less than the former, is but a series of impressions to the observer. The five-legged calf is a five-legged calf and the four-legged calf is a four-legged calf. Whatever good or bad there is in nature is supplied by the judgment of the observer and has no ontological status in *rerum natura.*

But if one persists in believing that positive and comparative adjectives—good, excellent, noble, etc.—depend for their present here-and-now signification upon the ontological status of certain superlatives, it certainly ought to follow that *all* adjectives which are capable of comparative and superlative degrees have ontological counterparts, likewise. Bad, therefore, yields an absolute badness. If the response be that all *being* is good, that there can be no superlative antecedents for evil or bad for they are negatives, the question then turns upon the issue of where the *empiricist,* who claims *tabula rasa,* and is shut up to the flux of nature, has located this evidence that only being is good. To the candid observer the bad seems to be just as ontologically real as the good. One either admits that all adjectives have their objective superlatives—mean yields the meanest, weak the weakest, etc.—or he denies this and leaves his empiricism. If one is empirically justified in hypostatizing *some adjectives,* there seems to be no logical stopping point short of empirically reifying them all. But this would prove too much.

5. *Teleology and government.* This is the most impressive theistic proof, for even the most crass logical positivist must

confess that the symbols he uses in correlating nature take on a pattern of symmetry and order, despite his effort. Unless one is to be completely blind to the empirical evidence, he must confess with Kant that there is an order to the world which evidences such an astonishing conformity to ends that one can hardly resist the temptation to postulate a self-subsisting something behind it as a cause.[25]

Granted the validity of the argument from perfection, however, one must be careful to stay within empirical evidence when he reasons *tabula rasa.* Conscientiousness in empiricism indicates that life is a mixed affair: partly good and partly bad. Shall we then reason from this to an *absolutely* good God? It is difficult to see how this follows. The presence of evil is indisputable.

> Look round this universe. What an immense profusion of beings, animated and organized, sensible and active! You admire this prodigious variety and fecundity. But inspect a little more narrowly these living existences, the only beings worth regarding. How hostile and destructive to each other! How insufficient all of them for their own happiness! How contemptible or odious to the spectator! The whole presents nothing but the idea of a blind Nature, impregnated by a great vivifying principle, and pouring forth from her lap, without discernment or parental care, her maimed and abortive children![26]

When one beholds the history of humanity, the struggle of animals, the untold waste and destruction in nature, the ruthless slaughter of human values, and the death of the universe under the hand of the second law of thermodynamics, it is

---

25. "The world around us opens before our view so magnificent a spectacle of order, variety, beauty, and conformity to ends, that whether we pursue our observations into the infinity of space in the one direction, or into its illimitable divisions on the other, whether we regard the world in its greatest or its least manifestations — even after we have attained to the highest summit of knowledge which our weak minds can reach, we find that language in the presence of wonders so inconceivable has lost its force, and number its power to reckon . . .The universe must sink into the abyss of nothingness, unless we admit that, besides this infinite chain of contingencies, there exists something that is primal and self-subsistent." Kant, *Critique of Pure Reason,* Transcendental Dialectic, III, VI.

26. Hume, *Dialogues,* Part XI.

difficult *empirically* to affirm that the universe is as perfect as the defenders of Aristotle's arguments must have it for the arguments to be significant.[27] Is it not evident that when we reason after the pattern of the relation between the artist and his work, the poorer the work the less perfection we attribute to him? A chip on the statue or a flaw on the canvas makes the artist inferior. Is not God, then, less than all perfect? One can think of an endless number of ways to improve the universe, ranging from the removal of mosquitoes and ants at picnics to the placing of two hearts in man, one to pump blood while the other is being repaired. In short, the universe evinces too much evil in it to bear the weight of the teleological argument.

D. Conclusion

One more point. Even if we should set up the notion of infinite mind, Hume wonders how much empirical worth such a concept has. "A mind, whose acts and sentiments and ideas are not distinct and successive; one, that is wholly simple, and totally immutable, is a mind which has no thought, no reason, no will, no sentiment, no love, no hatred; or, in a word, is no mind at all. It is an abuse of terms to give it that appellation."[28]

Let us conclude our challenge of empiricism at this point by reminding our readers that if truth is to be universal and necessary, it cannot be derived from an analysis of sense perception, for from flux only flux can come. Empiricism's conclusions are always subject to another look. Thomism cannot succeed in solving the problem of the one within the many because of its fatal empirical epistemology.

---

27. "A thousand vital germs but one remains alive; the others perish during the different stages of development from a lack of favorable conditions of growth, though they are in themselves capable of life. Destruction is the rule, preservation and evolution, the exception." Paulsen, *Introduction to Philosophy*, p. 166.

28. Hume, *Dialogues,* Part IV. The reader may construe that our arguments against Thomas apply to the conservative also, but this is not so. The solution to Christianity and the problem of evil will be dealt with below under the chapter of the same heading. To anticipate, the conservative starts with God, not external sensation, thus preserving him from the slough of flux.

Chapter VIII

Starting Point: Nature (Continued)

To whom then will you liken me, that I should be equal to him? saith the Holy One. Behold, the nations are as a drop of a bucket, and are accounted as the small dust of the balance: behold, he takes up the isles as a very small thing. And Lebanon is not sufficient to burn, nor the beasts thereof sufficient for a burnt-offering. All the nations are as nothing before him; they are accounted by him as less than nothing, and vanity.—Isaiah.

THERE is another way to lay bare the inadequacies of empiricism to solve the problem of the one within the many. It is by an exposé of the classic Scholastic-Aristotelian doctrine of the 'analogy of being.' We shall be very brief here, for the analogy is far too technical a question to go into with any thoroughness in a book of this type. Furthermore, we feel quite sure that we can lay our finger on the whole trouble in a very few pages.

I. The Structure of the Analogy of Being

A. No Innate Knowledge

Following the philosopher, Aristotle, Aquinas rejected the Platonic doctrine that the criteria of truth are innately implanted in the mind of man, thus marking an epoch in the history of Christian thought. Before 1225, Plato's theory of knowledge, under the influence of the bishop of Hippo, Augustine, dominated the epistemological scene; but after 1225, Aristotelianism, through Thomistic and Arabian prestige, came into that position of power which it today enjoys in Catholic theology. It may seem gnat-straining to point out that in Aristotle universals are lifted out of sensation and enjoy no antecedent existence in a world of Ideas, as in Plato; but history has proved that this teaching made the difference between the Western Church's preference of Christian empiricism to that of Christian rationalism. We contend that the gesture, if carried to its logical conclusions, is fatal for Christianity. The end of empiricism is positivism; and the end of positivism is Cratylus, who could not as much as speak, but only waved his hands.

Every empiricist is in a dilemma. The one who does not believe in God is troubled to find normative knowledge which holds good for tomorrow; while the one who does believe in God has that difficulty to face, *plus* the problem of locating concepts which may be predicated of God. All concepts must come from experience, but experience can only tell us what is not-God. The latter predicament is the lot of the Thomist. He defends the position that we have no innate knowledge of God, and thus is obliged to face the problem of how we finally manage to know God at all. "I say that this proposition, *God exists,* of itself is self-evident, for the predicate is the same as the subject, because God is His own existence as will be hereafter shown. Now because we do not know the essence of God, the proposition is not self-evident to us, but needs to be demonstrated by things that are more known to us, though less known in their nature—namely, by His effects."[1] This is our first observation. There is no efficient knowledge of God innate in our minds.

B. Problem of Predication

When we take a good look at what sense perception affords us, the plot thickens. All concepts seem useless when applied to God, for God occupies a different realm of being than do the facts from which our concepts have been drawn. Univocal predication of God, therefore, is impossible. "We can easily see the reason. All judgments applied to both the Divine and the human nature, employ the copula 'est.' But it has been

1. Aquinas, *Summa,* I. Q. 2, A. 1.

established that God 'is' not in the same sense in which creatures 'are.' The created being owns such perfections as it may possess, inasmuch as it has received them, while, on the contrary, in God there is nothing which is not His own being."[2] If empiricists are closed up to sensation for knowledge, where can they find any *rationes* (genera, universals, class-concepts) which may meaningfully be applied to Deity?

> Are we therefore to conclude that a proposition about a creature loses necessarily all meaning when applied to God? Such a conclusion would be inaccurate, and moreover dangerous. For to accept it would be tantamount to admitting that, taking our starting-point from creatures, we can know nothing of God nor prove anything concerning him without continual equivocations.[3]

C. *Via negationis*

May we not come to God by way of negation? Is it not as meaningful to say 'God is not this or not that' as to say that God is eternal—nontemporal, perfect—not imperfect, simple—not complex, and the like? Surely we can begin with sensation and know God.

But *negatio* in and by itself is not sufficient. First, we must know God to be able to say He is *not* this or that. How could we tell Him from 'this' or 'that' if we did not first know Him? Secondly, to say a piano is not a rhizome is to give us no clues to the principle of individuation in the piano which separates it from all other things which are likewise not rhizomes. For example, we know that a piano is not a rhizome, but that does not distinguish it from a nautilus which is also not a rhizome. We need more than the way of negation to help us. "We must accordingly admit, a certain analogy or proportion between the creature and the Creator, the basis of which is not hard to discover."[4]

---

2. Gilson, *The Philosophy of St. Thomas Aquinas*, p. 108.
3. *Ibid*, p. 109.
4. *Loc. cit.*

D. *Analogia entis*

Although we have not succeeded in getting from sensation any concepts which can be predicated about God, the Thomist has a ready solution to our predicament.

> Effects which are inferior to their causes, cannot be described in the same terms as the causes, nor especially in terms of the same meaning. Nevertheless, a certain resemblance between cause and effect must be conceded. Every productive thing produces naturally its like . . . Consequently, in a cause superior to its effect, the form of the effect may be traced in a certain sense, but not in the actual mode in which it occurs in the effect . . . For the same reason, and because God confers upon all things all their perfections, we are able to discover in all things their resemblance and unlikeness to God.[5]

The conviction that a cause imparts to the effect either all, a part, or a proportion of its perfections forms the basis of analogy of being. "From the knowledge of sensible things the whole power of God cannot be known; nor therefore can His essence be seen. But because they are His effects and depend on their cause, we can be led from them so far as to know of God *whether He exists*."[6] Let us here expend some effort to understand the analogy, since Thomists claim that "not a question can be asked either in speculative or practical philosophy which does not require for its final answer an understanding of analogy."[7]

As a preparation for the understanding of the analogy of being, let us review the relation between meaning and use of terms. Language is formed by the juxtaposition of names or terms, terms which may refer to different things while remaining unchanged themselves. For example, we say there is a 'lamb' in the field eating clover, and Christ is the 'Lamb' of God that takes away the sin of the world. Our term, 'lamb,' like all other names, may be used in three ways: univocally, equivocally, and analogically. Let us see what these three

---

5. *Idem.*
6. Aquinas, *Summa*, I. Q. 12, A. 12.
7. Phelan, *St. Thomas and Analogy*, p. 1.

senses are. A term is employed univocally when it "is predicated of things simply in the same sense. Thus 'man' is predicated univocally of various men, as 'animal' is predicated of the horse, the wolf, and the lion. For by these names is meant either the species that is simply the same in individuals of the species, or else the genus which is likewise simply the same . . . Thus the univocal concept admits of complete logical separation from the different subjects to which it is attributed."[8] "An equivocal term is one that is predicated of things in an entirely different sense. Thus 'lion' is predicated equivocally of the quadruped and one of the signs of the zodiac. Similarly 'dog' is predicated of the animal and of a certain constellation."[9] An equivocal term is an ambiguous term. The fallacy of 'equivocation' arises from the use of a word that may be taken in more than one meaning. Finally,

> An analogous term is one that is predicated of different things neither in simply the same sense nor in an entirely different sense, but according to a certain proportion or proportionality. An example of analogy of proportion or of attribution is the following: health is predicated primarily of the animal; and then proportionately, as referring to the healthy animal, the urine is said to be healthy (as a sign of health), the air, the food (as being the causes of health), medicine. . . . There is a proportion among these analogates, and extrinsic denomination suffices for this, as health is intrinsically in the healthy animal, and only extrinsically in the air, the urine. . . . Hence this analogy is also called analogy of attribution, because extrinsic attribution suffices for such analogy. An example of analogy of proportionality is the following: what the head is to the organic body, such is the general to his army, and the king to his kingdom.[10]

To review, terms may be used in one of three ways: with but one meaning (univocally), with different meanings (equivocally), and with a proportional meaning—partly the same, partly different (analogically).

---

8. Garrigou-Lagrange, *The One God*, pp. 395-396.
9. *Ibid.*, p. 396.
10. *Loc. cit.*

The empiricist, as we have seen, must abstract all of his terms for predication from sense perception. The question now becomes, which type of term may be used when predicating about God—univocal, equivocal, or analogical? How, in other words, may I say 'The stone is good' and 'God is good,' and mean anything by it? Do I use the term 'good' univocally? No, for it is impossible to relate two different orders of being by the same terms with exactly the same meaning to each. "Univocal predication is impossible between God and creatures."[11] Equivocally? Only in a very loose sense. "Therefore whatever is said of God and of creatures is predicated equivocally."[12] Analogically? Yes.

> Therefore it must be said that these names are said of God and creatures in an *analogous* sense, that is, according to proportion. This can happen in two ways: either according as many things are proportioned to one (thus, for example *healthy* is predicated of medicine and urine in relation and in proportion to health of body, of which the latter is the sign and the former the cause), or according as one thing is proportioned to another (thus, *healthy* is said of medicine and an animal, since medicine is the cause of health in the animal body). And in this way some things are said of God and creatures analogically, and not in a purely equivocal nor in a purely univocal sense. For we can name God only from creatures. Hence, whatever is said of God and creatures is said according as there is some relation of the creature to God as to its principle and cause, wherein all the perfections of things pre-exist excellently. Now this mode of community is a mean between pure equivocation and simple univocation. For in analogies the idea is not, as it is in univocals, one and the same; yet it is not totally diverse as in equivocals; but the name which is thus used in a multiple sense signifies various proportions to some one thing: *e.g., healthy,* applied to urine, signifies the sign of animal health; but applied to medicine, it signifies the cause of the same health.[13]

Univocation would (presumably) destroy the creature-Creation relationship, while equivocation would render meaningful

11. Thomas, *Summa,* I. Q. 13, A. 5.
12. *Loc. cit.*
13. *Loc. cit.*

predication impossible. "Between equivocation and univocation is analogy . . . it is a relation based on a comparison, a proportion, a relationship of two or more things to some one thing . . . analogous relations can obtain only when there is neither complete agreement nor complete disagreement between two things; there must be a union of agreement and difference."[14] In this mean between univocation (same term with same meaning) and equivocation (same term and different meaning) we lodge our predication about God and creature. When we say, 'The stone is good,' for example, the term 'stone' is used analogically, *i. e.,* partly the same and partly different. The being of the stone is to the stone as the being of God is to God. Both relationships are good, though the being of the stone and the being of God are not ontologically confused.

After this pattern we complete all of our predication of God, for "because God confers upon all things all their perfections, we are able to discover in all things their resemblance and unlikeness to God,"[15] as we have earlier shown. Univocation is rejected, because God and man belong to two wholly unique orders of being: God is necessary being and man is contingent being. Equivocation is rejected because by it "nothing at all could be known or demonstrated about God; for the reasoning would always be exposed to the fallacy of equivocation."[16] If we fuse the realms of being, we are back to Parmenides, while it we separate them completely we have the flux of Heraclitus. The *tertium quid* is supplied by the analogy of being, in which "names are said of God and creatures in an *analogous* sense, that is, according to proportion."[17]

II. A Critique of the Analogy of Being

The conservative sees two glaring fallacies in the analogy which prevent it from being a way out for the empiricist as he

---

14. Meyer, *The Philosophy of St. Thomas Aquinas*, pp. 128-129.
15. Gilson, *op. cit.*, p. 109.
16. Thomas, *loc. cit.*
17. *Idem.*

attempts to predicate about God those concepts which are abstracted from experience. Let us examine these two problems.

A. Built on a Contradiction

The contradiction is simply this: Thomas admits that there is no univocal element of relation existing between God and creation, and yet he turns to the analogy to lead us to the Almighty, *when the very thing which saves analogy from being sheer equivocation is its univocal element.* In the analogy, 'The mind is to the soul as the eye is to the body,' the univocal element is 'light' or 'guide.' When we say, 'The foundation is to the house as the heart is to the organism,' the univocal element is 'sustaining basis' or its equivalent. The success of *any* analogy turns upon the strength of the univocal element in it. If I tell some tribe in Africa that a steamship is like a canoe, they can understand the analogy only for the reason that there is a univocal element present—'force propelled conveyance for water transport.' If there is no univocal element, it is just like comparing wooflewumps with ear-pitchers: no *meaning* is conveyed. Without meaning there is no truth, for truth is properly construed meaning.

Without fear of confutation we may say that the basis for any analogy is non-analogical, *i. e.,* univocal. If we say, 'The boiler is to the engine as the muscle is to the body,' the univocal unit here is 'source of motive power.' If the analogy has no univocal element in it, it is simply an equivocation, and we object to ambiguity. If all of our *rationes* must be abstracted from sense perception, and if it be admitted that no name is predicated univocally of God and of creature, it follows that significant predication about God is impossible and we are no better off than the positivists. Where, in the whole gamut of our sensory experience, can we find that univocal element which a successful analogy requires, that we may use it in making a comparison between God and man? If the principals of proof originate in sense perception, how can the finished *rationes* be anything but sensible? How may the non-spatial be abstracted from the spatial? The spiritual from the material? The eternal from the temporal? The changeless from the flux? The intellect may be Oh so active! but it certainly cannot take from sensory experience what is not there.

There is but one way to complete an abstraction from nature: it is by setting aside the differentiating aspects of each item investigated and retaining the aspects which are common. For example, if I examine all animals—cats, cows, worms, elephants, sardines, and paramecia—as long as I examine vertebrate animals, I can only arrive at the abstract idea of 'vertebrate animals,' common to cats, elephants, cows, etc. But when I take in the worms and paramecia, I obtain a more abstract idea, perhaps of 'animal' in general. And if I include plants, I arrive at the still further abstract notion, 'living being.' But as long as 'animation' is common to all of the items examined, I cannot discard it. Similarly, if all I know of being is by way of examination of, and abstraction from, *sensible being,* I can never discard from my final abstract *rationes* the element of sensible being, for all my knowledge is freighted with it. By Thomistic abstraction, therefore, I have no basis for believing that from sense perception I can rise to a knowledge of the eternal and spiritual in the Almighty. By no act of philosophical legerdemain can the *rationes* which are abstracted from the time-space universe be applied meaningfully to God, for wherever the *rationes* go, there trails along the notion of *sensible being*—it is common to all concepts abstracted from sensation and cannot be discarded.

To admit simultaneously that we have no univocal knowledge of God, that all our knowledge comes from sensation, and that we can avoid ambiguity and equivocation by referring predication to the analogy of being, is a contradiction in terms; since the only element in analogy which preserves it from being equivocation is the univocal. If the univocal element is admitted, then, how do we account for it when *nihil est in intellectu nisi prius fuerit in sensu*? And if the univocal element is denied, how is equivocation avoided? We either give up the force of our empirical starting point or we admit that predication about God is impossible.

B. The Analogy Makes God Unknowable

When Thomas admits that essence and existence in God are the same, but that we do not know the essence of God, he gets himself in another difficulty. Gilson explains both the difficulty and his proposed solution. We shall attempt to show how he fails.

> But His essence remains unknowable to us; hence it should be the same with His existence. Lastly, is it not true, as we have suggested, that the principles of proof originate in sense-perception? And does it then not follow that all that exceeds the sense and sensible world, is unamenable to proof? Yet we are assured of the contrary by the word of the Apostle: *Invisibilia Dei per ea quae facta sunt, intellecta, conspiciuntur* (Romans 1:20). It is indeed incontestable that in God essence and existence are identical. But this is true of the existence in which God subsists eternally in Himself; not of the existence to which our finite mind can rise when, by demonstration, it establishes that God is. We are consequently able without attaining to the essence of God or the fulness of the infinite being which He possesses, to demonstrate this existence, expressed in the conclusion: God exists. Again it is certain that God exceeds all our senses and all sensible objects; but His effects, whence we start to establish His existence, are, on the contrary, sense-objects. The fact accordingly remains that our knowledge of the supersensible takes its origin in the sensible. But we must remember that in the argument whereby we prove the existence of God, we cannot take as principle the essence or quiddity of God, which is unknown to us. The proof *propter quid* being impossible, we are left with the proof *quia*. The only road which can lead us to a knowledge of the Creator must be cut through the things of sense.[18]

---

18. *Op. cit.,* p. 64. The Thomist's appeal to Romans 1:20 as support for his right to be an empiricist is *petitio principii.* If the view of Paul can be coherently explained in such a way that it is not peculiar to Thomism, then the argument from the apostle loses all of its force. Paul truly taught that God is known through sense perception, but that does not involve us in empiricism. May it not equally be that, *knowing* God (by innate knowledge, which Paul teaches) we are *reminded* of Him in His works? This may not seem forceful at once, but the implications of it will become clearer as we proceed.

Let us observe what is here admitted. God has two sides: as He is eternally in Himself and as He appears to us in an examination of the content of our sense perceptions. With this admission, two problems haunt us. First, how can we possibly know *that* a thing exists when we do not know *what* it is? What *is it* that we are talking about? What is the *Him* in the proposition, 'We know *Him* not as He is in Himself, but as He appears in His works'? If we do not first know *Him,* how can we possibly establish any relation between the *Him* and the as-He-appears-to-us God? If we do not know God's essence as it is in itself, it does not seem meaningful to speak of this essence, for we have no known means of ascertaining what the meaning of the term 'God' is. Without meaning, we repeat, truth is absent, for truth is systematically consistent meaning. The position of Thomas, therefore, is epistemologically impossible.

Secondly, the Thomistic empiricism throws both philosophy and religion into turmoil. Philosophically, the sluice gate is opened to unknowables when one defends an 'unknown God.' If we can continue to talk of God whose essence we do not know, we can also talk of snark, gobble-de-gook and splinth, whose essences are also mysteries.

> It should be perfectly clear that no man knows enough to assert the existence of an object of which he knows nothing. And not only so, but the assertion that an object exists of which nothing can be known reduces to skepticism, as the history of religion in France and the logic of the matter in Hegel demonstrate. The right of each man to assert the kind of unknowable he chooses throws all objectivity into confusion; and the implicit contradiction contained in asserting that something cannot be known cuts the foundation out from under any and all knowledge.[19]

Again, religiously speaking, we are forced on Thomistic epistemology to a place where, when we worship God, we have no way of knowing whom it is we worship. Because God is un-

---

19. Clark, *A Christian Philosophy of Education,* p. 177.

known, all we worship is a phenomenon—an object of appearance as distinguished from ultimate reality. This is hardly a sufficient basis for religion. On these three counts—epistemology, philosophy, and religion—we feel certain that there are fewer difficulties which attend Christian rationalism than attend Christian empiricism. Having rejected the latter, the onus is now on us to establish the former.[20]

---

20. Inasmuch as the word 'rationalism' seems to be attended by many unpleasant connotations, it is necessary to define what we mean by *Christian* rationalism.

We do not mean the ideal of classical rationalism, as in Descartes, for example; namely, that all knowledge is the same throughout and consists solely in combining what is self-evident. This ideal is patterned after the model of geometry: the passage from self-evident assumptions to necessary conclusions by way of valid premises. Classical rationalism is bottled up in what we have in an earlier connection called 'horizontal self-consistency.' We reject it as a theory of knowledge because reality has been ordered by the will and pleasure of a personal God, not by an abstract principle of rationality. Not all of our knowledge can be learned by logical anticipation.

According to Christian rationalism, however, a *part* of our knowledge can be learned by such anticipation. Since every human being is born with *a priori* equipment as part of the image of God — an endowment which belongs to man *qua* man — our first acts of knowledge in nature are possible because we already know other truths prior to sense experience. Christian empiricism denies this, contending that man must learn his first truths through sense experience.

This is the crux: Christian rationalism accepts the presupposition that the image of God in man means *at least* that we are born with a clear knowledge both of God and of His law. Rather than building up a knowledge of God through a patient examination of the content of sense experience, we proceed to such experience *equipped* with an awareness of God. Christian empiricism counters by insisting that the mind of the child is *tabula rasa* and that any knowledge we have of God comes either through sense perception or revelation. This is the issue which is in contest.

Chapter IX

Starting Point: God

The fear of Jehovah is the beginning of wisdom.
—Solomon.

THUS far we have been concerned with effable *external* experience. Let us now turn our attention to effable *internal* experience. In this gesture we are turning our affections from Christian empiricism to Christian rationalism. The story of empiricism, from Heraclitus to Hume, is a short history of skepticism. If *nihil est in intellectu nisi prius fuerit in sensu,* it is impossible to bring universality and necessity into truth, for from flux only flux can come. Cratylus, who would not so much as wave his hand to express his philosophy, was perhaps the only consistent empiricist; but one wonders how even 'hand waving' can be defended as normative by a *tabula rasa* epistemology. Empiricism, however, is a good thing to have around, for it has the 'nuisance value' of reminding us that "for experience to provide the mind with all the ideas it must have, there must already be in that mind certain other ideas which the experience itself could never provide."[1]

I. Transition to Christian Rationalism

The rationalist is convinced that the truths which we possess depend for their validity upon the prior existence of certain innate criteria of knowledge. Thus, as Augustine, a flaming Christian rationalist, taught, the mind, by natural endowment from the Creator, enjoys immediate apprehension of those standards which make our search for the true, the good, and the beautiful meaningful. The Christian, therefore, following

1. Martin *et al.*, *A History of Philosophy,* p. 483.

the *a priori* method, is careful to point out that "instead of beginning with facts and later discovering God, unless a thinker begins with God, he can never end with God, or get the facts either."[2]

A. Human Values and Epistemology

A value is anything which we prize or regard with worth, as, for example, the life of a little child or honesty and decency in character. Our entire intellectual, volitional, and emotional experiences revolve around what we conceive to be the valuable. The mind is drawn by the true, the will by the good, and the feelings by the beautiful. He who sees values in life, therefore, will tingle with zest for living, while he who does not may be tempted to commit suicide. To speak *meaningfully* of the true, the good, and the beautiful, however, we must have criteria; but criteria that are universal and necessary must be found other than in the flux of sense perceptions. We suggest, therefore, that to be significantly talked about, human values must be supported by value-standards which exist, not in the flux of nature, to be apprehended by sensation, but rather in the intelligible soul, to be perceived by an analysis of the content of rationality itself.

1. *The true.* We say a thing is true when it is systematically consistent. But where has this standard of coherence come from? How do we know that a thing must be coherent to be true, if the soul, by nature, is not in possession of the conviction? We cannot learn this piece of information from sensation, for it cannot give us truth which is normative for *tomorrow.* But truth *is* valid for tomorrow.

2. *The good.* All men know that whatever conduces to their well-being is the good, but how is it that we are able confidently to say that what is good today will be good tomorrow, unless we lodge our theory of the good in something outside the process of history? Perhaps what is good today will be bad

---

2. Clark, *A Christian Philosophy of Education,* p. 38.

tomorrow. But this conclusion we cannot tolerate. Butchering helpless infants must always be wrong!

3. *The beautiful.* The beautiful is that condition of symmetry and harmony which elicits a feeling of contented response from our soul when apprehended. But, without a changeless standard of art, what is to keep the Brandenburg Concertos of Bach from being neither more nor less beautiful than the howling of a timber wolf? Without a criterion of the beautiful, which can reach across the ages, the Phidian original is no better than its imitation.

B. Values, Metaphysics, and Human Conduct

Herman Bavinck has clearly stated the case for the Christian when he indicates that there is no morality without metaphysics. "Either norms of truth, goodness, and beauty have developed historically by evolution, and therefore are not absolute and the good of today may be evil tomorrow, or they have an absolute character, but then they are transcendent, metaphysical, and have their origin in divine thought and will. If everything resolves itself into a process, ideal norms of truth, goodness, and beauty lose their absolute character."[3]

1. *General observation.* Our theory of the true, the good, and the beautiful must be linked to the general character of the universe, or we have no means of telling what constitutes that which will conduce to our own well-being. As there is a 50/50 chance that we will fall into judgment before God, it is important that we weigh carefully the character of the universe, lest our actions bring severer judgment down upon us.

2. *Christianity and criteria.* What the Christian thinks of God controls what he thinks of the true, the good, and the beautiful, for God gives being to truth, content to the good, and permanence to beauty. The law of God is truth; keeping the law is good; and meditation upon, and enjoyment of, the law is the beautiful. The good is what God rewards and the bad what He punishes. Hence, only the true can be good, and

3. Jaarsma, *The Educational Philosophy of Herman Bavinck,* p. 102

only the good can be beautiful. The Christian rejects as spurious good or beauty, therefore, all things which cannot meet with the approval of God's law. The dance, for example, a form of recreation provided by God for human beings (II Samuel 6:14, Ecclesiastes 3:4), has been turned by the modern man into a mecca of lust, where soft lights, secluded corners, and emotion-stimulating music combine to reduce man to a passion-driven animal. This the Christian looks upon with disdain.

3. *Non-Christianity and criteria.* A typical paradigm of those who settled upon a false theory of truth, and were consequently led into a false theory of the good and the beautiful, are the Nazis of World War II. The memory of that horrible holocaust is fresh in our minds. Believing that Hitler's *Mein Kampf,* with its doctrine of the superiority of the so-called Aryan or Nordic race and the *Lebensraum* (living space) dogma, was the truth, the Germans patterned their concepts of the good and the beautiful after this *Weltanschauung.* The good was the exterminating of the inferior races, the slaughtering of the weak and the timid, and the subjugation of the recalcitrant. The beautiful was the swastika, the goose step, the screaming of those being cremated or excoriated, and the vicious program of state-sponsored motherhood. Truly, "how man conceives of his relationship to the Infinite and to the whole of reality vitally effects his conscious relationship to his fellow human beings."[4] If you want to know whether you ought to trust a man, or run from him, just ask him what he thinks of Him that is called the Christ, for a man is and does what his philosophy of life dictates.

C. *Values and the Necessity of Revelation*

It surely "is a matter of vital concern to the moral life of man whether reality recognizes and supports his ethical values and ideals or is totally indifferent or perhaps hostile to his ethical endeavors,"[5] but how can we know what the character

4. Jaarsma, *op. cit.*, p. 104.
5. *Idem.*

of all of reality is, so as to act wisely, unless God tells us? Will I be better off in the judgment if I turn to the left or to the right? "How can a man be just with God?" asks Job. Man has come on the scene without any original initiative of his own and he will fall into God's hands at the end of the process in the same manner. It is He that has made us and not we ourselves. Unless, therefore, He who made us tells us how He will dispose of us, happiness cannot be perfectly enjoyed. Revelation, then, is a condition *sine qua non* for our soul's well-being.

Since, however, the word 'revelation' is freighted with many clerical and ecclesiastical connotations which are foreign to the modern mind, it is well that we point out here what we mean by revelation. The Christian teaches that all insight into truth is an illumination by God of the heart, be that insight that two times two are four or that the grape is a fruit of the genera *Vitis* and *Muscadinia*. The Christian prays with a Kempis, "Send out Thy light and Thy truth, that they may shine upon the earth; for until Thou enlighten me, I am but as earth without form and void."[6] Revelation, then, is simply the disclosure by God of truth which was previously unknown. Truth is seen in light and this light is from God. "In thy light shall we see light" (Psalm 36:9). "Man can see light only in the Light; that all truth is the reflection into the soul of the truth that is in God; in a word, that the condition of all knowledge for dependent creatures is revelation, in the wider sense of that word."[7] By appealing to this structure of revelation, the Christian not only makes it licit for him to appeal to revelation, but also he makes it necessary for his opponent to do so too. Without revelation, there is no truth; for revelation is the light in which we see light.

Because he speaks of both 'natural' revelation, *i. e.,* the revelation of the meaning of reality in the facts of time and space, and 'special' revelation, *i. e.,* the propositional content of the Bible, the Christian can meaningfully speak of the 'incompetence' of the human reason. The reason of man, in addi-

---

6. *Imitation of Christ,* III. xxiii.
7. Warfield, *Studies in Tertullian and Augustine,* p. 161.

tion to being by nature corrupted through sin, is incompetent to work out a complete view of God and man because it, in its unaided state, is not supplied with enough information to complete its philosophy. The data which special revelation supplies is needed to supplement the data which natural revelation displays.

> Though the light which presents itself to all eyes, both in heaven and in earth, is more than sufficient to deprive the ingratitude of men of every excuse, since God, in order to involve all mankind in the same guilt, sets before them all, without exception, an exhibition of his majesty . . . yet we need another and better assistance, properly to direct us to the Creator of the world.[8]

Just as the intellect of man is incompetent to demonstrate that there is another side to the moon, because of the inaccessibility of the data, so also it is incompetent to complete a philosophy of life without special revelation from God. Because of our sinful hearts, which vitiate the evidence of nature, a more sure voice is needed to lead us into a theory of reality which is horizontally self-consistent and which vertically fits the facts.[9]

II. The Knowledge of God from the Self

Admitting that there are two types of revelation, then, natural and special, let us explore them one by one and see if we can be led into a more coherent proof for God than is the Thomist with his empirical epistemology. The first topic we shall discuss is the knowledge of God through general revelation. Every possible source that man has for knowing, save that of reading the Scriptures, is general revelation. The first source that we shall investigate is the knowledge of God from the

---

8. Calvin, *Institutes,* I, 6, 1.

9. This notion of incompetency is sharply to be distinguished from the Barthian doctrine that there is no point of univocity to unite the revelation from God to man. Revelation is an offense to man only because the latter is a sinner and not because the former is not propositionally veracious. The intellect of man is darkened, but it is not extinguished. If this were not so, the mind of man would be quite incompetent to distinguish the voice of God from the voice of the devil.

knowledge of the self. "We lay it down as a position not to be controverted, that the human mind, even by natural instinct, possesses some sense of a Deity."[10] After we have searched out what we can find from natural revelation, we shall return and explore the possibilities of knowing God from special revelation.

A. The Knowledge of God in the Cogito

Augustine, in refuting the skeptics of his day, turned to what has now come, through Descartes, to be a famous argument from the soul's thinking about thinking. It is, *cogito, ergo sum*—I think, therefore I am. When Augustine faced the sensationalists of his day who insisted that no changeless truth could be known, since all comes from flux-sensations, he asked them, "Do you exist?" If they said, "No," Augustine's position was correct, because there was no one there to dispute it. If they said, "Yes," then Augustine reminded them that they refuted their own position by admitting that *this* truth—that they knew that they existed—could be known. This is the argument from the *cogito.*

The *cogito* establishes four things. First, it succeeds in drawing our attention from sensationalism to the mind, the source of knowledge to which rationalists appeal. By it we are successfully carried into our starting point, 'internal effable experience.' Secondly, it is a rebuttal to all who say that there is nothing in the intellect which was not previously in the senses. Here is a piece of information that *is* found in the soul without any external sense perception. "Even he who says, 'I do not know,' thereby evinces not only that he exists and that he knows that he exists, but also that he knows what knowing is and that he knows that he knows it. It is impossible to be ignorant that we are; and as this is certain, many other things are certain along with it, and the confident denial of this is only another way of demonstrating it."[11] Thirdly, the *cogito*

---

10. Calvin, *op. cit.,* I, 3, 1.

11. Warfield, *op. cit.,* pp. 138-139. Sense perception and intuition are not to be confused. We never smell or taste our soul. We know it immediately.

provides us with a knowledge of God. Knowing what truth is, we know what God is, *for God is truth.* God is perfect consistency. In Him we move and have our being, physically *and* intellectually. This argument for God does not constitute a demonstration; rather, it is an analysis. By the very nature of the case, a fulcrum able to support the weight of a proof for God would have to be God Himself. God gets in the way of all demonstration of Deity, for His existence is the *sine qua non* for all demonstration. Proof for God is parallel to proof for logic; logic must be used to prove logic. Fourthly, the *cogito* allows us to make univocal predications about God, for we are not limited in our *rationes* to those which can be abstracted from sensation. In properly knowing ourselves, we know truth; and God *is* truth.

B. *God Involved in the Knowledge Of Our Finitude*

Now that we *know* that we exist, and that the truth of this existence leads us to meditate upon perfect Truth, which is God, further examination of the state of our existence leads us into a richer knowledge of the Almighty. For the *locus classicus* of this argument for God's existence, we turn to the oustanding theologian, John Calvin.[12]

> Our poverty conduces to a clearer display of the infinite fulness of God. Especially, the miserable ruin, into which we have been plunged by the defection of the first man, compels us to raise our eyes towards heaven, not only as hungry and famished, to seek thence a supply for our wants, but, aroused with fear, to learn humility. For, since man is subject to a world of miseries, and has been spoiled of his divine array, this melancholy exposure discovers an immense mass of deformity: *every one, therefore, must be so impressed with a consciousness of his own infelicity, as to arrive at some knowledge of God.*

Let us observe the movement of this argument carefully. Without the aid of sensation, man knows that he is finite, dependent, and wretched; but these adjectives would be absolutely meaningless without a prior knowledge of their correlatives, infinity,

---

12. *Op. cit.*, I, 1, 1.

independence, and felicity. These belong to God alone. "To know self implies, therefore, the co-knowledge with self of that on which it is dependent, from which it derives, by the standard of which its imperfection is revealed, to which it is responsible."[13] We know God as that Being over against Whom we are perpetually set, upon Whom we completely depend, and to Whom we are finally responsible. All of this we know from a knowledge of our own finite, sinful, infelicitous condition. This explains why the dog does not worry about death, while man does; the latter, unlike the former, has in his very heart the *sensus divinitatis* (sense of divinity). "Thus a sense of our ignorance, vanity, poverty, infirmity, depravity, and corruption, leads us to perceive and acknowledge that in the Lord alone are to be found true wisdom, solid strength, perfect goodness, and unspotted righteousness; and so, by our imperfections, we are excited to a consideration of the perfections of God."[14]

This structure blends nicely into the Christian doctrine of creation, for man is made in the image and after the likeness of God. Christ is the true Light which enlightens every man. The Christian shares the conviction of Descartes, therefore, that "one certainly ought not to find it strange that God, in creating me, placed this idea (God) within me to be like the mark of the workman imprinted on his work; and it is likewise not essential that the mark shall be something different from the work itself."[15] When man jumps in fear because of the crashing of the thunder about him, it is not simply because of irritated nerve endings: it is also due to a fear of God.

> For the most audacious contemners of God are most alarmed, even at the noise of a falling leaf. Whence arises this, but from the vengeance of the Divine Majesty, smiting their consciences the more powerfully in proportion to their efforts to fly from it? They try every refuge to hide themselves from the Lord's presence, and to efface it from their minds; but their attempts to elude it are all in vain. Though

---

13. Warfield, *Calvin and Calvinism*, p. 31.
14. Calvin, *loc. cit.*
15. *Meditation*, III.

> it may seem to disappear for a moment, it presently returns with increased violence; so that, if they have any remission of the anguish of conscience, it resembles the sleep of persons intoxicated, or subject to frenzy, who enjoy no placid rest while sleeping, being continually harassed with horrible and tremendous dreams.[16]

This is not mere wish-thinking; it is a sober appraisal of the facts of life. Observe the death of the Nazi war chiefs. After all of their years of indescribable cruelty and boasting that there was no God who would judge them, when it came to the dangling from the noose, they wept like babies, prayed with the priest, and asked the Judge of all men for forgiveness. The positivist may shrug his shoulders in the presence of this evidence, but perhaps he ought to reserve his judgment until that moment when the cold breath of death blows over *him*. It may be that he will change his mind. In the meantime the Christian *has* an hypothesis which can explain why men fear death.

III. The Knowledge of God through the *Rationes aeternae*

Further to show man's affinity to God and his distance from the brutes, let us turn to an analysis of what Augustine denominates the *veritates* (truths) or *rationes aeternae* (eternal concepts). "Along with his reason, it is now said, every man possesses by nature, that is, by his constitution as man, a body of ideas: they belong to his nature as a rational being. In making this step we have definitely passed over from Sensationalism to Rationalism."[17]

A. Logic

The first indubitable truth which Augustine located in an analysis of the act of reason itself is found in the field of logic or dialectics. "I am certain that the world is either a unit or not a unit, and that if it is not a unit, it is either finite in number or it is infinite."[18] From this, Augustine concludes that

16. Calvin, *op. cit.*, I, 3, 2.
17. Warfield, *Studies in Tertullian and Augustine*, p. 143.
18. *Contra Acad.* III, 10, 23.

"through dialectic I have learned that these things are true—as well as many other things, which it would be very tedious to enumerate—true in themselves, however our senses may be affected."[19] This innate character of the principles of dialectic was the same sort of a conclusion that Plato arrived at when he interrogated the little untutored slave boy that phenomenally did geometry. "If he did not acquire the knowledge in this life, then he must have had and learned it at some other time . . . And if there have been always true thoughts in him, both at the time when he was and was not a man, which only need to be awakened into knowledge by putting questions to him, his soul must have always possessed this knowledge."[20] In like manner Kant argued for the *a priori* character of the categories, reasoning that if science is to be possible, there must be more to knowledge than sensation can supply. But science *is* possible; therefore the categories are innate in the mind. Experience cannot supply them. In the same spirit, the Christian argues for the innate knowledge of logical consistency as the basis for truth.

First, the law of contradiction (and the laws of being and excluded middle, too, of course) must be innate if meaningful *sense perception* is to be possible. The 'telephone pole,' which I observe, cannot at the same time and in the same sense be the 'grass,' which I likewise observe. But, without the axiom of contradiction, this perception is impossible. Man thinks in concepts or universals; yet, until these universals receive the go-ahead sign from the law of contradiction, they cannot refer to anything. 'Telephone-poleness' cannot apply to anything until I see it as equal to itself and different from non-self. The law of contradiction thus permits me to separate the telephone pole from the grass, cows, and pigeons around it. If they all blurred together into some ethereal 'being,' obviously *significant* sensation would be impossible. A thing cannot be sensed until it is 'this' and not 'that.' But a *conditio sine qua non* for

---

19. *Ibid,* III, 13, 29.
20. *Meno* 86a.

the mind's so seeing things as 'these' and not 'those' *is* the law of contradiction.[21]

Secondly, the law of contradiction must be innate if *truth* is to be possible. Truth is a property of right judgment, but right judgment is already a condition to which the law has been applied. The process that man follows when learning is called 'discursion,' the running to and fro of the mind between facts until a coherent pattern of meaning is achieved; as opposed to God's changeless knowledge, by an eternal intuition, both of all the facts and their implications in every direction. When man relates subjects and predicates carefully, long enough, behold out comes a body of information; if it is coherent, we call it truth. But discursion, to be significant, must be *according* to something, else it would have no direction. Now, if man is ever to get started in discursion, he must have the guide for discursion within him; otherwise he would never succeed in rising above the brutes. "The animal lives in a world of perception; its thought on the whole is sense-bound; it expressly recalls no past and expressly anticipates no future."[22] If we have not innate knowledge of the rules for right thinking, right thinking cannot start; but right thinking *can* start: therefore, the rules are innate.

Thirdly, the law of contradiction must be innate if *speech* is to be possible. At some time the random sounds of the child change from a state of meaninglessness into a system of communication, such as the 'da da' to call for attention. The child learns to use certain signs to express certain wants, and, in the act, is engaged in conceptualizing. But a sign, to be meaningful, must stand for *something,* otherwise it would be a sign of no *thing,* and would consequently be no sign at all. Before the

---

21. It may be objected here that the brutes can tell things from one another, but do not know the law of contradiction. First, we are not prepared to say that the soul of the dog does not have a limited use of the law. Secondly, the imagination of the brute cannot rise to organized conceptions because full rationality is lacking. If the dog applies the law of contradiction to eat a bone, he cannot apply the law of contradiction to worship God because he is not made in God's image. Thus he does not have the *rationes* in that full sense that human beings do.

22. Blanshard, *The Nature of Thought,* I, p. 257.

first sign could have been used, however, the mind must have been aware of the axiom of contradiction which permits us to think of one being, one object, or one idea at a time. The child could never start speech without knowing *things;* but things can be known only by the law of contradiction. Therefore, since the child *does* begin to communicate, the law must be innate.

From this awareness of the soul of its own endowments it knows God, for only a transtemporal, trans-spatial Mind can sustain the timeless character of logic. We have not elected to be logical; another has made us that way. The smoothest hypothesis to account for this making is, not the brute bumping of undirected atoms, but the creation of man in the image of God. This is the structure the Christian chooses to follow, for he believes the postulate of a rational God to be a workable hypothesis in the light of the evidence.[23]

B. Ethics

There is yet more in the intellect which was not first in the senses. All men know by nature the difference between right and wrong, the obligation of virtue, the responsibility for character and conduct, and the culpableness of evil deeds. First, there is the conscience, that voice within us that drives us away from doing things that we might otherwise do. How often we could cheat or steal but are saved from such acts by the knowledge within us that those who do such deeds are worthy of shame and punishment. We say, "Let you conscience be your guide," or "Haven't you any conscience?" and in either case we are appealing to something which is part of man *qua* man. The fear that the thief in the night has of being apprehended can hardly come from criteria abstracted through sensation. A more plausible hypothesis to account for the universal fear of the consequences of right and wrong is that God, in creation, made man in His moral image.

---

23. Let us remember that we are not attempting a *demonstration* of God's existence; we are simply pointing out the presence of data which make the hypothesis of God's existence coherent.

Secondly, there is the universality of ethical codes. Every tribe and nation under heaven is governed by moral laws. The cannibal who eats another will not touch those of his own tribe; that would be unethical. The thief who steals from others makes it very plain to his fellow culprits that there may be no stealing of his things. "Where, then, do these rules stand written, whence even the unrighteous may recognize what is righteous; whence he that has not may learn what he ought to have? Where can they stand written save in the book of that Light which is called the Truth, whence every righteous law is transcribed, and transferred into the heart of man who works righteousness, not by a process of transportation, but by a process of imprinting, as the device from a ring while it passes over into the wax, yet does not leave the ring."[24] Not all men may know how to apply their knowledge of right and wrong consistently, to be sure, but this does not destroy the criteria themselves. "As thinkers may differ in their conclusions and all seek the truth in distinction from error, so in general ethical norms men may differ, yet all seek the good in distinction from evil."[25] A good coherent hypothesis is to suppose that it is the very presence of the changeless standards in the heart of man that makes speaking of ethical relativity possible.[26]

Thirdly, there is the basic and obvious distinction between man and animal. Though *both* enjoy sense perception, only the former knows moral laws. The laws, then, cannot have come from sensation, for the animals have better senses than man does, yet they lack a moral sense. Observe the difference between man and animal. Man's wearing of clothing is a universal testimony to the sense of nakedness which God put in his heart at the time when our first parents, Adam and Eve, disobeyed Him and fell into guilt and condemnation. The inability of men to make the nudist colony a normal condition in life is further evidence of the sense of shame that is universal in the hearts of rational beings. Man may be just as

24. Warfield, *Studies in Tertullian and Augustine*, p. 148.
25. Jaarsma, *op. cit.*, p. 105.
26. We shall analyze the problem of ethical relativity in Chapter XVIII.

promiscuous as the animal, but he, unlike the latter, seeks seclusion and darkness before leaving the path of what he knows to be the right.[27]

We shall have occasion in a later chapter to point out that the principle of individuation which distinguishes man from the animal, is not his bone structure, but his moral, rational nature. It is important to note this as a key to unlocking the problem of organic evolution.

Fourthly, the Scriptures teach that the law of God is written in the heart of every man. "They *know* God's decree that those who do such things deserve to die . . . They show that what the law requires is *written on their hearts,* while their conscience also bears witness and their conflicting thoughts accuse or perhaps excuse them on that day when, according to my gospel, God judges the secrets of men by Christ Jesus" (Romans 1:32; 2:15-16). [Although we are still dealing with natural, rather than special revelation, it is not inappropriate at this point to show how natural and Biblical lines of evidence stand related.]

The only convincing hypothesis to account for this phenomenal evidence which we face when we look at man, is that God has made us in His image. We say to man, 'Have you lost your sense of common decency?' or 'Haven't you any self-respect?' or 'Where is your sense of honor?' and in so doing we speak in a manner which is significant only on the position of Christian rationalism. Apart from the God Who has revealed Himself in Scripture, we could not *meaningfully* say that murder will be wrong tomorrow; but we *can* so speak: therefore, God, the Author of our moral nature, exists.

---

27. While this volume was being written, a boxing fight was 'fixed' in New York City by some racketeers. This gesture threw the sports world into a temporary revolution, for it was such a 'low' deed. Now, 'low' in relation to what? Why is 'fixing' fights any more evil than refraining from so doing? It would not bother any of the animals, so why does it bother man? The Christian contends that it is meaningful to speak of fights being 'fixed' only if man is a creature made in the image and likeness of a rational, moral God.

C. Aesthetics

Some think that the aesthetic experience lies beyond the interests of truth, but this judgment is superficial. In life we *do* talk significantly about the 'beautiful' and the 'ugly' and, unless all culture and niceness are to be destroyed and man is to be lowered to the level of a beast, there *is* such a thing as art. Joad states the case well.[28]

> That a Mozart quartet is better than a chorus of cats; that it is right to say that 2 and 2 make four and wrong to say that they make 5, and that a philosophy which *refrains* from introducing absolute standards of values represents a closer approximation to the nature of things and is, therefore, truer than one which is still cluttered with these figments of the scholastic imagination. In these ways and in a hundred others, supporters of the view that is under criticism do persistently suggest that some things are better, higher, truer, more beautiful, more civilized, more moral, more edifying than others, and that civilization progresses in so far as it embodies or realizes or approximates to or brings forth a greater number of these better, higher, truer, more beautiful, more civilized, more moral, or more edifying things. And they make this suggestion, because they cannot help themselves. Granted, then, the necessity under which we all labour of making judgments of moral and aesthetic import, I do not see with what logic we can avoid the implications of our necessity by seeking to deny the existence in the universe of certain absolute standards and values in terms of which alone our moral and aesthetic judgements have meaning and content. These standards and values cannot, as I have tried to show, be part of the process which they are invoked to measure.

Three things strike us here. First, without eternal standards of the beautiful, it is meaningless to say that the Golden Gate Bridge is prettier than a crushed cigar-box. The Hermes of Praxiteles is then no lovelier than mud pies made by a sleepy idiot. But the fact that men *do* continue to speak of the beautiful is patent evidence that they have a standard in their heart

---

28. *God and Evil,* p. 158. The sad ending that this book has is testimony to what happens to one who cannot accept Jesus Christ as the ontological Son of God.

by which to judge. If there is no distinction between Mozart and a chorus of howling cats, let us cease wasting words on such things as culture, loveliness, and beauty. But this is social skepticism.

Secondly, when we speak of the beautiful, we do it intending to communicate truth. "Clearly the assertion falls in the domain of truth or falsity and our thinking may correspondingly be right or wrong. For to mean 'beautiful' is to mean something real and definite about the object of our thought, even though it is a more difficult quality to verify than such qualities as colors or shapes."[29] This links the criterion of the beautiful with our metaphysical world-view, for only the true can be good and only the good can be beautiful.

Thirdly, aesthetic criteria lead us to a knowledge of God. God is the Author of the true and good, and thus supports the beautiful. God is beauty, for He is perfect harmony and symmetry. His law is good. "Finally, brethren," admonished Paul, "whatever is true, whatever is honorable, whatever is just, whatever is pure, whatever is lovely, whatever is gracious, if there is any excellence, if there is anything worthy of praise, think about these things" (Philippians 4:8). This advice was possible only on a Christian metaphysics, for "a humanistic, atheistic, purposeless universe provides no basis for art."[30] There is no ultimate loveliness if the end of man is the second law of thermodynamics.

IV. The Knowledge of God through Nature

Though the Christian rejects empiricism, he is yet vitally interested in the world of flux, for he is part of that flux. But it is only *with* the *rationes* securely in hand that meaning can be made out of the flux of history at all. Let us now turn to our sensory experience and see what it yields.

---

29. Burtt, *Right Thinking,* p. 13.
30. Clark, *A Christian Philosophy of Education,* p. 59.

A. The RATIONES AETERNAE *and Sensation*

Without a knowledge *a priori* of the *rationes,* sense perceptions cannot report to us anything meaningful. But with our innate knowledge of logic we can tell the deception of the magician from the natural growing of the wheat, since the former sensory witness breaks the law of contradiction. With the *rationes* we are able to separate the true from the false, the bad from the good, the ugly from the beautiful. We stress this to show that instead of Christian rationalism leading to a neglect of nature, it is the only form of epistemology which *can* make our sensory experience intelligible.

B. God and Nature

The two things that awed Kant—the starry heavens above him and the moral law within—will awe any man who will take time carefully to analyse the *rationes* within and the remarkable concourse of nature without. It is here that all of the evidences from contingency, order, efficient cause, and motion, which Thomas abortively introduced, have relevance. To be sure, the world *is* regular; it *is* conducive to our happiness; and it *is* harmonious; but it will do little good so to speak until we first possess those standards in relation to which such statements are significant. Yet if our mind is *tabula rasa,* by what right do we call things harmonious, regular, and symmetrical? If we know not the truth before coming to sensation, the world is neither rational nor irrational, for the terms are meaningless. If we know not the standard for good, the world is neither good nor bad. So with beauty: it is neither lovely nor ugly. But these criteria depend for their existence upon the mind of God.

How, then, can Paul say that all men know the power and deity of God *from the things that are made* (Romans 1:20)? In this manner: Because we *know* God's existence and nature in our heart, we *recognize* Him in His handiwork. Thus the heavens declare the glory of God, for they constantly remind us that God exists. The limited perfection of nature is a reminder of absolute perfection; the mutability of nature is a reminder that there is absolute immutability. If man did not know what to look for when he observed nature, it would be pointless for Paul to look upon nature as a means to bring all men under condemnation. "But since the meanest and most illiterate of mankind, who are furnished with no other assistance than their own eyes, cannot be ignorant of the excellence of the Divine skill, exhibiting itself in that endless, yet regular variety of the innumerable celestial host,—it is evident, that the Lord abundantly manifests his wisdom to every individual on earth."[31]

Summer and winter and springtime and harvest,
   Sun, moon, and stars in their courses above,
Join with all nature in manifold witness,
   To Thy great faithfulness, mercy, and love.

Great is Thy faithfulness, O God my Father,
   There is no shadow of turning with Thee.
Thou changest not, Thy compassions, they fail not.
   As Thou has been Thou forever wilt be.

This is not a formal demonstration of God's existence: it is simply proof by coherence. The existence of God is the self-consistent hypothesis that the mind must entertain when it views all of the evidence which experience provides.

An example may serve us here. Suppose that Hans Mueller makes a special type of shoe, a shoe with his own unique marks on it; and suppose that one were to come from Mars where shoes are unknown; when he beholds the shoes of Hans Mueller, they will be but an unintelligible datum to him—they may be 'African betties' for all he knows. He can see no meaning to what is before him, because he lacks the criterion. In like

---

31. Calvin, *op. cit.*, I, 5, 2. One thing is certain. Paul could not have based Gentile responsibility upon men's ability to find God through the arduous causal proofs of Aristotle and Thomas, for, not only are the arguments logically invalid, but also it is doubtful if the ignorant millions would know what a man was talking about when the proofs were called for. The knowledge of God from nature must be made accessible to men to be a basis for responsibility. If all men know God by nature and are immediately reminded of Him in nature, then there is meaning to say that by observing the things that are made, we are held responsible for knowing God. Otherwise the words are quite inappropriate.

manner, without the standards of truth, goodness, and beauty in us, it is impossible for us to see truth, goodness, and beauty in the universe. Apart from these criteria we would lack a knowledge of what to look for in a world that has been made by God. Thomas thought that he could demonstrate God's existence upon a *tabula rasa* epistemology, but we object. Until we first know God within, all appeals to truth, goodness, and symmetry in the universe without, fall on deaf ears. It would be similar to proving to a dog that there is a moral order in the universe. The dog would pay no atention to you because he lacks the *conditio sine qua non* for appreciating it. But it is meaningful to say to a child, "Now, aren't you sorry? You know you should not have done that!" In like manner it is futile to take a weasel to hear Tschaikowsky's Fifth Symphony or teach a horse higher calculus. These animals have all the sense perceptions that are needed; they just lack the *rationes* in the mind with which to make cognitive sense out of their sensations.[32]

But let us press our illustration further, to provide a transition to the next chapter. Suppose that our man from Mars *was* aware of the meaning of shoes. Then he could significantly reason from the shoes to a shoemaker. But, being ignorant of the marks which Hans Mueller put on *his* particular shoes, he could not successfully reason from the existence of the shoes to the existence of the particular shoemaker, Hans Mueller, as distinct from all other shoemakers. In the same manner, all men have the *rationes* by which means they know that God exists. But, being in defection by their sins, what they see is vitiated. Thus, they are not able to see and appreciate that one of the peculiar characteristics of this God is that He is the Creator of the world and the Savior of men. God, therefore, gives men up, for they "exchanged the truth about God for a

---

32. Paul expresses this thought as follows: "For what person knows a man's thoughts except the spirit of the man which is in him? So also no one comprehends the thoughts of God except the Spirit of God" (I Corinthians 2:11). The lack of a spiritual faculty makes the things of the Spirit foolishness to the natural man in the same way that moral standards are foolishness to a dog.

lie and worshipped and served the creature rather that the Creator, who is blessed forever! Amen" (Romans 1:25). To give us knowledge unto salvation, we must have special revelation. General revelation "ought not only to excite us to the worship of God, but likewise to awaken and arouse us to the hope of a future life . . . But, notwithstanding the clear representations given by God in the mirror of his works, both of himself and of his everlasting dominion, such is our stupidity, that, always inattentive to these obvious testimonies, we derive no advantage from them."[33]

---

33. Calvin, *op cit.,* 1, 5, 10-11.

Let us remind the reader again that it is not part of the responsibility of a volume on philosophical apologetics to list the standard evidences for Christianity based on nature — the beauty of a rose, the marvelous parts of the human body, etc. This type of study must be delivered over to the specialists who are trained for such work. But if we were to insert a hundred pages of evidences, it is precisely at this point where they would be placed. When an apologist has formulated a *philosophy* of evidences, he may then turn to the more mechanical task of their listing and detailing.

Our omission of evidences does not mean that we consider such labor of less value than the topics which we choose to discuss. We rather believe it inadvisable to mingle apologetics in general with the problem of evidences in particular. Evidences form a subordinate field, lying under the wider and more comprehensive heading of apologetics.

Chapter X

Starting Point: God (Continued)

The rich man also died and was buried; and in Hades, being in torment, he lifted up his eyes, and saw Abraham far off and Lazarus in his bosom. . . . And he said, 'Then I beg you, father, to send him to my father's house, for I have five brothers, so that he may warn them, lest they also come into this place of torment.' But Abraham said, 'They have Moses and the prophets; let them hear them.' And he said, 'No, father Abraham; but if some one goes to them from the dead, they will repent.' He said to him, 'If they do not hear Moses and the prophets, neither will they be convinced if some one should rise from the dead.'

—*Luke*

BECAUSE we have come some distance since we set out to solve the problems of happiness, truth, and a rational view of the universe, it may appear that we have philosophically arrived in Canaan, and that we may now repose and eat the fruit of the land. But we must not be too hasty, since, as a matter of fact, we have only succeeded in escaping from the empiricism of Egypt. Although we have solved many problems, there are yet more ahead in the wilderness. For example: What is the nature of God? What is His relation to the process of history? What is His relation to our *rationes*? And what must we do to be saved? These questions, which we must answer to claim a consistent world-view, wait for their solutions upon the information detailed in Holy Writ. We have defended our right to appeal to the Bible; now the time has come for us actually to utilize this prerogative. "God, foreseeing the inefficacy of his manifestation of himself in the exquisite structure of the world, hath afforded the assistance of his word to all those to whom he determined to make his instructions effectual."[1]

I. The Appeal to Special Revelation

When Plato said that one must "take the best and most irrefragible of human theories, and let this be the raft upon which he sails through life—not without risk, as I admit, if he cannot find some word of God which will more surely and safely carry him,"[2] he nicely stated the alternatives any philosopher must face. One either constructs his opinions from experience and then runs a risk that they will be invalid for tomorrow, or he has claim to some sure word of God as an external reference point at which he sets his lever. The Christian claims that he owns this sure word of prophecy that can tell him the meaning of the world, while no other has a guide like it. Even "Plato himself, the most religious and judicious of them all, loses himself in his round globe."[3]

By special revelation we mean not part nor piece, but the full and whole sixty-six canonical books which make up the Bible. "The books of Scripture are therefore called canonical, because they had their prime and sovereign authority from God Himself, by whose divine will and inspiration they were first written, and by whose blessed providence they have been ever since preserved and delivered over to posterity, so have they been likewise received, and in all times acknowledged by His church to be the infallible rule of faith, and the perfect square of our actions in all things that are any way needful for our eternal salvation."[4] These specific books make up the Christian's major premise, since, when added to or subtracted from, one is left with a less coherent world-view than if the manipulation is not undertaken. There is thus nothing strange about this conviction; it is an hypothesis that has been chosen with the same diligence as that of a scientific hypothesis. Like any hypothesis,

1. Calvin, *Institutes*, I, 6, 3.
2. *Phaedo* 85b.
3. Calvin, *op. cit.*, I, 5, 11.
4. Cosin, *A Scholastic History of the Canon of the Scripture*, pp. 1-2.

it is verified when it results in an implicative system which is horizontally self-consistent and which vertically fits the facts.

Let us be clear about our transition. When we leave natural for special revelation, we are not bifurcating epistemology; the Christian operates under *one* major premise—the existence of the God Who has revealed Himself in Scripture. We are not exchanging reason for faith, as did Thomas; rather we are seeking to strengthen the faith which we already have, for faith is a resting of the heart in the worthiness of the evidence. The Bible is needed to give us more evidence. Therefore, when we say that, though the light of nature is sufficient to bring man to a knowledge of God, God has been pleased "for the better preserving and propagating of the truth, and for the more sure establishment and comfort of the Church against the corruption of the flesh, and the malice of Satan and of the world,"[5] to commit wholly to writing the full counsel of His will for our salvation, we are not abandoning that spirit of verification which we have defended up to this point. Truth is systematically construed meaning, and if the Bible fulfills this standard, it is just as true as Lambert's law of transmission. Any hypothesis is verified when it smoothly interprets life.

A. The Fact of Special Revelation

Although few really think about it, no cogent philosophic argument can be introduced to preclude the possibility of revelation. One can know whether God has revealed Himself or not only after an examinatoin of all of the facts in reality, for any one fact overlooked may be the very revelation itself. But God Himself is one of these possible facts. Significantly to say there is no God, therefore, one must first look under every flat rock on the planet Earth. When this source is exhausted, he must then go to Mars and do the same thing; and then on to Jupiter and Venus, until every inch of the entire universe has been exhaustively worked over. But, when our explorer has gone to Mars, perhaps God will have gone to Venus, and while he is on Venus, perhaps God—Who is the Almighty—will

5. *Westminster Confession of Faith,* I, 1.

have suddenly come back to the earth. To track God down, therefore, one must at least be everywhere at the same time, which is to say, he must be God Himself. If a man says there is no God, he simply makes himself God, and thus revelation is made actual. If he says there is a God, the only way he can know this is by God's having revealed Himself, for the Almighty is powerful enough not to give any clues of His existence if He so elects; and again revelation is actual. And if a man says he does not know if there be a God or not, he is certainly in no position to know if this God, Whom he does not know, has revealed Himself; and even in this extreme position, revelation is possible. If we have succeeded in showing that generic revelation is possible, the same arguments hold for special revelation.

B. The Necessity of Special Revelation

The fundamental reason why we need special revelation is to answer the question, What must I do to be saved? Happiness is our first interest, but this happiness cannot be ours until we know just how God is going to dispose of us at the end of history. Remember, that He Who made us by the freedom of His own will may also dispose of us within the framework of that same sovereignty. Thus Paul asks,

> For who has known the mind of the Lord,
> Or who has been his counselor?
> Or who has given a gift to him,
> That he might be repaid?[6]

Until we have definite information on the subject, we have no sure guarantee that He Who made us will not also destroy us.

It will do little good to say, "But haven't we established through the *rationes* that God is good? How, then, can He destroy us?" In answer, though God is good, that attribute does not close to Him the avenue of destroying us, since He, not some abstract standard of good, is the standard of what is

6. Romans 11:34-35.

good. God is the *Almighty*. As one expresses it, He is either God of all or He is not God at all. The famous illustration of the philosopher's chicken will help us here. The chicken each day receives corn and water from the farmer; from this bit of empirical evidence the chicken deduces (possibly by Thomas's fifth argument?) that the farmer is good, for all the latter does for the chicken is for the chicken's welfare. Content with this induction, the chicken knows that the nature of the farmer is good; therefore, nothing evil can come from his hand, for the farmer cannot act contrary to his nature. But, alas! there comes a sunny day when the man of the fields greets his chicken, not with the usual handful of grain, but with a hatchet to chop its head off. We can hear the chicken protesting with a loud cackling against such an unethical act, but the complaints soon die away as its head is separated from the neck. The farmer, not the chicken, happens to be the standard of good and bad in such a situation, even as God, not the farmer, is the standard of good and bad in the universe. In vain therefore do men plead that, since God has given us rain and sunshine, He must also save our souls at the end of history. *Non sequitur*. God may send His showers, but He is under no antecedent necessity to save our souls; if He is, He is not God, for there is some law over and above Him. To appeal to His nature to help one out of the difficulty is as bad an argument as that of the chicken, for the nature of God is determined by a description of what He does. If He damns us, that is the way His good nature expresses itself. For these reasons, the Christian's major premise is not just an appeal to a *good* God; rather it is to the God Who has revealed Himself in Scripture, and to Him alone. Without the data outlined in Scripture, we are no better off in our world-view than the chicken was in the barnyard, Thomas's empirical proofs notwithstanding. We simply point this out to call to the attention of all who reject the infallibility of Scripture what a sorry plight they are in. "Will you yet say before Him that slays you, I am God? but you are man, and not God, in the hand of Him that wounds you" (Ezekiel 28:9).

C. *Which Revelation?*

Granted that we need revelation from God to learn how He will dispose of us at the end of our lives, are there not many revelations which vie for our approval? How shall we make a selection, when we are not God? We can answer this in a sentence: Accept that revelation which, when examined, yields a system of thought which is horizontally self-consistent and which vertically fits the facts of history. When viewing the Bible, the Christian says, "I see a series of data in the Bible. If I accept the system as it is outlined, I can make a lot of problems easy." Bring on your revelations! Let them make peace with the law of contradiction and the facts of history, and they will deserve a rational man's assent. A careful examination of the Bible reveals that it passes these stringent examinations *summa cum laude*. Unlike all other religious volumes, the Bible speaks of, and gives a metaphysical basis to, the unity and solidarity of the entire human race under God. Christ's message has nothing clannish, tribal, esoteric, or racial about it. Christ was not only in sympathy with the building of a bridge or brotherhood that would wipe out all class distinctions, but He expressly lived and died to make all men one in Him by His cross. Christ is not, like Mohammed, Socrates, and Buddha, a defender of principles which have only the approval of either an oriental or an occidental culture; He came as the ideal Son of Man, the Alpha and the Omega. He combines in Himself all of the best virtues of the East and the West. His promises were to whoever will, to all, to each, everywhere, always. The ritual of His gospel is so simple and unadorned that it is applicable everywhere: it makes no peculiar demands upon a culture; it only asks for faith. Its law is sublime, bearing with it, as it contacts all tribes under the sun, these elements of moral elevation which man needs to keep him from descending to the level of the animal. The Bible may be translated into any tongue without fear of moral offense. Its literature is the finest; its expressions the sublimest. Whatever good elements the other religions of the world may contain, Christ's embraces them all, surpassing each as day surpasses night in light.

D. The Bible as Revelation

The authors of Scripture speak with authority. Their words are punctuated with peals of thunder: "Thus saith Jehovah "that rules heaven and earth." Were these individuals who wrote the Bible merely *witnessing* to what they believed was the covenantal working of God in history? Were they like reporters on a great city newspaper, trained, efficient, alert, but in possession of no other equipment that what was resident in them as men? Did they possess the inspiring, superintending Spirit of God in a stronger form, but qualitatively no different from, that which is enjoyed by other men who have not written Scripture? Hardly. From Genesis through Revelation, these men wrote sober truth. One self-consistent, historically accurate, plan of salvation runs through their hundreds of pages of manuscripts which, astoundingly, were written by men that were relatively ignorant of the existence of each other. Moses gave the plan of salvation in Genesis 3:15, hundreds of years before its fulfillment: "I will put enmity between thee and the woman, and between thy seed and her seed: he shall bruise thy head, and thou shalt bruise his heel." The prophets passionately unfolded it; the gospels carefully outlined it; and the epistles immaculately completed it. Toward the end of special revelation, Paul said, "The God of peace will soon crush Satan under your feet" (Romans 16:20), pointing to the last jot-and-tittle fulfillment of Genesis 3:15. In this entire system of salvation there is nothing repulsive to the reason of man; there is nothing impossible, immoral, absurd, nothing inconsistent with the corpus of well-attested truth.

What volume can even begin to compete with Scripture? Its truths are the highest known: truths of the nature of God, the origin and the end of the world, and the nature and destiny of man. So powerful has Christianity's influence been, that it has set the pattern for Western culture. Scripture has satisfied the scholar, broken the sinner, comforted the oppressed, and encouraged the weary.

> Read Demosthenes or Cicero; read Plato, Aristotle, or any others of that class; I grant that you will be attracted, delighted, moved, and enraptured by them in a surprising manner; but if, after reading them, you turn to the perusal of the sacred volume, whether you are willing or unwilling, it will affect you so powerfully, it will so penetrate your heart, and impress itself so strongly on your mind, that, compared with its energetic influence, the beauties of rhetoricians and philosophers will almost entirely disappear; so that it is easy to perceive something divine in the sacred Scriptures, which far surpasses the highest attainments and ornaments of human industry.[7]

The Christian does not arbitrarily accept the Bible as the word of God; he feels he cannot be restrained from so making that hypothesis, for to elect any other position would be to fly in the face of the facts, a gesture more befitting an irrational ornithoid than a rational man in quest of a rational explanation of the universe.

Let us now turn to the "revelation of the mystery which was kept secret for long ages but is now disclosed and through the prophetic writings is made known to all nations, according to the command of the eternal God, to bring about obedience to the faith" (Romans 16:25-26), and see if, after accepting it, we can make a smoother picture out of our philosophy of life with it than without it. The following enquiry contains but sample questions; if one were to set down all of the implications of Christianity, perhaps even the world itself could not contain the books that should be written.

II. The Benefits of Special Revelation

Before we can have a genuine reason for personal happiness, a rational understanding of the universe, and a basis for changeless truth, we must face the four questions which we alluded to earlier. They concern the nature of God, His relation to process, His relation to the *rationes,* and His relation to our salvation. Let us briefly show both why these are prob-

7. Calvin, *op. cit.,* I, 8, 1.

lems which all men must face, and also how the Bible nicely accounts for them.

A. The Nature of God

The *cogito,* the analysis of the self, and the *rationes,* all corroborate to remind us that God is truth. But religion needs more than this. For prayer to be effective, and for trust in providence to be meaningful and satisfying, God must be a Person. But we cannot make God a Person by simply taking thought; we must have evidence for the hypothesis. In the Bible we find such a coherent body of evidence. It assures us that God is triune, three Persons in one divine essence. Being personal, God can be an object of fellowship. The gods of the ancients—Plato and Aristotle—were too near abstract principles of impersonal intelligence to be of service to man in worship. In Christianity, God not only thinks about Himself: He thinks about us. As Bavinck expresses it, it is the Father *of* Whom, the Son *through* Whom, and the Spirit *in* Whom all things have their being. All religions need a personal God; Christianity provides Him.

B. The Relation of God to the Process of History

Though we may trust in God, it makes a difference whether He be conceived of pantheistically, deistically, or theistically. If God is identified with the process of history, as in pantheism, then we have no hope for salvation. By definition, God's history is eternal; therefore, there are no goals to which we can strive, for there is no *terminus ad quem* in an everlasting process of striving. Hence, salvation can be no goal. Furthermore, if God is the process of history with all its evil in it, he deserves our pity, not our worship. But if God is deistically conceived, *i. e.*, is wholly transcendent above the process of history, then He is too out of reach to be called upon as a loving Heavenly Father. He might just as well not exist as far as His being a solution to our personal happiness is concerned. "If God's dwelling lies somewhere far away, outside the world, and his transcendence is to be understood in the sense that he has withdrawn from creation and now stands outside of the actuality of this world, then we lose him and are unable to maintain communication with him. His existence cannot become truly real to us unless we are permitted to conceive of him as not only above the world, but in his very self in the world, and thus as indwelling in all his works."[8] If God is to solve the riddle of history's process, He must enjoy sovereign mastery over that process; otherwise who knows but what He will fail us at death? But He must also be related to the process of history; otherwise His sovereignty would have no relevance to the human situation. In the Bible we discover that God *has almighty power,* and yet *is our Friend.* God is related to the process as its Sustainer, and yet He is completely above the process as its Author. He rules the ponderous courses of the planets, marks the sparrow's fall, and numbers the hairs on our heads. Yet, neither the planets, the sparrows, nor our heads are part of God.

Another problem under this same head is the question of the origin of the world. Christianity teaches the doctrine of creation; no other cosmogony can give man happiness. If the world is as eternal as God, we have no hope for an end to history, for evil goes right along with process throughout eternity. As we will show below many implications of these observations, we will pass by the issue this time.[9]

C. *The Relation of God in the* RATIONES

All agree that human minds are rational and that what is true for the nature of one is true for the natures of all, but the Christian alone can suggest a coherent hypothesis to account for this astounding phenomenon. How does it happen, that out of all the possible arrangements, all men turn out to have the *rationes*? Kant, for example, assumed that all human minds possess the categories, but where was his proof? On any position, save the Christian, it is nothing short of millions of miracles that all minds agree. The Christian handles the

8. Bavinck, *Philosophy of Revelation,* p. 21.
9. See *infra,* chapters XVI-XVII.

problem with facility by his doctrine that man is made in the image of God. The rationality of God preserves our right to trust both in the validity of the *rationes* for tomorrow, and to believe that the universe will continue regular and predictive. Creation cannot fail in the ends for which it was made, for the wealth of heaven and earth belongs to a rational God. Indeed all men continue to act as if the minds of men and the universe about them will continue rational, but it is salutary to remind them that apart from the God Who has revealed Himself in Scripture, such optimism is rationally unfounded.

D. The Relation of God to our Salvation

While the gods of the heathen are interested only in themselves, the God of Christianity is interested in man—'for God so loved the world.' We have elsewhere outlined the Christian plan of salvation; so there is no virtue in repeating it. Christ, being God, took on the form of man and died in the human nature, as an expiation for the sins of all who will believe. What heathen tribe ever conceived of so sublime a theory of soteriology? "For God so loved the world that he gave his only Son, that whoever believes in him should not perish but have eternal life" (John 3:16). What more comforting words could fall upon weary ears than those of the Son of man? "Come to me, all who labor and are heavy-laden, and I will give you rest. Take my yoke upon you, and learn from me; for I am gentle and lowly in heart, and you will find rest for your souls" (Matthew 11:28-29). Who is more worthy of our trust than He who left His glories in heaven to deliver "all those who through fear of death were subject to lifelong bondage'" (Hebrews 2:15)? This One, the Christ, *is* the "mystery which was kept secret for long ages."

In Christ's cross we reach the summit of the Christian view of God and the world. The cross culminates our case for the logic of the Christian faith, for in it time and eternity, man and God, met and were reconciled forever. Words seem impertinent to laud this Lamb of God that takes away the sins of the world.

O sacred Head, now wounded,
With grief and shame weighed down;
Now scornfully surrounded,
With thorns, Thine only crown.

O sacred Head, what glory,
What bliss till now was Thine!
Yet, though despised and gory,
I joy to call Thee mine.

What language shall I borrow
To thank Thee, dearest Friend,
For this Thy dying sorrow,
Thy pity without end?

O make me Thine forever;
And should I fainting be,
Lord, let me never, never,
Outlive my love to Thee.

But to appropriate Jesus Christ presupposes a knowledge of the Bible, for that is our only document to tell of this blessed atonement. "No man can have the least knowledge of true and sound doctrine, without having been a disciple of the Scripture."[10] In meditating upon the grandeurs of Christ let us remember that one must consider not only those implications which attend the Christian hypothesis, but also those which flow from its denial. "For if we sin deliberately after receiving the knowledge of the truth, there no longer remains a sacrifice for sins, but a fearful prospect of judgment, and a fury of fire which will consume the adversaries" (Hebrews 10:26-27).

III. Objections to Christianity

A. Leads to a Neglect of Sensation

If we turn our attention to the eternal *rationes,* we shall tread the path of those rationalists and idealists who, enamored of their union with God, turned their back upon the world of sensation as a useless excrescency in their epistemology. We have earlier answered this, but, to refresh our memory, let

10. Calvin, *op. cit.,* I, 6, 2.

us recall that without the *rationes* there is no meaning to sensation at all. Hence, Christianity is a guarantee of, not a hindrance to, significant sensation.

B. What About Telescopes?

A variation of the above problem is the argument of modern science. If we have innate knowledge, how do we explain the fact that it was not until empiricism was taken seriously by science that accurate knowledge of nature arose? It seems that the more we repudiate innate ideas, the more our knowledge is advanced. In answer to this we say two things. First, science advanced, not when it gave up the *rationes*, for nothing would have meaning without them, but rather when it began using the *rationes* properly. By 'proper' we mean carefully applying our minds to the data of history. Secondly, it is part of the Christian system that we must so apply ourselves, for the Christian is commanded by God to subdue nature. But one cannot subdue something until he first knows what it is. Thus the need for telescopes and microscopes; we are not able to learn of nature's details without them. The use of them does not vitiate the *rationes;* rather, the *rationes* are *conditiones sine qua non* for the effective use of these instruments.

C. Leads to Mysticism

If we turn to an inwardness, mysticism follows. God is truth, and, when we interest ourselves with the truth, we metaphysically confuse ourselves in God. In answer we say, truly we know all truth in God, but God "is in the soul of man not *substantialiter* but only *effective*."[11] When we know truth in God, we are not confused with God. The creature-Creator relationship is inviolable. God's method of knowing will always be different from our method. God lets us see truth in His light, but He, not we, is the truth. We perceive truth; God's mind is truth.

---

11. Warfield, ***Studies in Tertullian and Augustine***, p. 145.

D. Not Christian but Platonic

Plato, not Augustine, thought of the *rationes* scheme; hence Christianity is founded on Platonism. In reply, Plato was formally right when he rejected empiricism; lacking special revelation, however, he did not succeed in completing his system with coherence. He did not know the meaning of the cross. But that Plato hit upon the right synoptic starting point can be explained by the Christian through the hypothesis that, being made in the image of God, he was given illumination to see more of the problem of epistemology than were others. The truth which Plato found was made possible because Christ was antecedently true. A much better way to state the issue, then, is to say that wherever Plato spoke the truth, he was Christian; rather than wherever the Christian is coherent, he is Platonic. The Christian can explain Plato, but Plato cannot explain the Christian.

E. What About the Atheists?

Countless men say they do not believe that God exists. How, then, can we square this with the supposed Christian truth that all men know God by nature? First, there are no real atheists, for the same reasons that we gave for a man's being unable to say there is no revelation. A man must be everywhere at the same time to say there is no God, which is nothing but a short way of making himself God. Secondly, the Christian can explain those who say there is no God. The corruption of sin vitiates and sullies a man's knowledge of the Creator. Thus the atheist is a fool, for he is using words to deny the only Being which can give validity to these very words themselves. Without God to sustain the *rationes*, the atheist's speech is meaningless and may be ignored.

F. Destroys all Philosophy

Gilson, arguing as a Thomist, says that this approach destroys philosophy, philosophy being the "speculation of the natural reason on objects which are accessible to it in the state of fact natural to it."[12] Because one teaches that illumination is required for all intellection, Gilson concludes that he should "renounce, once for all, speaking of a 'philosophy' of divine things, whether it be for the purpose of reserving its use for himself, since he no longer has the right to it, or of forbidding it to others as impossible."[13]

Gilson's trouble is that he has defined philosophy the way that he as a Thomist wants it, and then has turned that definition upon us. But philosophy, both etymologically and historically, is the 'love of wisdom.' Shall we then be bound by that definition of philosophy which was formulated by Hugo of St. Victor and Aquinas to suit their theology? Philosophy is the love and pursuit of wisdom, and where one obtains his data to work out wisdom is quite irrelevant. If the Christian can succeed in his doctrine of illumination to construct a system of meaning which is coherent, he has both truth and a proper philosophy.[14]

---

12. *Christianity and Philosophy*, p. 30.

13. *Ibid.*, p. 43.

14. We shall not pause to ask Gilson, a *tabula rasa* epistemologist, where he found this normative truth that 'All who build their knowledge on illumination are not philosophers at all;' but it would make an interesting question we feel, for from flux only flux can come.

Part III

IMPLICATIONS OF THE CHRISTIAN WORLD-VIEW

Chapter XI

The Problem of Biblical Criticism

Our beloved brother Paul wrote to you according to the wisdom given him, speaking of this as he does in all his letters. There are some things in them hard to understand, which the ignorant and unstable twist to their own destruction, as they do the other scriptures. You therefore, beloved, knowing this beforehand, beware lest you be carried away with the error of lawless men and lose your own stability.—Peter.

HAVING summed up the general over-all strategy of the conservative philosophy of life, it is now incumbent upon us to face courageously what amounts to probably the most forceful argument against the Christian system from within the text of the Bible itself. We have reference to the full century of Biblical criticism which has succeeded in bringing to light many difficulties in the narratives of Holy Writ. These efforts have left the conservative in a predicament. On the one hand, he admits that the Bible is the infallibly inspired word of God,[1] and yet, on the other, confesses that there are not a few difficulties in the present text. "The conscientious student has, therefore, great difficulty sometimes in resolving problems raised by apparent contradictions . . . and he may frankly confess that he is not able to explain an apparent discrepancy in the teaching of Scripture."[2] To the modern mind the conservative position seems like weasel-wording.

---

1. "The Church doctrine denies that inspiration is confined to parts of the Bible; and affirms that it applies to all the books of the sacred canon. It denies that the sacred writers were merely partially inspired; it asserts that they were fully inspired as to all that they teach, whether of doctrine or fact." Hodge, *Systematic Theology,* I, p. 165. By 'inspired' we mean 'moved by the Holy Spirit to write down only what God approved.'

2. *The Infallible Word* (Westminster Seminary Faculty, ed.), p. 6.

For two reasons we must face this problem. First, academically we must point out the coherence of the Christian philosophy of Biblical criticism, for we can accept only that system of philosophy which is free from basic contradictions. Secondly, since many have left the faith of the gospel for skepticism, we must carefully state our position in an effort to prevent others from following in their train. "It is a fearful thing to fall into the hands of the living God" (Heb. 10:31).

I. The Nature of Biblical Criticism

Before setting down our philosophy of Biblical error, however, let us set down the two types of Biblical criticism, plus a rejection of false havens of escape.

A. Lower Criticism

The first shock that every young Christian convert must face when he comes to close grips with the Bible, is that the text of the English versions, which he uses, is corrupt in very small details. Contrary to what the untutored may think, neither the King James Version nor the Vulgate is plenarily inspired, for plenary inspiration is an attribute which is reserved solely for the original writings, those autographs of Moses, the prophets, and the apostles which are now all lost. What we possess in our present Bibles today is a remarkably substantial copy of this first set of writings, the purity of which is determined by the research of lower criticism. The lower critic must study the hundreds of extant Hebrew and Greek writings to determine which documents proceed from the original sources and which are spurious, for only the original writers, not the copyists and transcribers, were inspired. In the hundreds of years which have elapsed since the Bible was written, a few transcriptional errors have crept into the text. To cull out these errors is the task of lower criticism. The original text is wholly inspired; the present text is in a state of substantial purity. The first writers of the Bible were immediately inspired by God, while the copyists were providentially preserved from disturbing the doctrinal content of Scripture while transcribing it. They were not preserved from textual errors, however. The monks were as subject to proof-reader's illusions as we are. If an epsilon was mistaken for an iota by a sleepy monk, it went into the text.[3]

Conservatives have historically led the research in lower criticism, being stimulated to restore the original text by a consideration of the doctrine of original inspiration. Unless some objective science of criticism can be set up, Christians are left without a norm by which to tell God's genuine revelation from a corruption which has crept in. The words in the Lord's Prayer, for example, "For thine is the kingdom and the power and the glory, forever. Amen." are a good illustration of what is probably a textual corruption, thus not deserving a place in our Bible.[4] There are several others. The work of lower criticism, however, has substantiated, not jeopardized, the hypothesis that there were original documents from which our present ones have come. The more dirt the spade of the archaeologist turns over, the more harmonious becomes our knowledge of the text.

B. Destructive Higher Criticism

Lower criticism is concerned with the *state* of the text, while higher criticism deals with the over-all questions of the *meaning, validity, coherence,* and *worth* of the text. " 'Higher' criticism, however, is the attempt to determine the meaning of the text, and to do so by the same methods that scientific investigation has found successful in dealing with secular writings."[5] Observe, that a fundamental presupposition of the higher critic is that the Bible is just another piece of human

3. "We will furthermore grant that God did not keep from error those who copied the Scriptures during the long period in which the sacred text was transmitted in copies written by hand." *The Infallible Word,* p. 139.

4. Thus, neither the American Standard Version nor the Revised Standard Version have this conclusion to the Lord's Prayer in the text. The author advises all who want the purest state of the New Testament in their hands to work solely with the latter version.

5. Burtt, *Types of Religious Philosophy,* p. 316. It is only *destructive* higher criticism against which the conservative argues, a method which *corrects,* rather than interprets, the Bible.

writing, a book to which the scientific method may safely be applied, not realizing that the Bible's message stands pitted in judgment against that very method itself. It does not occur to the higher critic that he has started off with his philosophy of life in a way that makes the consistency of redemptively conceived Christianity impossible. We shall comment upon this further.

Higher criticism has had damaging effects. It led quickly "to results inconsistent with the traditional view of the divine inspiration of the Scriptures, hence fundamentalists have not recognized it as legitimate."[6] It has "revealed fundamental discrepancies with traditional beliefs. Differences in style, contradictory accounts of the same event, conflicting commandments purporting to come from God, made the older Protestant view that every word and every point was divinely inspired and literally true, exceedingly difficult to reconcile with faith in the wisdom and rationality of God."[7] In sum, it "made it practically impossible for modern men to believe all that the Bible literally says."[8] Observe the salient fact that the Christian begins studying Scripture with faith in a world-view which allows for the possibility of such revelation, while the higher critic starts with his hypothesis that there has been no revelation.

---

6. Burtt, *op. cit.,* p. 316.

7. Randall, *The Making of the Modern Mind,* p. 536.

8. Lippmann, *A Preface to Morals,* p. 40. Since the modern theologians have a field day in Fundamentalism by labeling it 'literalism,' and the Fundamentalists, 'literalists,' it is well that we point out the straw-man character of this sport. When Isaiah says. "the mountains and the hills shall break forth before you into singing; and all the trees of the field shall clap their hands" (55:12), no conservative is to be charged with teaching that the mountains and hills shall literally sing and the trees shall literally clap their hands. The Fundamentalist interprets Scripture *naturally*: when the natural is the literal, he is literal; and when the natural is not, he is not literal. In this passage we have the obvious use of poetic language to express that state of joy and exhileration which will be enjoyed when the blessings of Jehovah are poured out upon all Israel. When one reads the works of Reinhold Niebuhr, for example, he must take *cum grano salis* all of his references to the 'literalists,' for such references are but *ad hominem* devices to obscure the issue of what the Bible *really* and *essentially* teaches.

C. *The Rejection of False Havens*

There is a temptation to avoid the difficulties of Biblical criticism by retreating to false havens of refuge. The conservative rejects them.

1. *Irrationalism.* Some say that the Bible, since it is from God, can be expected to be irrational, for God has said, "Are not my thoughts higher than your thoughts?" Such a structure has a boomerang effect upon the defender, however, for, if God's thoughts are different from man's thoughts, then, how do we know that they are thoughts at all, let alone that they are God's thoughts? If Scripture does not have the same meaning for God and for man, then the verse quoted by the defender of this view ("my thoughts are not your thoughts"), may just as well mean that the rainy season in Albania is detrimental to the Kansas wheat crop. To be sure, we do not understand everything God has revealed in Scripture, but that is not to admit that the obscure parts are intrinsically irrational; rather it simply means that we have not studied them long enough. Time and illumination alone stop us from understanding the entire revelation of God.

2. *Allegorizing.* When one leaves those allegories which Scripture itself confesses, as Galatians 4:24, "Now this is an allegory," there is no logical stopping point short of unbridled fanaticism and irrationalism. Allegorizing, favorite method of the church fathers, is little less than the imagination of holy men working overtime. The admission that we cannot trust the text as it stands, but must allegorize it, is another way of falling back on irrationalism.

3. *Authority.* Rome tries to solve Bible difficulties by introducing the sure voice of tradition. This only doubles our problem, however, for now we have not only the entire Bible to account for, but also the traditions of the elders, the decisions of the councils, and the *ex cathedra* pronouncements of all the popes. If we cannot successfully apply the law of contradiction to the simple words of Christ, "Come to me all who labor and are heavy-laden," where shall the Romanist stand?

D. The Basic Problem of Inerrancy

When we speak of the original documents being 'inerrantly inspired,' we mean that none of the Biblical writers said anything which was not coherent with everything else written in the Scriptures. In other words, the entire corpus of revelation was preserved free from logical and historical mistakes. But, though this may be so, the question naturally arises, in exactly what sense, and by virtue of what right, does the conservative make the leap from a text which is admitted not to be fully inspired to the original documents which were plenarily inspired? To aid the reader in the appreciation of Fundamentalism, let us set down some of the dialectic steps in its reasoning on this issue.

1. The first thing to take note of is the fact that the standing witness of the Biblical text itself is that in both part and the whole it is objectively and plenarily inspired. The writers presume to speak with such commanding authority that to approach their judgment critically through criteria gained on non-Christian presuppositions is itself an act of sin. The conservative accepts the Biblical witness as true until it can be shown to be otherwise.

2. Since the Bible does claim to be an originally inspired revelation from God, for "till heaven and earth pass away, not an iota, not a dot, will pass from the law until all is accomplished" (Matthew 5:18), the question now gravitates around the problem of whether God did actually give us an originally inspired set of documents, or whether He did not. The Christian, to preserve the rights of language in the Bible plus the sovereignty of God's goodness, accepts the hypothesis that the original autographs were plenary inspired.

If, however, we jettison the conservative's hypothesis that the Bible means exactly what it says and that God actually did unfold His will infallibly to men in divers manners, then, if we believe that the Bible is God's revelation in any sense at all, we must assume either that God could have given us a true-throughout Bible but elected to allow His name to be appended to documents which claim to be fully true but which are partially corrupted, or He desired to give us that perfect revelation but was hindered. Let us consider the former alternative first. If we suppose that God has not chosen to be related to us in such a way that His revelation can be subjected to the canons of coherence, our only notion of truth, then it must follow that our standards of truth cannot apply to God. In this case we can only be agnostic about what God requires of us since He has not elected to be related to us in such a way that the standards by which we judge realms of value in society apply to Him. In such a predicament we cannot solve the problem of the one within the many and we are left with the skepticism of empiricism. How can we tell the voice of God from the voice of the devil if God does not maintain a relation to us wherein the laws of rationality are applicable to His revelation?[9]

3. And if God originally willed to relate Himself to the world in such a way that coherence is applicable to His revelation, but was prevented, then something non-God is frustrating Him. In this case we cannot trust any portion of the Bible, since we have no way of knowing but what at that point where we put our most confident trust, there this finite God is being inhibited from telling the whole truth. What may appear coherent in the Bible may be incoherent in relation to that which God is being prevented from revealing. If a God who elects not to maintain a coherent relation to the world cannot be known because coherence is invalid, then a finite God can-

---

9. Some object that if God is sovereign over His own law He may repent of His promise to save all who trust in the shed blood of Christ. In this case what hope has the Christian? The answer is that the Christian is an adopted son. He is related to God filially. To ask for any stronger persuasion than the word of the Father is itself the reflection of a sinful heart. The Christian has the sure promise of God that he will be saved. To seek for a more powerful assurance is to sin. God has sworn by Himself and He will not repent. The Christian's hope is in God, not coherence. Coherence is a test to know whether God is speaking or not, but God, not coherence, gives significance to what is spoken.

not be known because He Himself is frustrated in His intentions to be coherent.[10]

4. If we try to come to the Bible with a principle of selectivity found outside of the Bible, we render the Bible needless, since we can accept of it only what coincides with the truth which we had before we ever came to Scripture in the first place. In this case, we do not need Holy Writ at all; all we need is the truth, and we already have that.

E. But Why is the Present Text not Inerrant?

Granted that the original documents may have been inspired, why, if God is sovereign both in goodness and in power, did He permit these original manuscripts to be lost? And why, if He had the power to do so, did He not extend inspiration to the copyists, that we might enjoy today the precision of the text which the original writers knew? These are two separate, but vastly important, questions; so let us treat of them in turn.

1. First, the clinching reason why the autographs are all lost is that God, the source of all wisdom and right decision, elected to have them lost, even as He decreed the dissolution of Noah's ark, the brazen serpent, the tabernacle, the original temple, and the holy vessels. God was under no antecedent compulsion to give man a revelation in the first place; so why should there be any external force upon Him to preserve this revelation inerrant?[11] Secondly, as the history of relic worship indicates, man is too depraved to be trusted with holy things.

---

10. Some think that God had to accommodate his revelation to man's sinfulness and inattentiveness and thus error in the Bible resulted. The Christian cannot be so easily persuaded by this way out. If God is God then He can surely superintend the minds of those who put into writing the whole counsel of His will. And if God is too finite to prevent men from writing down error, it is hard to see wherein He is competent to prevent them from writing down error at every point. The problem here is that God still signs His name of approval to a book which is half from the devil.

11. This may appear puerile, as if everything can be solved by calling in God's sovereignty. Let not the profundity be missed, however, for the point at issue is how God can be good and still withhold from man the perfection of the autographs when the latter were so important in reflecting His own perfection. The answer is that God elected to do it. The good is what God does.

Worship due to God alone is usurped by a piece of bone or iron. The same would happen to the original words of Paul.[12]

2. As to the more difficult question why God did not extend inspiration to the copyists, when He could have done so because He is the Almighty; first, He elected not so to do, even as He elected to let his perfectly created universe fall into partial corruption. Secondly, since Christ is the Living Word, and yet was broken by the belligerent actions of sinful men, is it logical that the written Word, which depends upon Christ as the effect upon the cause, shall suffer less? Is the servant worthy of more honor than the master? Thirdly, permitting man to fall into transcriptional error in so holy and religious an assignment as copying the originally inspired manuscripts, is the highest possible testimony to that complete penetration into our inward lives that sin enjoys, and shows that, no matter how hard a zealot may concentrate, pray, and petition for grace, he still falls short of the immaculate Son of God. "He committed no sin; no guile was found on his lips" (I Peter 2:22). Meditation upon the problem of transcriptional errors, therefore, ought to excite us to repentance, not to fleshly arrogance, for, if we are apt to sin in matters which demand so peculiar a reverence and caution, how much more do we need grace to be preserved from falling into the hands of the evil one in daily life? Fourthly, as the original creation of nature was perfect, to be proportional to the perfection of God, and yet, though presently defective through the introduction of man's sin, is sufficient to bring men to a knowledge of God's glory and power; so also the written Word was inerrant, to be proportional to the truth and wisdom of God, and yet, though partially defective today through man's inattentiveness in transmitting the original words, is sufficient to bring men to a saving knowledge of Jesus Christ. Nature, though

---

12. This very thing happened in the case of the brazen serpent. The good king Hezekiah "broke in pieces the brazen serpent that Moses had made; for unto those days the children of Israel did burn incense to it" (II Kings 18:4). The absence of idol-veneration in conservative churches is due to a sober consideration of the command of God not to make any graven image like unto Him.

stained with the curse of sin, is quite sufficient to bring all men to condemnation by displaying God's handiwork, power, and glory; so also Scripture, though today slightly less perfect than when given by God, through the mal-copying of some, yet contains clearly and unmistakably all of those doctrines which are necessary to deliver us from the curse which is against us and to lead us to Christ. If the glory which is found in nature, and the truth which is found in the Bible, were heeded, man would have all the information required to bring him to salvation. "Jesus did many other signs in the presence of the disciples, which are not written in this book; but these are written that you may believe that Jesus is the Christ, the Son of God, and that believing you may have life in his name" (John 20:30-31). Thus, though the Bible needed to be originally pure to be commensurate to the work of a pure God, the present text need only be substantially pure, for its task is to lead men to salvation.

Before leaving this, it may be well to pass a remark on a new issue which this last observation has raised. If God can presently save us through a text which is not wholly without problems, why could he not have done so in the first place, and thus there was no need for an inerrant text at all? In answer, we teach that the original documents were inerrant, not that the writers might be saved, for they could have been saved with our text; but rather that only a jot-and-tittle perfect revelation could be commensurate to the perfect nature of God. God could not be perfect and still sanction a revelation which claimed to be originally without error, but was not. But observe that this compulsion holds only for the original writings and not for the present text, for the purpose of the present text is to lead men to repentance, and a document preserved substantially pure is sufficient to accomplish this task.

Again, how do we know that the passages in which the Bible claims to have been originally inerrant are not the very places which have come to us with transcriptional errors? Very easily. The lower critic has restored for us the text, and we learn from it what places are and are not in dispute. There is no conjecture at this point. Lower criticism is an exact science.

II. The Basic Issue

The conservative is convinced that the question which separates his view of Scripture from that of the higher critic is more than simply the status of certain objectively verifiable facts. Rather, two basic philosophies of life are at issue. The conservative conceives of reality supernaturalistically and redemptively, while the higher critic views it naturally and mechanically. The Christian denies the competency of man's mind to know reality without revelation, while the non-Christian confesses it. Our trouble, once again, is philosophy.

A. Proof from History

Philosophy may not bake bread, but it has an almost unbelievably powerful effect of setting the perspective of a man when he comes to reality to look at the facts. Philosophy makes up the glasses one wears: if the glasses are green, all looks green; and if they are red, all is red. A study of history shows that one's presuppositions really do affect his coloring of the facts. This observation holds particularly true in the optimism of the critics to revise and correct, rather than submit to, the text of the Bible, is the mood of rationalism and the enlightenment. Kant defined this optimism as follows: "Enlightenment is the liberation of man from his self-caused state of minority, which is the incapacity of using one's understanding without the direction of another. This state of minority is caused when its source lies not in the lack of understanding, but in the lack of determination and courage to use it without the assistance of another."[13] What Kant is saying, in short, is that man's reason, unaided, is all that one needs to follow in working out his world-view. Is this not a presupposition that special revelation is unnecessary? Being unnecessary, the higher critics have concluded that it is not actual.

---

13. *Was est Aufklärung?* 1784.

But this conviction remains only a philosophic hypothesis, and is subject to the judgments of the law of contradiction and the facts of history.

Along with the rationalistic hope that man in his own strength could develop a complete philosophy of life was the emergence within science of what has come to be called 'the principle of uniformity'; namely, that the same laws which hold true at one place in the world hold true likewise throughout the entire universe.

It might appear at first glance that this is a quite harmless assumption on the part of the scientist. One is left with the feeling that the *critic of this law* is a worse sort of a fellow than the critic of Scripture. If we do not have law reigning in the universe, what have we but chaos?

But like all principles devised to serve as a working explanation, the principle of uniformity has been abused through misuse. Not content to apply the thesis in the very narrow sphere of the physical sciences, philosophers have set out to reconstruct all of history and religion in the light of uniformity. A perfect example of this work is the staggering idealistic structure of Hegel. Convinced that the dialectic is the clue to the way God's mind is searching for self-consciousness, he plotted the history of Spirit, starting with pure being and ending up with the superiority of the German nation. It was unneedful that Hegel humbly and modestly submit to the Bible to learn the mind of God, for 'the real is the rational.' Since the order and nature of mind is the same as the order and nature of things, what value is the opinion of Jesus Christ? Christ is but a stage on the way of the evolution of all religion—the highest stage, perhaps, but only the highest *thus far*.

Rationally convinced on the above grounds that the Christian world-view is superfluous, therefore, it was only natural for men to turn upon the documents of Christianity and seek for an explanation of them within this naturalistically conceived frame of reality. Since the Christian and the naturalist differ *toto caelo* in their evaluation of reality, the "problem of religious investigation became, not to discover historical evidences of revelation, but rather to explain how supernatural beliefs took their rise and secured wide acceptance."[14] The problem of the Christian is to understand how anybody can be so conceited as to try to solve the problems of history without resorting to revelation, while the problem of the higher critic is to understand how anyone can be so feeble-minded as to call for the necessity of revelation in understanding reality in the first place. Needing revelation, the Christian struggles with the documents of the Bible under the supposition that they are the word of God; the critic, however, says that "if the Scriptures were taken as the work of human minds profoundly moved by a sense of divine things, all difficulty vanished; and the sacred books became the record of early mythological and imaginative attempts to understand the world and its meaning."[15] Observe what separates the Christian and the higher critic. It is not the facts of Scripture, but two different philosophies of reality. Choice must be made between them on the grounds of which best provides for human happiness, a rational view of the universe, and a basis for truth. Christianity cannot be ruled out *a priori* as a possible choice.

B. Proof from Prejudices

To buttress our conviction that the trouble with the higher critic is philosophy rather than the facts of the Bible, let us indicate three basic prejudices which the critic labors under when he approaches the text of the Scriptures.

1. *Predictive prophecies.* Isaiah (39:6) spoke to the people, who were at ease in an alliance with the Chaldeans, warning them of the utter destruction of the city and the banishment of the people. But not leaving the matter here, Isaiah went on

14. Randall, *op. cit.*, p. 458.
15. Randall, *op. cit.*, p. 536.

to mention the name of Cyrus (45:1), well over a century before Cyrus was born, who would rise against the Babylonians to release the people of Israel from exile. Jeremiah, before the event ever took place, limited the captivity to seventy years (25:11-12). So, dozens of prophecies were made and fulfilled while the covenant of grace unfolded, even to the minute fact that not a bone in Christ's dying body should be broken. The Christian considers these prophecies evidences of the divinely conceived character of the Bible, for they are what he ought to find if Scripture is fully inspired. But not so with the higher critics. Convinced that all prophecies which go beyond scientific generalizations are but sheer guesses, all documents that claim to be prophetic are called 'late,' as the book of Daniel, for example. Or there is 'accommodation,' as when John said that Christ's bones were not broken, to fulfill the Scripture (John 19:33)—John just put that in to give the appearance of fulfilled Scripture, but we have no evidence that it ever happened. To the Christian, such distortion of the text deserves contempt, not intellectual refutation.

2. *Miracles.* Assured that the universe is governed by natural law, the critic explains Christ's walking on the water by a series of submerged rafts, and His resurrection as but a resuscitation of His dying body by oriental balms. "Since Hume's critique of miracles in the eighteenth century, religious liberals have refused to believe in any such interferences with the order of natural law. The records they explain as the product of the natural causes of human credulity, imagination, and legend."[16] To the Christian, this is nothing but blinded prejudice.[17]

3. *Bible books.* When the Christian supernaturalism juts out too far, the critic, in his bias, has no difficulty rejecting entire books of the Bible. John is the classic example. Assured that it is 'Platonic,' the critic assigns everything that John

---

16. Randall, *op. cit.*, pp. 537-538.
17. We shall establish this below in Chapters XIV-XV. A hypothesis passes into a prejudice when the facts no longer stand as a threat to one's attitude toward a given data-situation.

says to 'Logos-speculation extracted from Greek tradition.' This explains why the critic is concerned only with the synoptic problem. The Christian views this not only as prejudice, but also as a poor knowledge both of Christianity and of Plato. The redemptive Logos of John has no counterpart in Heraclitus, Pythagoras, or Plato; it was the Lamb of God, the mystery hid from the foundation of the world. "*None* of the rulers of this age understood this; for if they had, they would not have crucified the Lord of glory" (I Corinthians 2:8).

III. The Strength of the Conservative Hypothesis

There are two sides to any hypothesis, the negative and the affirmative. We regret that, due to lack of space, we cannot show the negative strength of the conservative's hypothesis. If it were possible, we would show how modernism has reduced to humanism and humanism to skepticism, on the one hand, while neo-orthodoxy is quagmired in irrationalism, on the other. A second volume would be required to complete the demonstration, that, when one leaves the conservative's position on textual inerrancy, there is no stopping point short of skepticism and irrationalism. Therefore, we must be content here, merely to show but a few of the positive features which attend the Christian hypothesis.

A. Based on the Evidence

We have stressed *in extenso* the fact that, unless a hypothesis vertically fits the facts, it fails to meet the requirements set up for all valid assumptions. The conservative alone can take the Bible as it stands and account for it. This is a mark of true science. If there is a tree in the yard, for example, one does not succeed in explaining it by calling it a horse. Likewise, when the Bible claims to be an inerrant revelation, it is no explanation of it to call it a report of the religious experiences of certain men. Only the conservative can accommodate his hypothesis to the overt supernaturalism which is stretched across every page of Holy Writ. So, let us not soon forget that the Christian, not the higher critic, has actually faced and conquered the facts as they stand. If one assumes that the Bible is a human product, it becomes meaningless; but if one assumes the existence of the God Who has revealed Himself in Scripture, he can explain, not deny, the basic facts of the text of the Bible.

B. Accommodation of Difficulties

Though holding to an inerrant original text, the Christian is able nicely to accommodate whatever legitimate difficulties Biblical criticism can succeed in raising.

1. *Admission of the difficulties.* "All things in Scripture are not alike plain in themselves, nor alike clear unto all."[18] The Christian is alacritous to admit that there are not a few difficulties in the text of the Bible. In the Old Testament, for example, certain oriental idioms make a few passages in the prophets unintelligible at our present state of knowledge. Again, Paul spoke of women having to wear veils because of the angels (I Corinthians 11:10), of the baptism for the dead (I Corinthians 15:29), and of Michael contending with the devil about the body of Moses (Jude 9). Confessedly we see that these are difficult passages. And we need not even mention the highly figurative book of Revelation.

2. *Minor character of the difficulties.* "Yet those things which are necessary to be known, believed, and observed, for salvation, are so clearly propounded and opened in some place of Scripture or other, that not only the learned, but the unlearned, in a due use of the ordinary means, may attain unto a sufficient understanding of them."[19] The radicals of Christianity—the Trinity, the deity of Christ, creation, the virgin birth, the atonement, the resurrection, the image of God in man, the fall, etc.—have not been successfully attacked by higher criticism. But, to refute Christianity, one must show, not only that there are problems in the text of minor character —such as the women wearing veils because of the angels—but also that the fundamentals of the system of Christianity can-

18. *The Westminster Confession of Faith,* I, vii.
19. *Loc. cit.*

not mutually support one another; just as, to refute Plato, one must show that the radicals of Platonism are incompatible. Let us observe the significance of this. Since the logic of Christianity is secure, the critic has more of a task on his hands than he thinks; it is not enough to show that Noah could not get all of the animals into the ark or that the genealogies of Christ in Matthew and Luke seem discrepant. "The errors in matters of fact which skeptics search out bear no proportion to the whole. No sane man would deny that the Parthenon was built of marble, even if here and there a speck of sandstone should be detected in its structure. Not less unreasonable is it to deny the inspiration of such a book as the Bible, because one sacred writer says that on a given occasion twenty-four thousand, and another says that twenty-three thousand, men were slain. Surely a Christian may be allowed to tread such objections under his feet."[20]

A relevant piece of contemporary scholarship is the testimony of those who drew up the beautiful, Revised Standard Version of the New Testament. "It will be obvious to the careful reader that still in 1946, as in 1881 and in 1901, no doctrine of the Christian faith has been affected by the revision, for the simple reason that, out of the thousands of variant readings in the manuscripts, none has turned up thus far that requires a revision of Christian doctrine."[21] When the radicals of a system are secure, it is a solid piece of evidence that the system is secure.

3. *Parallel to empirical science.* "The Bible is no more a system of theology, than nature is a system of chemistry or of mechanics. We find in nature the facts which the chemist or the mechanical philosopher has to examine, and from them to ascertain the laws by which they are determined. So the Bible contains the truths which the theologian has to collect, authenticate, arrange, and exhibit in their internal relation to each other."[22] There is a close parallel between science and Chris-

---

20. Hodge, *Systematic Theology*, I, p. 170.
21. *An Introduction to the Revised Standard Version of the New Testament,* p. 42.
22. Hodge, *ibid.*, I, p. 1.

tianity which a surprisingly few seem to notice. As Christianity assumes that all in the Bible is supernatural, so the scientist assumes that all in nature is rational and orderly. Both are hypotheses based, not on all of the evidence, but on the evidence 'for the most part.' Science devoutly holds to the hypothesis that all of nature is mechanical, though, as a matter of fact, the mysterious electron keeps jumping around, as expressed by the Heisenberg Principle of indeterminacy. And how does science justify its hypothesis that all of nature is mechanical, when it admits on other grounds that many areas of nature do not seem to conform to this pattern? The answer is that, since regularity is observed in nature 'for the most part,' the smoothest hypothesis is to assume that it is the same throughout the whole.

In like manner the Christian looks upon the Bible. As Butler wisely observed, there is no difficulty in revelation which has not its counterpart in God's ordinary providence. The Christian carefully surveys the facts in the Bible and discovers that the regular and consistent witness of Scripture is that it is from God, wholly without error, and sufficient for faith and practice. Therefore, constrained by the convergence of this uniform testimony to Scripture's supernaturalism, the Christian adopts the hypothesis of the uniform supernaturalism of the whole of the Bible, although, *de facto,* there are minor patches of Scripture which may not at times seem to fit into this pattern. Thus, just as the scientist does not abandon his hypothesis that all of nature is regular and mechanical when he comes upon data which do not appear to fall into this pattern, in like manner the Christian is not required to give up his hypothesis simply because he is not fully aware of how all of the data in the Bible can be harmonized into one consistent whole. Shall the scientist be allowed to have his Heisenberg principles when the Christian must abandon his hypothesis simply because he is not sure whether the flood of Noah was universal in scope or local? This observation is all the more interesting when we observe that the higher critic rejects the Biblical narratives on presuppositions guaranteed by science.

4. *Reality involves mystery.* Edison once remarked that we do not know one-millionth of one percent about anything, but his estimate was generous. In relation to the mystery which we face in every direction, we hardly know anything. From the photosynthesis of the leaf to the beating of the heart, all of nature is shot through with awe-provoking mystery. Now, if science admits that the electron, the basis of all nature, is a complex affair, *a fortiori* what of the Trinity, the Author of the electron?

> It might seem that this confession of his own inability to resolve seeming discrepancy is not compatible with faith in Scripture as infallible. This is, however, at the best, very superficial judgment. There is no doctrine of our Christian faith that does not confront us with unresolved difficulties here in this world, and the difficulties become all the greater just as we get nearer to the centre. It is in connection with the most transcendent mysteries of our faith that the difficulties multiply. The person who thinks he has resolved all the difficulties surrounding our established faith in the Trinity has probably no true faith in the Triune God.[23]

If the leaf is complex, might it not be that the higher critic has not begun to grasp the profundity of Holy Writ? In any case, he certainly does not succeed in refuting conservatism by showing that there are obscurities in the Bible: all reality is obscure. The very presence of mystery in the Bible is *prima facie* evidence for the fact that it is dealing with, not avoiding, reality. "Great indeed, we confess, is the mystery of our religion" (I Timothy 3:16).

IV. Concluding Observations

Christianity knows no contradiction of its radicals. All the work of the higher critic has fallen short of refuting the system from this perspective. As for the minor difficulties, we appeal to the complicated character of reality, the parallels to science, and the fact of our own finitude and ignorance. Before leaving this question, however, two final observations may be made.

---

23. *The Infallible Word,* p. 6. The obscurity of reality is only from the human perspective. To God all facts are exhaustively known.

A. Perpetual Presence of Minor Difficulties

It may be that there are those who just cannot comply with the Christian philosophy of error as outlined, contending that a system of philosophy must be absolutely free from difficulties before one can rationally accept it. To such we say that the objection is impossible. If one is to cavil at, and, finally, to reject Christianity simply because it contains minor contradictions, he has resorted to the application of a criterion which not only refutes Christianity, against which it is directed, but also succeeds in refuting the basis of the very objection itself. To be significant, the objection must itself be free from all difficulties, which, obviously, is impossible. There is no presently known system of philosophy which does not contain, not a few, but many, many minor problems. To search after perfection, while we walk by faith and not by sight, is a quest after the Holy Grail.

B. Christianity Solves Problems

The Christian, by assuming that the original Scriptures were without error and that the present text is substantially pure, is in possession of a philosophy of life which is horizontally self-consistent and which vertically fits the facts of life. And if he rejects the hypothesis of the God Who has inerrantly revealed Himself in Scripture, he is left with a system which is not horizontally self-consistent and which does not vertically fit the facts of life. Without the data given in the Bible, one cannot, for example, explain satisfactorily the history of the Jews, the person of the historical Jesus, the origin of the religion of Paul, and the reason for the founding of the Christian Church. And what is science, but the ability to explain facts systematically? To know is to judge, and to judge properly is to be systematically consistent; and systematic consistency, when analyzed, turns out to be truth. If the Christian, with his view of the inerrancy of Scripture, is able to construct a system of thought which is coherent, can any more be legitimately required of him?

Chapter XII

The Problem of Common Ground

What partnership have righteousness and iniquity? Or what fellowship has light with darkness? What accord has Christ with Belial? Or what has a believer in common with an unbeliever? What agreement has the temple of God with idols?—Paul.

A FRUIT of the redemptively conceived *einheitliche Weltanschauung* of Christianity is a doctrine which startles one when it is first seen, but which, when understood, is recognized as a legitimate implication of that world-view. The doctrine we refer to is 'common ground.' "Be it observed, there is no such thing as a common ground between Christianity and a non-Christian system. From a world naturalistically conceived, one cannot argue to the God of the Christians. From a world-view that denies all revelation, one cannot produce a Biblical revelation."[1]

At first glance this seems like foolishness, and reminds us of Berkeley, who said that philosophers first raise a cloud ot dust and then complain that they cannot see. If there is no common ground between the system of the Christian and that of the non-Christian, it would seem to follow that the Christian and the non-Christian could not even talk to one another. But this is preposterous, for they cooperate daily in even the most technical scientific research without pleading two sets of figures, two columns of data, and two separate truth-systems.

To clarify the issue, let us point out that we are here discussing the Christian *world-view's toto caelo* divergence from a non-Christian *world-view,* not the conduct of individual men

1. Clark, *A Christian Philosophy of Education,* p. 164.

in their systems. To say that we can talk together is no refutation of our thesis, for it may very well be that the non-Christian's words are significant only upon the Christian's major premise of the existence of the God Who has revealed Himself in Scripture. In an open universe it is impossible to speak meaningfully at all, for anything may be its opposite before a concept can be translated into a word. Men speak together because they are all made in the image of God, not because there is common ground between Christianity and non-Christianity. Technically speaking, whenever a man talks and expects something to be meant by it, he is resorting to a prerogative which belongs to the Christian alone. On an empirical flux system, one can only, like Cratylus, wave his hand to express his philosophy, for from flux and change only flux and change can come. But no one likes to cease talking, be he inconsistent for so doing or no.

The very nature of Christianity demands that there be no common ground between the system of the godly and the system of the ungodly, for a man's attitude toward what he considers to be the highest logical ultimate in reality determines the validity of his synoptic starting point, his method, and his conclusion. The Christian, having chosen as his logical starting point the existence of the God Who has revealed Himself in Scripture, is admonished, as an implication of this starting point, to hew to the implications of this decision in every phase of life. "And whatever you do, in word or deed, do everything in the name of the Lord Jesus, giving thanks to God the Father through him" (Colossians 3:17). The non-Christian, having rejected as his logical starting point the existence of the God Who has revealed Himself in Scripture, lives, not for the glory of Jesus Christ, but for his own lusts. "Their end is destruction, their god is the belly, and they glory in their shame, with minds set on earthly things. But our commonwealth is in heaven, and from it we await a Savior, the Lord Jesus Christ" (Philippians 3:19-20). What a man thinks of Jesus Christ, therefore, determines his entire view of God and man.

It is folly, therefore, for the modernist to speak of the 'brotherhood of all men' on the basis of Christianity. If men do not have the same Father, how can they be brothers? Christ makes it plain that those who reject God Almighty as their logical starting point, reject also the Almighty as their Father. "You are of your father the devil, and your will is to do your father's desires" (John 8:44). All men are neighbors in virtue of their common creation by God, but only those in Christ Jesus can truly be called 'sons of God,' and, consequently, brothers one to another.

I. The Three Levels of Meaning

The key to our structure of common ground is the distinction we have made thus far in our study between fact and meaning. The facts of life are any units of being which are capable of bearing meaning; meaning is what the mind entertains when it passes judgment upon the facts. When you ask a man what he thinks of a thing, you ask him what it means to him. Truth, we have seen, is properly construed meaning; its parts stick together in coherence. Where the Christian world-view separates from the non-Christian world-view is not with facts, but with their meaning. There are basically three levels of meaning; an analysis of them will open up the way to a solution of our problem of common ground.

A. The Personal Level

By the personal level we understand that stratum of meaning which depends for its existence upon one's individual feeling in the presence of a given fact-situation, as 'Do you like spinach?' But judgment on the personal level cannot be called true or false, since it is simply an expression of how one personally reacts to any fact, person, or thing. To the ape, a banana personally means something which takes the wrinkles out of his stomach, something to throw, or something to swing from.

Personal attitudes, feelings, and prejudices help blind one's appreciation of objective reality. Here Bacon's idols are in order. "Everyone, as it were, dwells in a den of his own, from which he looks out upon the world in distorted ways. For instance, men become attached to different interests and subjects, in the light of which they color everything they encounter. They acquire what we generally describe as 'one-track' minds; they are the 'special pleaders' whose prepossessions have made them unfit for the reception of ideas that do not touch their favorite themes."[2] A final illustration or two may help. A fern plant which is purchased at the local florist means more after it has been used at grandmother's funeral than it did before. A flower from one you love means more than an ordinary posy. All these lie on the personal level. There is no common-ground problem here at all, because there is no question of truth at issue.

B. The Scientific Level

Our fern is now removed from the home and is taken to the botany laboratory, where it takes on a level of meaning which is still fully common to both Christian and non-Christian. Science seeks for the natural meaning of a thing; whatever personal feelings a given botanist may have toward the fern are considered quite irrelevant in the laboratory. The fern is known as part of the impersonal order, *Filicales,* a group of flowerless plants that resemble seed plants in being differentiated into root, stem, and leaves and in having vascular tissue.

We say there is no problem of common ground here, for scientific conclusions as such do not depend for their meaning upon one's logical starting point. Water is H_2O for the Christian no less than for the non-Christian. It would be absurd to suggest that Christians have a science all their own, as if nuclear physics, *qua* physics, is different when explained by the Christian than by the non-Christian. As long as the scientist confines his judgments to an impersonal description of what objectively exists in the world of flux, the problem of common ground has no relevance.

---

2. *Knowledge and Society,* The University of California Associates, p. 19.

C. The Metaphysical Level

Although the line that divides scientific judgments from metaphysical judgments is almost invisible, we can assuredly assume that there is a point where science leaves off and metaphysics begins. Neutrality in metaphysics is impossible. One either believes God is the Author and Judge of the universe, or he does not; there is no *tertium quid*. The fern to the Christian is a unit of being which has been originally made and is now sustained by the power of the Almighty, while to the non-Christian the fern is a unit of being which has been made and is now sustained by other than the Almighty. On this level, the level of ultimate meaning, the system of Christianity and the system of non-Christianity have absolutely no truth in common. God is the logical starting point for the Christian, and non-God is the logical starting point for the non-Christian. The reach of metaphysics is absolute: it overshadows every level of meaning. Therefore, a proper logical starting point can give one a clue to the real meaning of all existence, while a faulty logical starting point can throw one off the track at every point. This is what makes the division between the Christian system and the non-Christian system significant, for

> There is a way which seems
>   Right unto a man;
> But the end thereof are the
>   Ways of death.[3]

But this is not the whole story. So penetrating is the metaphysical level of meaning that it succeeds in reflecting back upon the lower levels also.

II. The Reflection of the Metaphysical Ultimate

Up to this point we have said that as long as ultimates are not talked about, the Christian and the non-Christian enjoy common ground. Now, let us point out that as far as the motive for human actions is concerned, the metaphysical level

---

3. Proverbs 14:12.

succeeds in removing all common ground between Christianity and non-Christianity. At times, it even vitiates common ground between scientists in the laboratory. It may appear that we have contradicted ourselves in this chapter, for previously we admitted that common ground exists between the Christian and the non-Christian scientist, while we now suggest that at times it must be denied. The solution is this. If a scientist elects not to talk about metaphysics in the laboratory, H_2O is quite in common to both Christian and non-Christian alike. But, as soon as a chemical formula is viewed under the genus of ultimate reality, *i. e.,* is related to one's logical starting point, common ground disappears. The Christian and the non-Christian are no longer talking about the identical thing, for they no longer *mean* the same thing by 'water'; H_2O to the Christian means something wet made by the Almighty, not by forces resident within the universe itself, as it does to the non-Christian. If, however, the scientist in the laboratory can succeed in operating within an impersonal, nonmetaphysical realm of meaning, be he Christian or non-Christian, the question of logical starting point is so far irrelevant to the arrangement. All one must do in such circles is announce what level he is talking about.

But it may be questioned whether a man *can* elect not to talk about ultimates in the laboratory. Is not one's metaphysics implied in his every predication as well as his every act? When the non-Christian speaks of water, certainly he means water that is *not* related to the Christian world-view. In reply, to be sure, one's metaphysics is *implicit* in every formula, but common ground concerns only *explicit* metaphysical meaning. As long as I keep to myself my ultimate level of meaning, and as long as my opponent keeps to himself his ultimate level of meaning, we can hold our scientific meanings fully in common. The proof for this is that it happens every day. The Christian and the non-Christian alike worked on the atom bomb. The former, unlike the latter, saw the Almighty implied in all he did, but such an implicit meaning-level had no place in the final scientific report. When science becomes metaphysical, it is philosophy, not empirical science. Pure science is confined to an impersonal description of the phenomenal universe.

On the level of moral action, however, all common ground between the consistent Christian and the consistent non-Christian system ceases. If he is scrupulous about the principles of his philosophy of life, the Christian lives before God at all times. As God's prophet he interprets reality according to God's mind; as priest he dedicates the meaning of reality to God; and as king he rules over nature for God's glory. The marching orders of the Christian are clearly given in Holy Writ. "And whatever you do, in word or deed, do everything in the name of the Lord Jesus, giving thanks to God the Father through him" (Colossians 3:17). A Christian scientist in the laboratory must dedicate his conclusions to God, even as he must live in every area fully aware that he will some day give an account to the Almighty for every thought entertained and every deed done.

And if the non-Christian is consistent, he likewise will act according to the dictates of his metaphysical ultimates. Seeing no God at the end of history, he will find no need to relate his present scientific conclusions to the Almighty; and knowing no Christ, he will act as if he will not fall into God's judgment at death. Thus James admonishes, "Come now, you who say, 'Today or tomorrow we will go into such and such a town and spend a year there and trade and get gain'; whereas you do not know about tomorrow. What is your life? For you are a mist that appears for a little time and then vanishes. Instead you ought to say, 'If the Lord wills, we shall live and we shall do this or that'" (James 4:13-15).

To recapitulate, person to person, Christian and non-Christian can enjoy common ground on every level of truth, save that of metaphysical. System to system, however, Christianity and paganism have absolutely no common ground whatever on any level, for, when a world-view is seen as a whole, it necessarily evinces a metaphysic, a metaphysic which governs every level of meaning.

Thus, when a man accepts Jesus Christ, he shifts his interest from one world-view to another. "Therefore, if any one is in Christ, he is a new creation; the old has passed away, behold, the new has come" (II Corinthians 5:17). But one does not see the implications of the Christian view of God and the world at once; he must grow in grace and knowledge. This is the Christian doctrine of sanctification. When the Christian fails to give God the glory in the laboratory, and thus sins, he is living as if the Christian God is not the Lord over every realm of life; but, having sinned, when he confesses his sins, he is restored to full fellowship with God and a consistent relation to the Christian metaphysic.

Because of his enjoyment of 'common grace,' the non-Christian is not consistent in his world-view; he is honest, pleasant, and kind—attributes which are meaningful only under the Christian world-view. 'Common grace,' plus inconsistency among individuals, serves to make common ground a theoretic, not a practical problem. Practically speaking, the Christian is pagan enough and the pagan is Christian enough to allow for common levels of action between them. Theoretically speaking, however, the system of Christianity in the ideal and the system of paganism in the ideal have absolutely no area in common. Christianity *qua* system waits for every truth upon God; non-Christianity *qua* system waits for every truth upon non-God.

It may now be asked why we discuss common ground at all. The answer is twofold. As a theoretic question it drives one to think in terms of philosophic systems. This is the only unit in which the problem of a world-view may be cast. When we talk of Christianity as a system of objective truth, we speak of it in the dimensions of a world-view. And as a practical question it reminds us of two things. First, that our every thought and act must be made captive under Christ, that we may die daily unto sin and live unto righteousness. Secondly, to remind us that, in our appeal to the logic of conservative Christianity, we do not seek to establish a common ground for contact between Christian and non-Christian. The *rationes* and the facts of nature are our formal contacts with each other, but they, by themselves, are not enough to bring one to a new life in Christ. The power of repentance comes from the effective agency of the Holy Spirit, and apart from this power, no man can know Christ's saving grace. But this power is available to all who pray in faith, not wavering.

III. Objections

A. Many Believe in God But Reject Jesus Christ

Christians say that God is their logical starting point, and then turn around and deny common ground between the Christian world-view and the non-Christian, forgetting that many, who reject the Trinity, sincerely believe in a personal Creator and Sustainer of the universe. Although they may not agree upon details, it appears that both Christian and non-Christian begin with God, and thus the whole structure of common ground is quite out of order.

Indeed, it is difficult to draw a line between Christians and non-Christians, for the former admit that when the latter worship God, they are in reality worshipping the true God, but they do not know it. But, strangely, after this admission we are still faced with the problem of common ground. The reason for this is that God, the final arbiter in all matters, has elected to accept worship in and only through His crucified Son, Jesus Christ. So Paul, finding the Athenians energetically worshipping the true God, did not simply commend them and then leave them as they were; rather, he preached to them the resurrected Christ, in relation to whom acceptable worship before the Father is possible. "What therefore you worship as unknown, this I proclaim to you . . . because he has fixed a day on which he will judge the world in righteousness by a man whom he has appointed, and of this he has given assurance to all men by raising him from the dead" (Acts 17:23, 31). When Paul *did* preach Christ unto them, their paltry love for the true God showed itself. They mocked and left, while but a few clung unto Paul. The Christian, therefore, is careful to point out that it is not enough to believe in God. The devils do this also and tremble! *"Believe in God, believe also in me,"* pleaded Christ (John 14:1). When Paul left Athens, he went to Corinth, and there he preached the risen Christ, for God promised that He had "many people in this city" (Acts 18: 10). These "many people" were those who would believe not only that there was an undergirding power in the universe, but that this very power was Jesus Christ, the Logos of God. Thus, though a man believes in God, that does not give him any common ground with the Christian. While the Christian theology is built upon Jesus' blood and righteousness, the non-Christian system of theology is not.

To this structure it may be objected that the above response is arbitrary, for it gratuitously assumes the validity of the Christian system. We do not deny that our answer is valid only within our major premise, but we have prepared for many pages now for this right so to appeal to Christianity as truth. Apart from the Bible we are unable to construct a philosophy of life; but with the Bible's message we learn that God now receives worship in and only through His beloved, crucified and risen Son, Jesus Christ. Thus, instead of the line that separates the Christian world-view from the non-Christian being invisible, in reality a concrete wall separates them, the wall of worship in and through the atoning God-Man.

Therefore it *is* pertinent to ask a man what he thinks of Jesus Christ, for "He who does not honor the Son does not honor the Father who sent him" (John 5:23), and, again, "No one comes to the Father, but by me" (John 14:6). What a man thinks of Christ determines what he thinks about the world, and the nature and destiny of man.

What will you do with Jesus?
  Neutral you cannot be!
Some day your heart will be asking,
  'What will He do with me?'

To trifle with Christ is suicide. "If anyone's name was not found written in the book of life, he was thrown into the lake of fire" (Revelation 20:15).

B. Logic and Mathematics are Common to All

All men have the *rationes;* therefore, they must be common. But the *rationes* are only common as facts. When the Christian accounts for these formal facts, he relates them to his logical starting point, God, while the pagan does not. It is a Christ-controlled universe versus a Christless universe, for Jesus Christ *is* the Wisdom of God, the Logos of reality, the Author of the *rationes.*

C. The Natural Law is Common to All

"Does not nature itself teach you that for a man to wear long hair is degrading to him?" asks Paul (I Corinthians 11:14). Surely this piece of information is independent of a man's metaphysical commitments. The natural law is therefore common to all men. In answer, the law is common by creation, and is a fact which all possess alike. But *explaining* this fact is not in common, and common ground is concerned with meaning not with facts. The Christian conceives of his moral nature as coming from a moral God Who redeems lost men in Christ, while the non-Christian does not. Once again, "He who does not honor the Son does not honor the Father that sent him."

D. Final Truth Leads to Intolerance

The church of the middle ages claimed final truth and a result was the burning at the stake of heretics. This will follow from any claim to finality. On the contrary, it is the finality of Christianity which preserves tolerance for tomorrow. If all truth is relative, then the truth that we should be tolerant is also relative; this leaves the horrors of the inquisition open as a possibility for tomorrow. Is it not evident that without final truth, it cannot be shown that one must love his neighbor today, and tomorrow?

E. The Inconsistent Lives of Christians

If the Christian has this final truth, why is it that on a bus one cannot tell the Christian from the non-Christian by his dress and actions? Distinguish between the system of Christianity and the actions of Christians. One that follows Christ ought to live without sin, but in daily life he fails to live up to this ideal. But this fact does not render the ideal superfluous, for it is only in relation to that ideal that we are able to speak of things as being more or less consistent. If there were not a changeless standard in the light of which we judge one another, it would be meaningless to speak of the 'inconsistency' in the lives of the followers of Christ. But once again we remind ourselves that the problem of common ground concerns systems of ideal thought, not the actions of feeble men within the systems. Until men are confirmed in righteousness they will struggle in inconsistency. This is not to be interpreted as an excuse to be indolent; it is rather an admission that wise men may continue their struggle for happiness, though it will never be obtained on earth, for they look "forward to the city which has foundations, whose builder and maker is God" (Hebrews 11:10).

The blindness of inconsistency due to sin is reciprocal, however. The non-Christian is so blinded by sin that he is ignorant of the fact that he uses Christian presuppositions to give frame and support to his pagan ultimates. Because of his sinfulness, the non-Christian continues to believe and teach things which are true only on the Christian system. For this reason there exists a genuine common ground between the inconsistent Christian and the inconsistent pagan. It is only when the non-Christian consistently articulates his facts and their meanings to ultimates other than the mind of the self-contained God as revealed in the Bible, that the relative truth, which he inconsistently and without right possesses, passes from inadequacy into absolute error. For example, the pagan who collects money to give to the poor as a philanthropic gesture does a good, but inadequate and incomplete, thing; good because it is what God commands to be done but incomplete because it is done without glorifying God. But when the money is collected in the name of a false religion, then the incomplete truth passes over into diabolical error.

Chapter XIII

The Christian Faith and the Scientific Method

When it is evening, you say, 'It will be fair weather; for the sky is red.' And in the morning, 'It will be stormy today, for the sky is red and threatening.' You know how to interpret the face of the heaven, but you cannot interpret the signs of the times.—Jesus Christ.

HISTORICALLY considered, the most successful opponent to the Christian method of verification is the scientific method, if we dare refer to a thing so manifold as a 'method.' Since its inception, the scientific or empirical procedure in proof has met with very little failure, until today most men are intoxicated with its promises and pledges. Under the steady direction of science, the world has been transformed from the darkness of medieval backwardness to the present mechanical age of dazzling light. What formerly took a thousand slaves a hundred weeks to perform, can now be achieved by the mere flick of a switch. From the motions of the ponderous planets above to the molecular construction of the most humble clump of mud below, science has interwoven nature with a system of empirical laws by means of which reality may be controlled and predicted.

It may not seem that Christianity has anything to fear from science, for the latter, not unlike the former, is in search of truth. But let us not be deceived. As historically conceived, empirical science is founded on an epistemology which undercuts the entire Christian metaphysic.

I. Transitional Material

A. The Cause for Friction Between Science and Christianity

It is not surprising that the empirical method revolted from the superstitious theology of the middle ages. Finding truth in superstition is like digging for gold: for every nugget pocketed, a mountain of slag must be carefully sifted and discarded. Legion are the myths, old-wives's tales, and charlatan fancies which were pawned off on a credulous public by the clergy of the church as veraciousness. Wandering vagabonds bore tales of wonderful beasts, strange plants, fountains of youth, and miraculous healings throughout the world, all of which fructified into an awed submission to the church and a witch-burning of the heretics. No one ever paused to verify these tales of tall giants, devils in caves, visions of virgins and crosses on hillsides, and visits with demons in valleys, for they were of a 'religious' nature. Hume classically expresses this fervor.[1]

> With what greediness are the miraculous accounts of travellers received, their descriptions of sea and land monsters, their relations of wonderful adventures, strange men, and uncouth manners? But if the spirit of religion join itself to the love of wonder, there is an end of common sense: and human testimony, in these circumstances, loses all pretensions to authority. A religionist may be an enthusiast, and imagine he sees what has no reality: he may know his narrative to be false, and yet persevere in it, with the best intentions in the world, for the sake of promoting so holy a cause: or even where this delusion has not place, vanity, excited by so strong a temptation, operates on him more powerfully than on the rest of mankind in any other circumstances; and self-interest with equal force. His auditors may not have, and commonly have not, sufficient judgment to canvass his evidence: what judgment they have, they renounce by principle, in these sublime and mysterious subjects: or if they were ever so willing to employ it, passion and a heated imagination disturb the regularity of its operations. Their credulity increases his impudence; and his impudence overpowers their credulity.

B. The Revolt of the Scientific Mind

Believing that superstitious theology resembles the mind of the savage which believes "perhaps as a result of some dream about a deceased parent, that dead ancestors were somewhere

1. *Inquiry,* Section 10, Part II.

living the same kind of life they had lived here,"[2] the scientist determined to clean house. To him a thing is not verified because a council or a church prelate declares it, but rather when it terminates upon a carefully prepared inductive experiment. Humility before the facts, not prostration before the pope, was the way to learn what the real world was all about. To foster this ideal, science set down certain canons to guide itself.

1. *Intelligibility of the entire universe.* Men in the medieval period had been taught that they should not pry into nature too closely or they would be overpassing the rights of human beings. Nature has patches of mystery through which finite minds are not to perambulate. For science, however, there are no areas in the entire structure of reality that are not completely rational throughout. Blind, churchy, credulous faith has no part in the scientist's apparatus.

2. *The reign of law.* The scientist means by 'intelligibility' the presence of natural law behind every phenomenon. Thus, nothing happens in the universe without having a sufficient, natural reason behind it, a reason which can be located if patient inquiry is carried on long enough to find it. "The boldness of the faith of modern science lies precisely in the fact that it insists on an ideal of intelligibility that spurns all limitations; for its implicit conviction there is absolutely nothing in nature, however capricious to ordinary observation, that is not at bottom reducible to universality of law. Every relation is regular if we but penetrate to its determining conditions."[3]

3. *No need for revelation.* A concomitant presupposition is that there is no need to appeal to special revelation to explain reality. Science sees no value in presupposing the existence of God. "Since the divine purposes are recognized as inscrutable to human minds, nothing can be deduced from such an idea; we cannot say that if God has created something, then such

---

2. Burtt, *Right Thinking,* p. 57
3. Burtt, *Religion in an Age of Science,* pp. 45-46.

and such specific facts will be found in it. It is primarily for this reason that modern science, while not denying the validity of a religious attitude toward the world, has found it necessary to abandon appeals to God to explain this or that particular occurrence."[4] Observe, that, by appealing to but one presupposition—the character of all reality as natural, mechanical, and self-contained, in the whole, and in the part—the scientist by definition precludes the possibility of miracles; he eliminates the need for the Christian God; and he renders superfluous the appeal to special revelation. For this reason, we are assured that Christianity may ally itself with the scientific method only with caution. In a rational universe, the presuppositions of naturalism and the presuppositions of supernaturalism cannot simultaneously be true.

C. The Capitulation of Modernism

Not all men immediately saw that one cannot have his cake and his penny, too; one cannot succumb to the scientific method as the only way of knowing reality, and still cling to Christian supernaturalism. Yet, large blocks of Protestant theologians were talked out of their faith in the inerrancy of the Bible by those self-imposed ideals of science. Whatever parts of the Bible science rejected, modernists believed were no longer necessary to the modern man's creed; if God is rational, truth cannot contradict itself, be it from the Bible or from science, they reasoned. By this surrender to science, however, liberalism has reduced Christianity to an ephemeral, normless, this-worldly, tentative religion. In its abortive zeal to harmonize Christianity and the empirical sciences, it has given the conciliatory olive-branch to the latter. It has made Christianity empirical and scientific, rather than science Christian—the difference is vast! It has socialized and modernized Christianity rather than Christianizing science and modern thought. The end of liberalism, which we are now observing in this very day, has come because of its own internal weakness; it lacks a metaphysics which can solve the prob-

4. Burtt, *Right Thinking,* pp. 86-87.

lem of the one within the many and provide us with a basis for changeless truth. It has covered up this deficiency by employing conservative terminology. "To an impartial observer there does seem, in the liberal positions, much confusion and lack of precise thinking, as well as the appearance at least of a lack of frankness and a fondness for esoteric 'reinterpretation' that may approach in its effects actual hypocrisy."[5]

D. The Resistance of the Conservatives

The conservatives, like the Roman Catholics, saw the handwriting on the wall, as science came into its own. If all was to be made relative and tentative, then there was no way to keep Christianity itself from descending to the status of flux and change. Furthermore, if there are no miracles, then Christ is not risen from the grave. But,

> If Christ has not been raised, then our preaching is in vain and your faith is in vain. We are even found to be misrepresenting God, because we testified of God that he raised Christ, whom he did not raise if it is true that the dead are not raised. For if the dead are not raised, then Christ has not been raised. If Christ has not been raised, your faith is futile and you are still in your sins. Then those also who have died in Christ have perished. If in this life we who are in Christ have only hope, we are of all men most to be pitied.[6]

To comment upon these beautiful words would be to try to improve upon the grandeur of a freshly blossomed American Beauty rose. Only the blind can fail to see that there can be no Christianity without miracles. Remove Christ's bodily resurrection, and you have removed one of the basic supporting pillars of our salvation.

E. The Contemporary Dilemma

So wide is the rift between science and Christianity today, that hope of harmony has been abandoned by practically

---

5. Randall, *The Making of the Modern Mind,* p. 527.

6. I Corinthians 15:14-19. We shall face the problem of verifying miracles shortly.

all. Having so departmentalized our fields of learning that they completely lack a coordinating principle of harmonization, the scientific method forces the modern student to wander from classroom to classroom, armed with no metaphysical principle to unite the disciplines he studies. Having been taught a smattering of ethics and sociology, combined with a piecemeal interpretation of history, our contemporary university student follows the pattern of an animated robot, for, though he can recite the canons of quantum physics, he has little or no idea what the divine sanctions in the decalogue are. Consequently, although able to classify the bugs in Borneo, he cannot solve that problem of personal happiness which harasses millions of groveling human beings.

> The confusion is deep because the substituting of unrelated aims for a single comprehensive aim in education is both the result and the example of the absence of any ultimate aim for human life as a whole. If the educators had any view of the chief end of man, they would find it easier to locate the proper place of liberal education. Whether it be the views of an individual professor or the policy of a faculty, all will be confusion unless founded on an unambiguous world-view. But this is what modern education does not have.[7]

The shift of man's interest from the resurrection of Jesus Christ to the nervous system of the frog has not been without its repercussions. So adept in technology and so weak in moral virtue is modern man, that he faces potential extermination by another world war through the fruits of the very method which science has embraced *ex animo*.

> Our predicament is a commentary, not on instruments and instrument makers, but on the human inability to employ both scientific knowledge and technical achievement to bring about the good life and the good society. Man is an animal who is peculiarly in need of something to buttress and to guide his spiritual life. Without this, the very capacities that make him a little lower than the angels lead to his destruction. The beasts do not need a philosophy or a religion, but man does.[8]

---

7. Clark, *A Christian Philosophy of Education,* pp. 17-18.
8. Trueblood, *The Predicament of Modern Man,* p. 17.

Science's power is truncated. It can produce buzz bombs without difficulty, but it has no means of controlling the hearts of the men who get a hold on such bombs. Yet "out of the *heart* come evil thoughts, murder, adultery, fornication, theft, false witness, slander. *These* are what defile a man" (Matthew 15:19-20). It is important that we enjoy technological improvements, for all good things are given by God for man's usage; but "it ought to be clear as a flare and as emphatic as a bomb that *who* uses these for *what* is a tremendously more important matter than their invention . . . Every mechanical aid, by which Thorndike judges that a society is good, can be used by bureaucrat or dictator to make his society bad."[9] What scientific experience can change the vile heart of man? What chemical formula can prevent man from plotting that last war which shall destroy all life? Man, as ever, needs God to give his moral life direction and reason.

In an age of atom power, will the scientist continue to support the archaic, benighted hypothesis that Christianity lies outside the pale of verification? Christianity *must* be true unless science itself is to be destroyed by the few Frankenstein monsters that it has created. Only the moral law of Christ can save us now.

II. The Proposed Rapprochement

The Christian needs the scientist, and the scientist needs the Christian. Since Christianity must fit the facts of nature to be true, it waits upon the maturity and precision of the scientific methodology to amass and screen the data of history. The inductive examination of the evidence is the best scheme thought out yet to show the veracity of particular historical events. If the resurrection of Christ did or did not occur, for example, one must turn to the verdict of the carefully plotted grammatico-historical method. But the scientist needs Christianity, too, though he may not at first appreciate its offer to help. To show this mutual interdependence better, let us

9. Clark, *ibid.*, pp. 22-23.

examine three disciplines which are ***sine qua non*** for science, but which can be defended only by a philosophical-theological method. These disciplines are metaphysics, epistemology, and ethics.

A. Metaphysics

Science assumes that nature is regular throughout but, not having seen the whole, how does it account for this grandiose assumption? It seems that, unless we know on other grounds that the Author of the universe has elected to keep it rational, we cannot meaningfully anticipate nature at any point; for, in an open universe, there is always a 50/50 chance of anything, or its opposite, happening. It is not enough to base one's metaphysical hypothesis, that the universe is regular throughout, upon the simple fact that with this hypothesis we are able to predict and to control nature; for the possibility always remains that tomorrow's experience will be *totally different* from what we have had today. Unless the scientist can succeed in showing how today and tomorrow are organically united he must admit that his optimistic hypothesis that the universe is regular is quite without compelling rational basis.

It is evident that we *need* the hypothesis of the universe's regularity, but the Christian reminds the scientist that only he can *account* for that regularity. By wisdom God founded the heavens and by understanding He laid out the earth. It is part of the coherence of Christianity that nature can be rationally relied upon to keep her steady course. The Lord Almighty swore to Noah and his children forever that He would not again destroy the world by flood, and that "while the earth remains, seedtime and harvest, and cold and heat, and summer and winter, and day and night shall not cease." (Genesis 8: 22). Thus, as long as there is an earth here at all, the Christian is able to guarantee for the scientist that there will be maintained that order of sequence which the latter requires for the success of his method.

B. Epistemology

Science is empirical in its theory of knowledge, but we have learned from David Hume that out of the flux of nature nothing but skepticism can come. Now how can the scientist, who says he finds all of his data in the laboratory, claim normative validity for his conclusions, or for anything else, when the very method he employs can produce nothing but skepticism? There can be no normative truth on the ledger unless we have a theory of knowledge that makes normative predication possible. Take, for example, the proposition, 'All of our scientific conclusions are tentative.' What laboratory experiment can establish the validity of this? No inductive experience can settle the truth of this or any other universal proposition. Induction, to be successful, must be supported by a non-inductive epistemology which allows some changeless truth to be possible.

Once more the success of science is contingent to the antecedent truth of Christianity for it is the latter's world-view which is able to come forth with those universal and necessary propositions that make significant inductions possible. We have previously outlined the nonempirical arguments for the existence of the *rationes.* Christ is the Wisdom of God, the Logos of nature. Having this structure clearly in mind, we understand the vision of science to know all reality. But deny the Christ, Who supports the *rationes,* and nothing that science says has any meaning at all.[10]

C. Ethics

The success of any scientist's reputation depends upon the honesty and thoroughness of his work. But why is it that the scientist believes that being honest will be the best policy *tomorrow?* Has he had a private revelation on the subject? Perhaps lying in scientific journals will be the vogue five seconds from now. Yet the scientist persists in his conviction that

10. We feel justified in this relatively superficial statement of the epistemological rapprochement between science and Christianity, for there is no need here to repeat all of the arguments against empiricism we have previously outlined, simply to clinch our point. We presuppose at this point everything that has preceded in the text thus far.

honesty is the right mood for all men of truth to follow, today, tomorrow, and forever. We would not trust that scientist who even remotely suggests that one week from today a cheat or a fraud might be a model scholar. But what we wonder is, where has this normative conviction on the part of the scientist come from? A chemical formula? A field trip to Albania? The intestines of an elk? The rings on Saturn?

When the empiricist persists in defending honesty and integrity in the laboratory as a normative truth for all times he is unconsciously leaving his inductive method and is turning to philosophy. And if he will examine the problems of philosophy very carefully, he will learn that it is only within Christianity that metaphysics and epistemology *are* so stated that changeless ethical norms are rendered possible. "I am Jehovah thy God . . . Thou shalt not bear false witness against thy neighbor" (Exodus 20:2, 16). With an atom-bomb war looming on the horizon, we are not surprised to learn that "a marked change has characterized the attitude of modern scientists, and (that) today science is no longer inclined to dismiss the deliverances of the moral and religious consciousness as necessarily illusory."[11] It ought to be clear to the most positive of the positivists, that if ethical conduct is to have meaning at all the rules that guide it cannot come from the flux of the laboratory.

This is what we mean by the rapprochement between Christianity and the scientific method. Without the help of the scientific method, Christianity cannot make accurate contact with the details of God's providential working in nature; and without Christianity, science has no metaphysical, epistemological, or ethical frames of reference within which to give world-view meaning to the facts it colligates.

Two strange revolutions have occurred in history. First, the church became arrogant and declared its independence of science, a blundersome gesture. "The battle was for the Church a series of almost continuous defeats. Rushing in where

11. Joad, *Philosophical Aspects of Modern Science*, p. 13.

savants feared to tread, an army of unprepared and uninformed clergymen were beaten off the field by the withering fire of fact with which the biologists, the geologists and the physicists bombarded them. Rarely have controversialists chosen their ground so unwisely. Rarely has there been such a humbling of spiritual pride."[12] The church has repented of its rashness; it confesses humbly today that it cannot fulfill God's command to subdue nature without the precision of the scientific method. But, secondly, with the rise of the scientific method, science shook the dust of the church off from its heels and declared itself independent from theology, a likewise blundersome gesture. Now that science has displayed all of its power in the Second World War, observe its impotency in time of peace, when there is so much power vested in the veto. While outwardly professing their love for peace, the nations are frantically engaged in underground research for more awful weapons than have been dreamed of yet. Science can do almost everything but control the heart of man. And yet this is the one thing needful, the one thing that will save us from total annihilation. Only philosophy can get into the heart of man; and only Christian philosophy is attended by a power which is able to make philosophy work. It is time that the scientist repents of his rejection of Christ, lest a worse thing fall upon him than an atom bomb. Falling into the hands of the living God will make an atom war seem like a mild experience.

III. Concluding Problems

Though the conservative believes that he has the only metaphysical scaffolding which is strong enough to support the ideals of science, many, strangely, feel that orthodoxy is little likely to succeed for the very reason that it is contrary to the ideals of science at so many points. "Orthodox Christianity . . . cannot come to the aid of modern man, partly because its religious truths are still imbedded in an outmoded science and

12. Joad, *God and Evil,* p. 132.

partly because its morality is expressed in dogmatic and authoritarian moral codes."[13] It is difficult to follow this reasoning. We can see nothing in proper science which conflicts with the Bible. Let us look at some of the more frequently discussed objections.

A. The World-View of Jesus

The first thing that strikes the scientist as being wrong with conservative theology is the view of reality which Jesus Christ held.

> His theory of the world . . . is squarely opposed to the scientific naturalism that a frank assessment of experience increasingly compels modern men to accept. Far from thinking of nature as an objective, law-abiding order, to which man must patiently learn how to adjust himself while assuming responsibility intelligently to transform those parts of it that are amenable to human control, he believed it to be directly subject in all its details to the purposive care of a personal being. Every hair of our head is numbered; no sparrow falls without his supervision. Repent of your sins, love your neighbor, and have faith in God, is his counsel.[14]

This is an interesting twist to things. Let us not forget that all that science actually observes in nature is a sequence of regularity; but this regularity is compatible with either Christianity, where God keeps it regular, or with blind naturalism, where (goodness knows what!) keeps it regular. Since the order of nature can be accounted for by both Christ's teleology and the mechanical system, one is to choose between these world-views by seeing which shows itself to be more horizontally self-consistent and more able to fit the facts of history. Christ can account for metaphysics, epistemology, and ethics; science cannot. Thus, rather than reject Christ for science, a rational man, if he must make an either /or choice, will reject science for Christ. If Christianity is true, we find here a good case of a mouth biting the hand that feeds it. The Father of Jesus Christ is He Who keeps the universe

---

13. Niebuhr, *An Interpretation of Christian Ethics*, p. 4.
14. Burtt, *Types of Religious Philosophy*, pp. 359-360.

regular, and yet it is this very Deity-directed regularity which the scientist seizes upon to show there is no need for Deity at all.

Furthermore, science may scoff at Christ's salvation, but, as a matter of fact, man, if he is in his right mind, is more interested in being saved than in having new flame-proof curtains invented by science. Even in so practical a thing as economics, spiritual well-being is considered more important than having enough food to eat. "We have not yet learned how to prevent business depressions, but we have at least come to see that the moral injury of prolonged unemployment for workmen and of closed opportunity for youth is a more serious and difficult problem than that of bodily hunger."[15] As man fears insecurity more than hunger, so he fears God more than the failure to have his new automobile delivered. When science looks askance upon Christ's theology, it is treading under foot the only system of meaning which can keep man from becoming a manic-depressive.

B. The Incarnation and Astronomy

In chapter one we indicated that science has pushed the boundaries of our universe out almost to infinity. A strange conclusion has been drawn from this premise. Since the universe is so big, it seems unlikely that God chose this planet on which to become incarnated. Therefore Christianity is impossible. First, what possible connection is there between the ***size*** of the universe and *Christ's redemption*? God, Who made reality, certainly can dispose of it in any way He elects. The larger we see the universe to be, the more marvelous it should make our salvation, not the more impossible.

> O what a wonder that Jesus found me,
> Out in the darkness, no light could I see.
> O what a wonder, He put His great arm under,
> And wonder of wonders, He saved even me!

---

15. *Twentieth Century Philosophy,* (Runes, ed.), p. 36.

Secondly, *we* are the ones that are in spiritual trouble. Speculating as to whether there are people on Mars will not help *our* plight here on earth. *We* are in the process, *we* need to be saved. To declare glibly that God has no awareness of us because the universe is so big, is to throw us to the mercy of the second law of thermodynamics. On this scheme man is but a jest or a joke, not a creature of infinite dignity. God must be interested in us, or we are above all most to be pitied.

C. Geocentricism and the Old Testament

From such passages as Joshua 10:12, where Joshua says, "Sun, stand thou still upon Gibeon," and sundry passages where reference is made to the "four corners of the earth," some conclude that the Bible rejects the heliocentric system of astronomy. This is a prize example of forcing a natural meaning into an unnatural mold. These utterances no more commit the writers of the Bible to a specific view of astronomy than do the statements of our radio commentators, that the sun rose this morning at five-forty, commit them to a given scientific judgment. The Bible is written by very ordinary men. They employ what is called the optical point of view; they describe nature just as it appears to the observer, not as it may look to the disciplined scientist. Take, for example, the statement that "the sun was risen upon the earth when Lot entered Zoar." This is pure optical language. *It is a true description of an event from the point of view of the observer.* Translated scientifically, it would read — as another has put it — "that Palestine had revolved, when Lot entered the city, until its tangent plane coincided once more with the solar azimuth." The inconvenience of this is self-evident.[16]

D. Genesis and Evolution

Let us conclude our study with a brief analysis of that touchy question, evolution. The fact of evolution is here to

---

16. We could, though we will not here press it, make it clear that all motion is relative, anyway. Whether the earth moves around the sun or the sun moves around the earth, then, depends upon what one elects as his frame of reference.

stay; so we must treat of it, even though it be with extreme reserve and caution. Scientists claim that from Darwin's day to the present, not "a single fact has been discovered to shake the conclusions of Darwin that all living beings have evolved from earlier simpler forms; rather the mass of cumulative evidence has grown mountain high, so that no intelligent man can possibly deny to-day the *fact* of organic evolution."[17] Furthermore, in dealing with evolution, we are coming close to the prerogatives of empirical science, and the church has been warned on every hand that "her unfortunate conflict with modern cosmology in the seventeenth century" is proof enough that "it is under no circumstances advisible for her to affiliate with any scientific system."[18]

Yet we feel constrained to say something on the issue, for the Bible account seems to lean over backward to tell us that man is not genetically related to the lower animals. The problem of evolution is not parallel to that of geocentricism, for Moses is clearly committed to a theory of man's origin which is other than that of modern science. If the carefully detailed account of man's origin in Genesis is part of an inerrantly inspired word of God, and not simply one small section of a pious volume which adorns our tables when the priest or minister calls, then this hypothesis of man's origin must be taken seriously—God's judgments are never to be trifled with. Furthermore, we feel assured that we here deal with a problem which is more philosophical than scientific; and when a philosophy is set up in competition with Christ's world-view, we believe we are under obligation to investigate it. Finally, it is incumbent upon us to show that when a theologian charges orthodoxy with toying with an 'outmoded science' he succeeds in so doing only by attributing to conservatism certain propositions which that system does not require.

Just exactly what *has* science found that gives it its right to defend 'total' evolution? First, there is the mountain-high pile of data which proves beyond doubt that the structural and

---

17. Randall. *op. cit.*, p. 474.
18. Paulsen, *Introduction to Philosophy*, p. 159.

functional sides of men and certain animals are similar. But, let us not forget that similarity does not necessarily mean genetic kinship, for God may have elected to create man and the higher animals with similar frames. Secondly, there is the equally imposing mass of data to prove that the time-honored doctrine of the 'fixity of species' must be scrapped. Paleontologists have demonstrated that 'species' in many cases have come from common ancestors; this evidence is too secure to be questioned. From these, and other facts, science assumes the truth of 'complete' evolution.

And exactly what does Moses teach? First, that the unit of life which God originally created, which is expected to remain 'fixed,' is not the 'species' of science, but, rather, the 'kind' of the book of Genesis, such as 'herbs yielding seed,' 'trees bearing fruit,' 'birds,' 'cattle,' 'creeping things,' and 'beasts.' Observe, therefore, that the conservative may scrap the doctrine of the 'fixity of species' also, without jeopardizing his major premise in the least. The Christian, thus, can accommodate a 'threshold' evolution, *i. e.,* a wide and varied change within the 'kinds' originally created by God. We shall return to this in a moment. Secondly, man is one of these original 'kinds,' and consequently is not genetically related to the lower 'kinds.' Man was made out of the dust by a special, *ab extra,* divine act, with a body which is structurally similar to the higher Vertebrata, and a soul formed after the image and likeness of God.[19]

Now, observe that both Christianity and science can accommodate the datum that the functional and structural aspects of man and of certain animals are similar. The problem, therefore, cannot turn upon this issue. Next, the doctrine of the 'fixity of species' is not required by either structure. The real crux, we feel, is the Bible's rejection of the evolutionary hypothesis that the basic 'kinds' of Genesis are related to still

19. Another reason why we cannot construe the words of Moses to suggest man's evolution, is that Adam was created temporally prior to Eve, thus eliminating that contemporaneity of the sexes at the first appearance of man, which is required on the 'complete' evolutionary scheme. We shall not press this, but it is salutary to point it out.

more primitive orders by their having evolved from them. On the 'threshold' evolution view, there are gaps which exist between the original 'kinds,' while on the 'total' evolution view, each 'kind' can be traced back to a more primitive type, and that, to a still more primitive, *ad infinitum.*

But let us challenge the validity of the 'total' evolution scheme. Paleontology reveals that *there are actual gaps* in our knowledge of the relation between the 'kinds,' a datum which 'threshold' evolution can account for more smoothly than can 'total' evolution. "There are no fossil animals to connect the order of insectivores (containing moles and shrews) and the order of rodents (mice, beaver). Not a single order of mammals (hairy animals) has transitional forms between it and any other order."[20] When science is faced with these gaps, it resorts to such hypotheses as 'missing links' (which are still missing!) and 'mutations,' while the Christian needs only to point to the fact that God, in the original creation, decreed that gaps should exist to mark off the original 'kinds'—herbs yielding seed, creeping things, beasts, etc.[21]

Lecomte du Noüy lists the Archaeopteryx as an intermediary link between reptiles and birds (*Human Destiny,* p. 67), and yet even *this* instance is in doubt. "In spite of the fact that it is undeniably related to the two classes . . . we are not even authorized to consider the exceptional case of the Archaeopteryx as a true link." (pp. 71-72)

Let us not fail to grasp the logic of the argument. Both the scientist and the Christian admit there *are* gaps between the orders or 'kinds' of plants and animals. But, while the scientist, on his scheme of 'total' evolution, must resort to the tenuous fabrications of 'missing links' and 'mutations,' the Christian, with his 'threshold' evolution, can accommodate both the gaps which paleontology reveals to exist between the orders, and the development of the multitudinous 'species' within these orders. "It is conceivable, then, that the 'orders'

20. Mixter, *Genesis and Geology,* in *Christian Opinion,* Vol. III, No. 4, p. 120.

21. Whether the 'kinds' of Genesis correspond exactly to the orders of science, only further exhaustive research can tell us. The Bible simply sets forth natural divisions; it is the job of the scientist to locate them.

of the paleontologist correspond to the 'kinds' of Genesis. Christian opinion holds to the derivation of certain types directly from the original activity of God in commanding the earth to 'put forth grass, herbs, and trees,' 'bring forth living creatures after their kind, cattle and creeping things,' and in telling the waters to 'swarm with swarms of living creatures.' This creative activity would produce kinds separated by gaps from other kinds. Is it not probable that the gaps of Genesis and the gaps of geology are the same?"[22]

Let us also observe that the Bible teaches that what distinguishes man from the lower 'kinds' is not the structure of his organism, but, rather, *his having been made in the image and likeness of the Almighty.* Yet science tries to base its case for human evolution upon the structural similarity between man and the other Primates or Vertebrata, when, as a matter of fact, this need not be the key to unlocking the mystery of man's origin. The Christian teaches that though Pithecanthropus may have had a frame which evolved considerably within the appointed limits of 'threshold' evolution, even to the point where he resembled the other Primates more than does modern man, that structural deviation does not relieve Pithecanthropus of his membership in the classification *Homo sapiens.* Even science admits that all of the fossil men that it has discovered are still *men,* despite their structural peculiarities. Since the individuating principle in man is not his bone-structure, but rather his rational nature and his qualifications to worship God, the *fact* that the bodies of the primitive men have evolved in this way or that, is neither here nor there. We *expect* organic evolution within the 'kinds,' for God has only promised the 'fixity' of the broad 'kinds,' not of the infinite 'species' that can develop out of them. All sentient beings that are qualified to worship God are *men,* no matter what their bone structure, be they Pygmy or Nordic. The point of the Bible is that no matter how much the structure of man may vary within the 'kind,' such as pigmentary changes in the skin and physical compensations of one sort or another,

22. Mixter, *loc. cit.*

a man cannot develop into a hog or a bird, nor can a bird or a hog develop into a man. The bird is a bird; the hog is a creature; and man is a sentient being qualified to worship God. They belong to different, not-to-be-confused 'kinds.'

We say our problem is philosophical, because both 'total' and 'threshold' evolutionists resort to hypotheses which go beyond the facts. When the way becomes dim for the evolutionist, he appeals to his imagination; and when the way becomes dim for the Christian, he appeals to the structure of the Bible. Obviously we have two world-views here in conflict. "Here, then, are two choices open to one who meditates on the origin of living organisms. In one case, reliance is placed upon a natural process which changes one or a few early forms into the multitudes of our present flora and fauna. Whenever there are lost pages in the evidence, they are supplied by the hopeful beliefs in speculations. On the other hand, the orthodox Christian puts his confidence in a supernatural Being who has endowed water and earth with life and mind. He believes the gaps exist as natural breaks in the plan of God and these gaps are spaces between the kinds of Genesis."[23]

Since our problem is philosophical, recall from chapter five what we must do when two competing world-views vie for acceptance. A rational man must elect to accept that one which can make the most coherent picture out of the *total* character of our experience, within and without. Now, since both 'total' and 'threshold' evolution can account for the basic findings of geology and paleontology, we may cancel out this level. Our decision must be made between them on broader considerations. When viewed as a whole world-view, 'total' evolution cannot begin to compete with 'threshold' evolution. We have earlier traced how empiricism leads to skepticism. But supernaturalistic Christianity, in addition to accounting for the fundamental facts of nature nicely through the doctrine which we call 'threshold' evolution, can coherently solve the problem of immortality, establish the rational character of the universe, and locate a basis upon

23. Mixter, *op. cit.*, p. 121.

which changeless truth may rest. Reject the words of Moses in favor of the 'total' evolution structure, and you are left with a view of things which cannot better handle the findings of geology and paleontology than the 'threshold' evolution, cannot solve the problem of personal immortality, cannot establish a rational view of the universe, and cannot locate a scheme of changeless truth. Not without relevance, then, did Christ castigate the scientists of his day. "When it is evening, you say, 'It will be fair weather; for the sky is red.' And in the morning, 'It will be stormy today, for the sky is red and threatening.' *You know how to interpret the face of the heaven, but you cannot interpret the signs of the times*" (Matthew 16:2-3). It appears that there is more to the job of detailing a world-view than examining and classifying clouds and sky.[24]

The relation between science and Christianity is like the relation that subsists between the parts of the body. The arm cannot say to the foot it has no need of it, nor the eye to the heart it has no need of it. The body of classified knowledge, like the church of Christ, cannot be harmoniously knit together until all of the parts cooperate to maintain a corpus of thought which is horizontally self-consistent and which vertically fits the facts of life. The scientist may locate the facts, but he cannot make them stick together without the pattern of the mind of Christ; and Christianity, while it may be self-consistent, cannot enjoy perfect tangency to the data of nature until it relates its system to the empirical data of science. In union there is strength; in division there is weakness.

We have deliberately avoided a thorny question in this chapter, that we might give it separate attention. We refer to the problem of miracles. Miracles have been under fire for so long now, that we must give a careful statement of our attitude toward them. This, then, is our next problem to face.

---

24. This structure provides food for thought on another subject. Noah, instead of having to round up, and put in the ark, all of the 'species,' had only to locate representatives of the original 'kinds' of Genesis. They were stock out of which, through 'threshold' evolution, all of our present types have evolved. This observation mitigates the problem of the ark considerably.

Chapter XIV

The Problem of Miracles and Natural Law

Why is it thought incredible by any of you that God raises the dead?
—*Paul.*

PERHAPS the conflict between Christianity and the scientific method shows itself no more perspicuously than in the latter's unequivocal, uncompromising judgment against the possibility of miracles. "For, obviously, the real existence of miracles, which are contraventions of the normal course of things, would turn the world from a system into a chaos, would wrench it from human control, and would place it at the whim of some supernatural being, whether deity or devil. Such a world would respond to witchcraft but not to science. The sorcerer would triumph over the physicist."[1] By examining this admission, we detect that there are two diametrically conceived world-views behind the Christian's insistence that miracles are *sine qua non for truth* and the scientist's insistence that miracles are *sine qua non for confusion.* In deciding between these two philosophic approaches, let us covenant to accept that one which, when viewed from all directions, is attended by the fewer difficulties.

I. Background Data

A. The Scope of the Issue

The problem which separates Christianity from a mechanically conceived world-view is not simply whether or not a miracle, such as the virgin birth of Christ, actually occurred, but rather whether miracles at all are possible. If we cast our

1. Dunham, *Man Against Myth,* p. 28.

problem in any lower dimensions than a strife between a supernaturalistically conceived and a naturalistically conceived *einheitliche Weltanschauung,* we can be assured that we are not grappling with the issue of miracles in its true proportions. To state the crux of the issue in boldest relief: Is the *Almighty* in sovereign control of all reality or are the *immanent laws*? Is the *mind of Christ* the *Logos* of things, or the *mind of autonomous man* the basis for all meaning? These questions state our problem in its proper breadth of importance.[2]

B. Spiritual Values and the Historicity of Miracles

When the conservative speaks of Christ's resurrection from the grave, he means that the phenomenon is as much a part of the actuality of history as Hannibal's military exploits or barnacles in Boston's harbor. The reason why we stress this is to uncover what is regarded by both conservatives and scientists as a truism, but which is not acknowledged by modern neo-orthodoxy.[3] We speak of the relation between spiritual values and historical facts. They cannot be separated in a rational world. If Christ was not literally, bodily, and em-

---

2. Orr sums up the problem succinctly. "A good deal of controversy has recently taken place in regard to certain statements of Professor Max Müller, as to whether 'miracles' are essential to Christianity. But the issue we have to face is totally misconceived when it is turned into a question of belief in this or that particular miracle—or of miracles in general—regarded as mere external appendages to Christianity. The question is not about isolated 'miracles,' but about the whole conception of Christianity—what it is, and whether the supernatural does not enter into the very essence of it? It is the general question of a supernatural or non-supernatural conception of the universe. Is there a supernatural Being—God? Is there a supernatural government of the world? Is there a supernatural relation of God and man, so that God and man may have communion with one another? Is there a supernatural Revelation? Has that Revelation culminated in a supernatural Person—Christ? Is there a supernatural work in the souls of men? Is there a supernatural Redemption? Is there a supernatural hereafter? It is these larger questions that have to be settled first, and then the question of particular miracles will fall into its proper place." *The Christian View of God and the World,* pp. 10-11.

3. Neo-orthodoxy clings to what is known as the dialectical relation between time and eternity. This encourages it to separate history from super-history, placing Christian truth in the super-history and science and philosophy in history.

pirically raised from the grave as a proof for our justification before the Father, it is futile to speak of the 'values of the resurrection.'

We say that this observation is not appreciated by all, however, for Niebuhr, as an example, teaches that "the idea of the resurrection of the body can of course not be literally true," but that it is a myth, the symbol of which may express "conceptions of a completion of life which transcends our present existence."[4] If a miracle—which never occurred—can be the basis for a real spiritual hope, then the time has come at last when we can put a square peg into a round hole and make it fit snugly. Shall one take courage from the moral acts of Caesar if he was a wicked man and never did a moral act in his life? Is Washington's courage a worthy symbol for our religious faith if historians can establish that he was a jealous, raving coward? How, then, can a rational man accept the resurrection of Christ—which never happened at all—as a symbol for his hope because it expresses "a dark and unconscious recognition of the sources of individuality in nature as well as in spirit?"[5] If we can divorce spiritual values and historical data, there does not seem to be any compelling reason why *Christ's resurrection* should be honored by being a symbol of our faith any more than should the story of Little Black Sambo. Furthermore, the latter has the virtue of not being literally true, plus enjoying freedom from conservative connotations.

C. *Christianity and Miracles*

Just as the Haydn Society would be meaningless if there had never been a Haydn, so also Christianity would be without meaning if the miraculous life and death of Christ are but a myth. The covenant of grace, the basis for our hope in personal, immortal felicity, rests its entire weight upon the historicity of the miraculously conceived, miraculously endowed, and miraculously resurrected Christ, the God-Man.

---

4. *Beyond Tragedy*, p. 290.
5. Niebuhr, *Human Nature*, p. 63.

Remove miracles from the Bible and you relieve it of all its supporting pillars. The Bible teaches that the apostles were willing to be crucified for Jesus Christ, not because the resurrection, which never happened, was a lovely religious symbol of their hope. On the contrary, they *saw* the resurrected Jesus; they *ate* with Him; they put their *hands* upon Him and *felt* Him; they *talked* with Him and were *instructed* by Him. "Then he said to Thomas, 'Put your finger here, and see my hands; and put out your hand, and place it in my side; do not be faithless, but believing.' Thomas answered him, 'My Lord and my God!' " (John 20:27-28). This is but a typical sample of the unequivocal manner in which all of the disciples personally and empirically came into contact with the resurrected Christ during those forty days of added grace before Jesus ascended to the Father.

At this point the principle of uniformity joins forces with the optimism of the enlightment to produce a revised version of the Christian narratives. Shackled to science, modernism has been forced to substitute rationalistic explanations of the miracles, supposing, *e. g.*, that the miracles of Christ in healing were due to Christ's influence over people. He got them to believe in themselves. Neo-orthodoxy, less concerned with science and history, has used the miracles as myths or story forms to bear along superhistorical truths.

> Some of the modernistic attempts to explain miracles are no less than the most tawdry of intellectual dishonesty. The piety which defends Scripture by explaining the feeding of the five thousand on the ground that when the boy opened his lunch box the others were inspired by his example to open theirs, and thus a huge picnic resulted, is a piety which deserves contempt, not intellectual refutation. How people who propose such explanations can pose as religious and moral leaders is beyond honest understanding. Whatever a miracle may be this type of device does not explain it, because of its absurd distortion of the text. Average morality dictates either an open denial of the alleged event, or an attempt to explain what the narrative actually contains.[6]

---

6. Clark, "Miracles, History, and Natural Law," in *The Evangelical Quarterly*, 1940, Volume XII, p. 24.

D. The Argument of Science

Leaving the faults of modernism and neo-orthodoxy, we now turn to the argument against miracles by science. Here we meet a truly worthy opponent. Backed by centuries of success through inductive verification, the devotee of the scientific method, for better or for worse, is wedded to the major premise that all nature is girded about by inexorable natural law. Realizing that values cannot be based upon empirical phenomena which have no existence, the scientist rejects both the conservative doctrine of the resurrection and the liberal attempt to extract symbols of faith from it. Encouraged by this straightforwardness, the conservative is delighted to open up debate on the question of miracles again.

II. What Is a Miracle?

Since so much is made out of miracles, both by the Christian in his defense of Christianity, and by the scientist in his rejection of Christianity, it is well that we be precise in what we mean by a miracle. We must watch with care the definitions which our opponent advances, lest miracles be whisked out of sight before we have had a chance to draw up our chair. David Hume, for example, through his definition, succeeded in removing miracles from the realm of *possibility* without leaving his study. This relieved him of the arduous task of searching history for the *actuality* of miracles. Defining a miracle as "a violation of the laws of nature" or "a transgression of a law of nature by a particular volition of the Deity, or by the interposition of some invisible agent,"[7] Hume called three strikes against the Christian before the latter even had a chance to go to bat. If everything which happens, happens according to natural law, then, by definition, it follows that a miracle cannot happen, for it is contrary to natural law. That is simple enough. If miracles are not even possible, what value is a discussion of their actuality?

---

7. *Inquiry*, Section X, Part I.

A. The Denotative Definition

There are two ways to define something: denotatively, which we shall consider first, and connotatively. A denotative definition is "*one which attempts to give meaning to a name by indicating examples or citing specimens of objects of which it is the name* . . . Thus we might say 'the word *skyscraper* means denotatively (or indicates) what is denoted by the names *Woolworth Building, Empire State Building, Chrysler Building, R.C.A. Building, etc.*' "[8] This is the fundamental sense in which the Christian is interested in defining his miracles. Denotatively, a miracle means what is denotated by the names 'the crossing of the Red Sea,' 'the floating of the axe head,' 'the healing of Naaman's leprosy,' 'the changing of the water to wine,' 'the resurrection of the God-Man from the grave,' and the like. To satisfy the need for a definition of miracles, then, all the conservative is required to do is to produce an exhaustive list of all the events in the Bible which he believes to fall under that general caption. In this way, though he does not establish the actuality of miracles, he at least leaves open the question of their possibility; that is enough for the time being.

B. The Connotative Definition

A definition is connotative if it states the essential attributes of any member of a species, as, 'Man is a sentient being qualified to worship God.' This definition is connotatively phrased, because worship of the Almighty is "the only thing which renders men superior to brutes, and makes them aspire to immortality."[9] It is this type of definition which Hume resorts to in his efforts to disprove miracles. It is instructive to observe, thus, that attacks against miracles generally, if not always, are spirited by connotatively conceived definitions. The reason for this is easily appreciated when we realize with what facility the historical possibility of miracles can be disposed of by a carefully worded connotative definition. To

8. Frye and Levi, *Rational Belief,* p. 135.
9. Calvin, *Institutes,* I, 3, 3.

illustrate, if I define 'good generals in World War II' as 'all men having fifty-five ears,' I have proffered a valid connotative definition, but I just do not happen to refer to anything in reality. Consequently, there is no virtue in looking under stone piles in France for the skeletal remains of one of these wonderful generals, for such beings just are nonexistent. In like manner, if we are not careful, one may define miracles out of existence, if such a gesture is convenient to the fundamental postulates of his world-view.

Setting up a connotative definition for anything is very difficult. "The name 'man' may have the uniquely descriptive alternative connotations: (1) animal with two hands, (2) animal who uses language, (3) featherless biped, (4) animal with a sense of humor, (5) animal who cooks his food, (6) rational animal. Which of these states more nearly 'the essence' of the specimens denoted by the name 'man'? . . . There is no single, objectively determinable 'essence' . . . The connotation to be accepted depends simply upon the purpose for which it is to be used."[10] If we are troubled with connotatively knowing ourselves, whom we have to live with all of the time, whether we care to or not, we can appreciate how difficult it is to find a connotative definition of a miracle which is gone and past.

Let us venture a definition, however, so as not to be guilty of evading a fundamental problem. A miracle is an extraordinary visible act of divine power, wrought by the efficient agency of the will of God, through secondary means, accompanied by valid, covenantal revelation, and having as its final cause the vindication of the righteousness of the triune God. Observe the three parts. First, *God* is the author of the miracle. This sets our definition squarely in the center of the Christian world-view. Secondly, the means used are the same type He uses to order any phenomenon. This sets our definition squarely in the realm of science, and relieves the scientist of his false notion that miracles are inexplicable, mysterious, and beyond rational explanation. Thirdly, the end of a miracle

10. Frye and Levi, *op. cit.*, pp. 142-143.

is to seal and sign the whole counsel of God as found in Holy Writ. This sets our definition squarely in the picture of our need for personal happiness and immortality.

III. What Are Nature and Natural Law?

Since Hume has set a pattern for the modern man by disposing of miracles because they presumably break natural law, it is well that we immediately call into court the whole question of nature and of natural law for a careful cross-examination. Through this effort we hope to establish the fact that, just as our definition of miracles is possibly *true,* so the scientist's definition of miracles is possibly *false.*

A. Science and Natural Law

Science leaves us in indecision as to what it means by natural law, for it harbors two separate convictions. On the one hand, it teaches that all nature is bound by changeless, eternal law, while, on the other, natural laws are but hypotheses which we entertain to account for things, and are tentative and conditioned. The first conviction grows out of an ideally postulated mechanical whole, while the latter stems from actual laboratory practice. Now, since philosophic presuppositions are useful only as they give us a basis for explaining reality, and since Christ's resurrection is a problem which can be handled within the dimensions of actual history, the conservative is more concerned with the second conviction of science than with the first. He wants to know what science actually does with Jesus Who is called the Christ.

With this in mind, let us be informed that natural laws, rather than forming an irrefragable strait-jacket that keeps the universe eternally in order, in reality are little less than laws of physics which the scientist entertains as good hypotheses to account for the observed regularity of nature. As nature is but the totality of the moving universe, so natural laws are but approximate descriptions of the pattern that this moving universe follows. The so-called 'absolute laws' that make up the metaphysical, mechanical order of things, remain forever but philosophic hypotheses. They can never be known. The scientist *hopes* that the laws he formulates actually coincide with these absolute laws, but he has no way of knowing for sure whether his conviction is well grounded. Laws do not wear tags to give them identity. We point this out because it has an important bearing upon the scientist's ability to find a law—absolute *or* relative—which the resurrection of Christ breaks.

B. Christianity and Natural Law

The Christian defines nature as what God does with His creation, and a natural law as but a mathematically exact description upon the part of man of how God has elected to order His creation. For the Christian there are no 'absolute natural laws,' but only the mind of God. From man's point of view, the regularity of the universe is called 'law,' but from God's point of view it is 'will.' Here the Christian world-view conflicts sharply with the scientific method. *Almighty God,* not absolute impersonal law, is the power behind all phenomena. "My Father is working still, and I am working" (John 5:17), says Christ. The blueprints of an eternal, mathematical, impersonally ordered machine do not control nature, but, rather, it is the Christ, the Logos, He Who upholds "the universe by his word of power" (Hebrews 1:3), and Who "is before all things" and in Whom "all things hold together" (Colossians 1:17).

This means that everything which happens in the world is natural, God-governed, and wrought through secondary means. The Christian teaches that only creation and providence are direct acts of God. Therefore, properly conceived natural theology is possible, for the heavens genuinely show the handiwork of God by crying out continually that God is responsible for their beauty, grandeur, and order. The Christian, seeing his God through the things that are made, is daily thrilled, inspired, and encouraged to follow the Almighty in still deeper paths of righteousness; while the non-Christian, who believes that impersonal law is behind the daily course of things, though delighted with the grandeur of nature, is constantly harassed by the fact that he is a personal being, thrust into an impersonal universe, being without hope and eternal life. From a knowledge of the beating of his own heart, then, a man ought to know God; thus, "what an unpardonable indolence is it in those who will not descend into themselves that they may find him!"[11]

If everything is from God and is accomplished by the use of detectable secondary means, all phenomena are a cause for wonder. But a miracle, let us remember, is an *extraordinary* wonder of God's working in nature. "All *is* wonder; to make a man is at least as great a marvel as to raise a man from the dead. The seed that multiplies in the furrow is as the bread that multiplied in Christ's hands. The miracle is not *greater* manifestation of God's power than those ordinary and ever-repeated processes; but it is a *different* manifestation."[12] But extraordinary or no, *all events* that transpire in the time-space universe are wrought by God's use of specific secondary means which are theoretically discernible by a patient application of the scientific method.

On the Christian hypothesis, therefore, laws, being but descriptions of what happens in nature, cannot be thought of as excluding the possibility of miracles; for miracles, if they actually happened, rather than *breaking* the laws of nature, make up part of the data which the scientist must reckon with in his *original plotting* of the laws of nature. If Christ walked on the water and was raised from the dead, these, like any other phenomena of history, make up the actual limits of laws. If a scientist refuses to consider the possibility of the resurrection of Christ, when historians show that there is credible evidence for its historicity, we may be assured that the problem of miracles is moral and philosophical rather than scientific, for the scientist is using his laws, not to *explain* reality, but to *explain reality away.*

---

11. Calvin, *op. cit.*, I, 5, 3.
12. Trench, *Notes on the Miracles of Our Lord*, p. 8.

IV. Natural Law and the Resurrection of Christ

If the scientist can succeed in demonstrating that Christ's resurrection is actually contrary to truly verifiable natural law, we feel certain that he will have brought conservative Christianity to its knees; for the resurrection is linked peculiarly to the whole picture of Christ's soteriology. "If you confess with your lips that Jesus is Lord and believe in your heart that God raised him from the dead, you will be saved" (Romans 10:9). But let us nip the scientist's enthusiasm in the bud by pointing out several fundamental reasons why his efforts to disprove miracles are *a priori* destined to failure.

A. The Thresholds of Sensation

The only way the scientist can know what is going on in reality, that he may plot his laws of physics, is through the use of his five senses. To date, we know of no extra-sensory fields of perception to which the empiricists can appeal. Now, because the experimenter is limited to his senses, he cannot escape from making errors when he plots his laws of nature.

> The existence of error in physical experimentation is no peculiar fault of the apparatus used; on the contrary it is inherent in the meaning or at least in the performing of an experiment. To be explicit, errors arise from the presence of what the psychologists call thresholds. There are three such, the upper threshold, the difference threshold, and the lower threshold. The last would be illustrated if we could have a piano or harp with a few octaves still lower than the ordinary instruments. Running down the scale one note after another, one could hear every note until the string struck vibrated at a rate of, say, less than sixteen vibrations a second. Deeper strings might vibrate, but the human ear could not hear them. The upper threshold could be similarly illustrated on the other end of this enlarged piano. The difference threshold exists because it is impossible to distinguish two tones whose vibrations differ by only one or two a second. If the tones differ by five or six vibrations a second, they can be recognized as different tones.[13]

---

13. Clark, *op. cit.*, p. 30.

The relation between the thresholds and miracles is this. First, the difference threshold makes it impossible for the scientist to know nature absolutely. Despite all the precision instruments that he has at his control, by no presently-known means can the scientist ascertain what the absolute length of even a piece of string is. The best the experimenter can do is to repeat his measurement over and over, and take an average of his findings. But this average, let us remember, is *always* attended by a plus or minus variable error. What this means is that natural laws, which are based upon the scientist's evaluation of data, are attended by a plus or minus variable error which is just as strong or as weak as the original experiments themselves. Physical laws, then, are by no means so iron-clad as we are told. They are just as frail as the eyes of the scientist that does the looking. If we do not know the absolute length of the string before us, is the scientist *absolutely certain* that he has made a perfect induction when he says that Christ could not have been raised from the grave?

Secondly, the lower threshold, together with the difference threshold, reveals that laws, instead of being forced upon the experimenter by the indubitableness of the facts, are chosen for reasons which personally suit him.

> If one should measure the length of a string, the difference threshold would prevent one from determining the exact length of the string, but there is no question about the fact that it is a string which is being measured. In the case of the lower threshold, however, a scientist or a philosopher may ask and has asked: How do we know that every infinitesimal fraction of a region occupied by string is itself occupied by string? No experiment can show that lengths and volumes below the threshold of observation are filled with string. In other words, while the difference threshold leaves indeterminate the magnitude of the string, the lower threshold leaves indeterminate the existence of the string.[14]

If the difference threshold leaves open the possibility that physical laws do not apply to nature absolutely, *the lower threshold leaves open the possibility that physical laws do not*

---

14. Clark, *op. cit.*, p. 33.

refer to reality at all. Is it likely, then, that the scientist is in possession of that precise insight into the total gamut of reality which is requisite for one to assert *categorically* that Christ's resurrection cannot have occurred?

The presence of the plus or minus threshold of error proves that

> When the scientist comes to formulate his law, the empirical data, while they exclude many mathematical formulae, none the less open up a wide range of choice. The observations fix the limits within which the law must be formulated, but they do not discover to us any one law. Hence the definite mathematical law stated in the physics books is not so much discovered, as it is made or chosen by the physicist. When the results of an experiment are transferred to a graph, the average with its error indicates not a point but a region, and through the many regions obtained by many experiments, an infinity of curves may be passed. The one curve or law which the scientist may announce to the world is therefore not forced on him by the data, but is the result of his choice. He may choose a law for personal, or aesthetic, or moral reasons, but he chooses the law rather than discovers it.[15]

Because of this, it is not improbable that the scientist, since he does not have his laws of physics forced upon him by a consideration of the facts, chooses his formulations according to the spirit of his fundamental major premise that non-God is in control of the universe, thus supplying him with the comfortable feeling that he has *disproved* the possibility of Christ's resurrection. To refute this suspicion, the scientist must at least come forth with this indubitable law of physics which the resurrection contradicts. Is it Boyle's law of the volume and pressure of gases? Archimedes' law of the displacement of water by floating bodies? Newton's laws of motion? Gravity? Relativity? The second law of thermodynamics? Run the whole gamut of the known laws of physics and see if there is a law which even begins to approximate that canon which is required to disprove Christ's resurrection.

---

15. *Ibid.*, p. 31.

B. The Ideal Character of Laws of Physics

This last observation provides us with a transition to our second point. Here we point out that not only has the scientist not yet obliged us by coming forth with that law which Christ's resurrection breaks, but also that he cannot, no matter how he may try. No scientific law is more than an *approximation* of, never a perfect counterpart to, what happens in history. When this fact is understood, we will be in a position to force the scientist into a dilemma.

Our first illustration comes from Larrabee:[16]

> According to the Law of Charles, the volume of an ideal gas under constant pressure (or the pressure that it exerts at constant volume) is directly proportional to the absolute temperature. Since for each centigrade degree of temperature which the ideal gas drops at constant pressure, it loses 1/273 of its volume, at -273° C., the ideal gas would have zero volume. *But this has not been observed to happen, not only because absolute zero has never been achieved, but because a phase-change occurs before it is reached.* If we relax our control of the variables, as we do when we explore the earth's atmosphere by means of balloons, we shall find that the pressure-temperature curve drops smoothly enough as the altitude rises to 40,000 feet, where the barometer stands at about 5 inches, and the thermometer at -67° F. Yet, beyond that point, although the pressure continues to drop (to about 3.1 inches at 65,000 feet), *the temperature remains constant at* -67° F.

From this interesting admission, our dilemma begins to take shape. Either the scientist must admit that beyond 40,000 feet he has a real case of a miracle, for a miracle (on his definition) is a transgression of natural law, and the Law of Charles is broken; or he pleads that another law, yet unknown and unplotted, resumes where the Law of Charles leaves off. If he selects the former horn of the dilemma, he concedes the fact that miracles are actual. Then he cannot object to the conviction that Christ's resurrection is possible, since he already admits one miracle. And if he chooses the latter horn, then,

---

16. *Reliable Knowledge,* p. 365. (Italics ours.)

since laws yet unknown and unplotted may be called in to account for *some* areas of experience which have not yet been mastered, they may be called in to explain *all.* The Christian thus may scientifically plead the existence of a law, yet unknown and unplotted, which can cover the resurrection of Jesus Christ. If the scientist refuses to allow the latter the use of a prerogative which he assumes for himself, we have further evidence that the problem of Christ's resurrection is not so much scientific as moral and philosophical.

Our second illustration is provided by Brightman:[17]

> Webster's *New International Dictionary* defines the simple pendulum as 'a particle, or material point, suspended by a thread without weight and oscillating without friction.' *This is a perfect abstraction. In concrete experience, no such pendulum could ever be found.* It can be conceived only by abstracting from the real facts and considering, as it were, their ghost. *Every law of physics is formulated for just such theoretically ideal conditions, from which friction and the influences of other forces have been eliminated.* Concretely the application of any law is limited by all the real forces in operation.

What have we here: a miracle in every grandfather's clock? Perhaps not. But at least if "the swinging of the pendulum of a grandfather's clock occurs without being invalidated by a law of physics—a law well known and mathematically exact—why should the resurrection of Christ be adjudged impossible through a law entirely unknown and never even approximated? Rather, just as the law of the pendulum has its limits set by real occurrences, so this supposed law, if it ever is to be formulated, would have its limits set by the historical fact of Christ's resurrection from the grave."[18]

With this observation we are back where we started. Hume, let us recall, defines a miracle as "a violation of the laws of nature," and then with these laws excludes from possible history all of the Christian miracles, not realizing that if these miracles actually occurred they are to be part of the data which

---

17. *Introduction to Philosophy,* pp. 270-271. (Italics ours.)
18. Clark, *op. cit.,* p. 32.

set the limits to the laws of nature. Laws of nature are a description of what *happens,* not a handbook of rules to tell us what *cannot happen.* In choosing his laws of nature, therefore, the scientist "should first consult history, and after deciding by historical evidence what has happened, should then choose his laws within the limits of historical actuality. The non-Christian thinker, intent on repudiating miracles, proceeds by a reverse method. He chooses his law without regard to historical limits, and then tries to rewrite history to fit his law. But surely this method is not only the reverse of the Christian method, it is clearly the reverse of rational precedure as well."[19]

Before concluding our analysis of the relation between miracles and natural law, let us face and answer two questions that are of peculiar interest to the empirical scientist. They are, first, that miracles ruin the closed character of the mechanical universe and thus frustrate prediction, and, secondly, that Christ's resurrection happened but once and so cannot be an example of a natural law. Let us discuss these in turn.

First, miracles, rather than *ruining* predictions, are the very things which save it. Miracles are a sign and a seal of the veracity of special revelation, revelation which assures us exactly how God has elected to dispose of His universe. In this revelation we read that He Who made us, and Who can also destroy us, has graciously chosen to keep the universe regular according to the covenant which He made with Noah and his seed forever. If the scientist rejects miracles to keep his mechanical order, he loses his right to that mechanical order, for, without miracles to guarantee revelation, he can claim no external reference point; and without an external reference point to serve as a fulcrum, the scientist is closed up to the shifting sand of history. In such a case, then, how can the scientist appeal to the changeless conviction 'that the universe is mechanical,' when from flux and change only flux and change can come? The scientist simply exchanges what he thinks is a "whim of deity" for what is actually a "whim of time and space." Why the latter guarantees perseverance of a

19. *Ibid.*, p. 34.

mechanical world, when the former seemingly is impotent so to do, is not easy to see.

Secondly, when we ask how *often* a phenomenon must occur to be strong enough to establish a law of nature, the answer is once. Laws of physics are only man's mathematical descriptions of the way God does things: for God there are no laws, but only will. Whatever is an expression of His will in the time-space universe, therefore, deserves the place of a law. The phenomenon's frequency of occurrence is determined by God's plan. Rocks keep falling, planets consistently wander, and grass grows because of the role they play in sustaining the durational character which God has decreed to the time-space universe. In these cases there is a repetitiousness to which the scientist can appeal in plotting his laws. But the only reason why there is such a recurrence is that the will of God decrees it. In the case of Christ's resurrection, however, there is no need for repetition. The purpose of God for rocks and planets is fulfilled in their recurrence, but the purpose of God in Christ's resurrection is fulfilled by the one act. Christ's resurrection from the grave is the way God regularily works in a universe of this kind, where sin has entered by man's defection, and where a God-Man has paid for these sins by a perfect, substitutionary atonement on the cross. The regularity of grass growing shows itself in repetition, while the regularity of a God-Man dying for sins shows itself but once, for it need happen but once in eternity. The *frequency* of a phenomenon is irrelevant to the question of law; what is *sine qua non* is that it happens.

By its very nature, the atonement and resurrection of Christ could happen only once. If there were need for its recurrence, the need would arise out of a deficiency in the first atonement; but this is impossible, because the atonement was accomplished by a *perfect* Lamb. "Nor was it to offer himself repeatedly, as the high priest enters the Holy Place yearly with blood not his own; for then he would have had to suffer repeatedly since the foundation of the world. But as it is, he has appeared *once for all* at the end of the age to put away sin by the sacrifice of himself" (Hebrews 9:25-26). To demand a repetition of Christ's death on the cross and His resurrection from the grave, for laboratory convenience, therefore, is to ask an illicit thing. This single occurrence is as truly an expression of God's will as the daily rolling of rocks and the perpetual illumination of the sun. "Lo, I have come to do thy will, O God" (Hebrews 10:7), was the word of the Logos. This one act of atonement, then, is as genuine an expression of the regular working of God in this universe as the growing of the lilies in the field or the singing of the birds. Frequency of occurrence is not what makes a law; it is rather the working out of the teleological purposes in the mind of God.

Chapter XV

The Problem of Miracles and Natural Law (Continued)

If there arise in the midst of you a prophet, or a dreamer of dreams, and he give you a sign or a wonder, and the sign or the wonder come to pass, whereof he spoke unto you, saying, Let us go after other gods, which you have not known, and let us serve them; you shall not hearken unto the words of that prophet, or unto that dreamer of dreams: for Jehovah your God proves you, to know whether you love Jehovah your God with all your heart and with all your soul.—Moses.

HAVING disposed of the proposition that miracles are contrary to natural law, let us now face Hume's argument that "no testimony is sufficient to establish a miracle, unless the testimony be of such a kind, that its falsehood would be more miraculous than the fact which it endeavors to establish: and even in that case there is a mutual destruction of arguments, and the superior only gives us an assurance suitable to that degree of force which remains after deducing the inferior."[1] This shift in the weight of the argument forces us to examine the broad question of how to verify a miracle. The Christian teaches that a miracle is verified by systematic coherence, and requires no more testimony to establish its veracity than is needed to establish other historical facts; but Hume cannot accede to this conviction. Instead, he lists for us a series of tests which a story of the miraculous must meet before it may be believed. Let us take these criteria and apply them to another historical narrative in the same manner that the critic

1. *Inquiry,* Section X, Part I.

does to the documents of the Bible and see how they fare. This sort of argument is *ad hominem,* to be sure, but we feel it will be effective to show that Hume is either applying his maxims to Christianity arbitrarily, or he must confess that we can believe nothing of history at all.

I. Hume's Canons and Historical Phenomena

We cannot believe the miraculous stories in the Bible because they are passed on to us by either indirect witnesses that are unable to present demonstrable proof for their data, or by eyewitnesses that spoke with a hasty, passionate hysteria that was mingled with a distrustworthy, religious zeal. No rational man, thus, can give his assent to documents which are based on such weak evidence. They are obviously spurious. To this type of judgment the Christian responds by asking: If the testimony of the honest, humble men who penned the Bible is rejected, whom then *can* we believe? Let us illustrate the inadequacy of Hume's canons by reducing them to absurdity. Fortunately our work has been done for us by Whately in his famous brochure, *Historic Doubts Relative to Napoleon Buonaparte.* If we can show that not even the existence of the great Napoleon can be rationally affirmed by one who follows Hume's advice, we will have succeeded in suggesting reasonable evidence to suppose that the canons themselves are inadequate. "But I call on those who boast their philosophical freedom of thought, and would fain tread in the steps of Hume and other inquirers of the like exalted and speculative genius, to follow up fairly and fully their own principles, and, throwing off the shackles of authority, to examine carefully the evidence of whatever is proposed to them, before they admit its truth" (p. 15).

We are very grateful to Hume for his canons, since minute examination of the Napoleon documents does give evidence that different schools of thought are at work, thus assuring us that a rational man can hardly accept the corpus of accounts as it stands. Some sort of higher criticism must be devised. "This obscure Corsican adventurer, a man, according to some, of extraordinary talents and courage, according to others, of very moderate abilities, and a rank coward, advanced rapidly in the French army, obtained a high command, gained a series of important victories . . . there is almost every conceivable variety of statement" (pp. 2-3).

A. The Veracity of the Indirect Witnesses

1. Most of the evidence for Napoleon was gleaned by the multitudes from the daily newspapers, but "whence this high respect which is practically paid to newspaper authority? Do men think that because a witness has been perpetually detected in falsehood, he may therefore be the more safely believed whenever he is *not* detected" (p. 7)? What means have the reporters had of gaining their information? The readers of newspapers hear of their stories from correspondents that are supposedly reliable, but "*who* these correspondents are, and what means *they* have of obtaining information, or whether they exist at all, we have no way of ascertaining. We find ourselves in the condition of the Hindoos, who are told by their priests, that the earth stands on an elephant, and the elephant on a tortoise; but are left to find out for themselves what the tortoise stands on, or whether it stands on any thing at all" (pp. 8-9). Who shall vouch for the veracity of the reporters? And who shall vouch for the veracity of the reporters of the reporters? *Ad infinitum?*

2. And what proof is there that the ones who circulated this story did not conceal some personal interest? Why may we not assume that their reports were 'fixed' by political bosses in the interest of personal aggrandizement? Perhaps the more the threat of Napoleon was written up by this political machine, the more quantities of money could be extracted from those hapless tax payers who at any cost would gladly ward off an invasion by this fabulous Buonaparte. The newspapers may have had the same worth that the Soviet press has today. "Their selection, omission, treatment and mode of presentation of 'news' is in most cases, for one reason or another, so close to being worthless from a scholarly or scientific point of view that the

published stories must be approached with the most pervasive skepticism and an unremitting readiness to check against basic sources."[2]

3. When Hume warns us to reject the witness of those who either *contradict* each other, or who are of a *suspicious character,* or who have an *interest* in what they affirm, we are at a loss to believe anything of the Napoleon accounts. "It is by no means agreed whether Buonaparte led in person the celebrated charge over the bridge of Lodi . . . or was safe in the rear, while Augereau performed the exploit. The same doubt hangs over the charge of the French cavalry at Waterloo. It is no less uncertain whether or no this strange personage poisoned in Egypt an hospital-full of his own soldiers; and butchered in cold blood a garrison that had surrendered" (pp. 11-12). What *shall* we rationally affirm? Some label Napoleon a sincere, wise, humane, magnanimous hero, while others vow with religious fervor that he is a monster of cruelty, meanness and perfidy. To some, he is a military genius and a man of intrepidity, while to others he is a raving maniac and a poltroon. "What then are we to believe? if we are disposed to credit all that is told us, we must believe in the existence not only of one, but of two or three Buonapartes; if we admit nothing but what is well authenticated, we shall be compelled to doubt of the existence of any" (p. 13). In sum, what shall we say of the veracity of the indirect witnesses? "First, we have no assurance that they have access to correct information; secondly, that they have an apparent interest in propagating falsehood; and, thirdly, they palpably contradict each other in the most important points" (p. 14).

B. The Veracity of the Eyewitnesses

If a man who follows Hume's canons cannot repose in the veracity of the indirect witnesses to the effect that there was this wonderful man, Napoleon, he surely can trust those who went to such effort to see Napoleon in person. And what of all the soldiers that fought him?

2. *Twentieth Century Philosophy* (Runes, ed.), p. 478.

1. As for those who went to see him, we doubt not that they actually went out intending to see him, and that, rowing out into the harbor, they actually saw a man who, so they were told, was Buonaparte, but "this is the utmost point to which their testimony goes; how they ascertained that this man in the cocked hat had gone through all the marvelous and romantic adventures with which we have so long been amused, we are not told. Did they perceive in his physiognomy, his true name, and authentic history? Truly this evidence is such as country people give one for a story of apparitions" (p. 16). It is always possible that the eyewitnesses suffered from an optical illusion the very moment they believed they saw the general.

2. As for the legion of soldiers that were in hospitals from wounds received from battle with Napoleon, how do *they* know that they actually fought this terrible Buonaparte? "That they fought and were wounded, they may safely testify; and probably they no less firmly *believe* what they were *told* respecting the cause in which they fought . . . But I defy anyone of them to come forward and declare, *on his own knowledge,* what was the cause in which he fought,—under whose commands the opposed generals acted,—and whether the person who issued those commands did really perform the mighty achievements we are told of" (p. 17).

3. Hume carefully warns us also to be suspicious of any who testify with passion and exaggeration, for the more wonderful their tale becomes, the less likely are such eyewitnesses to be called veracious. But how does the Napoleon narrative read? *Great* armies, *total* victories, *astounding* reverses, *amazing* frosts, *hair-breadth* escapes, and *entire* subjection of *whole* armies in a *moment* of time. Nothing in the entire annals of military history can compete with this fabulous tale. Napoleon gained control over Germany, for example, while it was proud, wealthy, and powerful, an achievement which the mighty Romans in the zenith of their power, during a struggle over many centuries, could not achieve against the ignorant, half-savage people that then inhabited Germany. "Does any one

believe all this, and yet refuse to believe a miracle? Or rather, what is this but a miracle" (p. 21)?

> What sufficient *reason* is there for a series of events occurring in the eighteenth and nineteenth centuries, which never took place before? Was Europe at that period peculiarly weak, and in a state of barbarism, that one man could achieve such conquests, and acquire such a vast empire? On the contrary, she was flourishing in the height of strength and civilization. Can the persevering attachment and blind devotedness of the French to this man, be accounted for by his being the descendant of a long line of kings, whose race was hallowed by hereditary veneration? No; we are told he was a low-born usurper, and not even a Frenchman! Is it that he was a good and kind sovereign? He is represented not only as an imperious and merciless despot, but as most wantonly careless of the lives of his soldiers. Could the French army and people have failed to hear from the wretched survivors of his supposed Russian expedition, how they had left the corpses of above 100,000 of their comrades bleaching on the snow-drifts of that dismal country, whither his mad ambition had conducted them, and where his selfish cowardice had deserted them? Wherever we turn to seek for circumstances that may help to account for the events of this incredible story, we only meet with such as aggravate its improbability (p. 23).

4. If the spirit of religion joins itself to the love of wonder, says Hume, then there is an end to common sense. But "is it not just possible, that during the rage for words of Greek derivation, the title of 'Napoleon,' which signifies 'Lion of the forest,' may have been conferred by the popular voice on more than one favorite general, distinguished for irresistible valor? Is it not also possible that 'Buonaparte' may have been originally a sort of cant term applied to the 'good part' of the French army, collectively; and have been afterwards mistaken for the proper name of an individual" (p. 32)? It is not unreasonable to suppose, then, that the Napoleon documents are neither more nor less than an embodiment of the European urge for mythological perfection in those who lead the nation in martial combat. We may conclude, thus, that the accounts of the existence of Napoleon are too confused, too contradic-

tory, and too flimsily documented to be affirmed as true by a rational man.

At length! when real scientific verification of this fabulous Napoleon is about to be organized, the news greets us that the man is dead! Now, what more artificial, yet effective, way could be devised to conceal the fabrication of the whole story than to destroy the phantom? All we have now is a tomb!

We have no need to go further to show that Hume's canons are, first, arbitrarily chosen by a prejudiced mind as devices to discredit the Christian Scriptures, rather than seriously thought out rules for historians to follow when sifting and screening the records of the past; and, secondly, that historical data can be reconstructed and verified, not by formal demonstration which yields complete rational assurance, but, rather by probability through systematic coherence.

> I call upon those therefore who profess themselves advocates of free inquiry, — who disdain to be carried along with the stream of popular opinion, — and who will listen to no testimony that runs counter to experience, — to follow up their own principles fairly and consistently. Let the same mode of argument be adopted in all cases alike. . . . If they have already rejected some histories, on the ground of their being strange and marvellous, — of their relating facts, unprecedented, and at variance with the established course of nature, — let them not give credit to another history which lies open to the very same objections, — the extraordinary and romantic tale we have been just considering. If they have discredited the testimony of witnesses, who are *said* at least to have been disinterested, and to have braved persecutions and death in support of their assertions, — can these philosophers consistently listen to and believe the testimony of those who avowedly *get money* by the tales they publish, and who do not even pretend that they incur any serious risk in case of being detected in a falsehood? If in other cases they have refused to listen to an account which has passed through many intermediate hands before it reaches them, and which is defended by those who have an interest in maintaining it; let them consider through how many, and what very suspicious hands, *this* story has arrived to them, without the possibility of tracing it back to any decidedly

> authentic source, after all. . . . But if they are still wedded to the popular belief in this point, let them be consistent enough to admit the same evidence in *other* cases, which they yield to, in *this.* If after all that has been said, they cannot bring themselves to doubt of the existence of Napoleon Buonaparte, they must at least acknowledge that they do not apply to that question, the same plan of reasoning which they made use of in others; and they are consequently bound in reason and in honesty to renounce it altogether (pp. 33-35).

II. What Is the Point to Miracles?

Before turning to our next study, the Christian attitude toward evil, we must answer a question which we have assumed as self-evident up until now, but which may not be perfectly clear to all of our readers. It is the question: What is the whole point to miracles anyway? Why are we not able to construct a philosophy of life without bringing them into the overall picture? The Christian suggests the following reasons to support the need for miracles in a *Weltanschauung.*

A. The Theoretical Worth of Miracles

1. First, miracles are a *sine qua non* for special revelation. We need special revelation to complete our view of God and man, but how shall we recognize this revelation when it comes along? Well, one way at least is to demand from the one who bears the revelation proofs that he is actually from God. God is the Almighty, and, since He rules heaven and earth, we may reasonably expect some evidences of this power when He comes in contact with history in the deliverance of a revelation. Thus, Pharaoh commanded Moses to "show a wonder" as a proof that he was from Jehovah (Exodus 7:9), and the Pharisees requested of Christ, "Teacher, we wish to see a sign from you" (Matthew 12:38), as a proof that he was one sent from God. These demands were quite in order, for "credulity is as real, if not so great, a sin as unbelief."[3] When one comes aver-

---

3. Trench, *Notes on the Miracles of Our Lord,* p. 20.

ring to be from God, it surely is a man's duty to demand a proof that this is so.

Christ approved of the rightful demand for signs as he answered the disciples of John when they inquired if He was the One they looked for, saying: "Go and tell John what you hear and see: the blind receive their sight and the lame walk, lepers are cleansed and the deaf hear, and the dead are raised up, and the poor have good news preached to them" (Matthew 11: 4-5). This is the first reason why a world-view needs miracles. Without special revelation we cannot find a philosophic solution to reality's riddle; but without miracles we cannot be assured that he who bears a revelation actually is from God. As Christ assured the multitudes, "these very works which I am doing, bear me witness that the Father has sent me" (John 5:36), so also we are assured in this age that the Bible can make a veracious claim to being from God, for it has the earmarks of divinity, *miracles*.

2. Secondly, miracles are *sine qua non* for recognizing our Savior. In Chapter One we showed that the first thing man wants is happiness, and that the first ingredient for the cure of soul-sorrow to give him this happiness is the establishment of a rational hope for personal immortality. Later we concluded that, since we are closed up to the process of history, a Savior outside of this flux must step in and save us, or we may perish like the beasts without hope. The Savior that is qualified to bring us into eternal felicity must be distinguished from pseudo-deliverers by two characteristics. First, He must know exactly what we want when we seek eternal blessedness. We shall expect Him to have such an insight into the basic human dilemma that He can take all of our disconnected groanings and fabricate them into a well-organized pattern of desire. Secondly, a Savior must be intimately related to the Almighty. In order that He can be relied upon to direct not only heaven and earth, but also reality's eternal destiny, for our happiness, we shall rightly look for present manifestations of such power as prophetic samples of the state of felicity for which we groan and which He is able infallibly to secure for us. It is not

enough for one simply to *tell* promises; he must show by some palpable proof that he can make them good. As the musician must give a sample of his music and the poet of his poetry, so the Savior must show us samples of power to prove that He can actually save. These samples are the *miracles.*

The miracles which the Savior wrought are token-proofs of "what no eye has seen, nor ear heard, nor the heart of man conceived, what God has prepared for those who love him" (I Corinthians 2:9). The miracles are pledges and samples of power, advance fruits of our felicity to come. In each of them "the *word* of salvation is incorporated in an *act* of salvation."[4] What are the things in life that inhibit us from finding perfect happiness? They are the fruits of sin: sickness, poverty, hunger, and death. We shall expect a Savior from our miseries to be able to destroy these, especially sin and death. Miracles are evidences that the Savior Who does them is metaphysically aligned to a world-view which makes place for our eternal happiness. Thus, in healing the sick, restoring the needy to strength, feeding the multitudes, and raising the dead, Jesus Christ provided all of those emblems of power that we need in order to trust Him as the "Lamb of God, who takes away the sin of the world" (John 1:29). "Only when regarded in this light do they (miracles) appear not merely as illustrious examples of his might, but also as glorious manifestations of his holy love."[5]

B. The Practical Worth of Miracles

1. First, since we are continually lethargic, stupid, and dull by nature, our daily beholding of the glories of the lilies that surpass the glory of Solomon fails to bring us to repentance. Therefore, God, in His grace, charged history with extraordinary manifestations of His power and might to shake us out of our stupidity and negligence, in order to lead us to a more indubitable knowledge of Himself. This accommodation to man's weakness is a further display of God's beneficence and

---

4. Trench, *op. cit.*, p. 24.
5. Trench, *ibid.*

long-suffering toward vessels fit for destruction. The perfection of the rose is quite enough to bring man to God, but God, seeing our natural proclivity to the wonderful, the extraordinary, and the far away, dipped into the regularity of His working in history and studded nature with signs, wonders, and mighty powers to arrest man's imagination and to call him to reflect upon the state of the universe. When Jesus raised the dead, cast out demons, and restored the lepers to health, therefore, all the city went after Him. Instead of turning men to arrogance, the miracles of Christ ought to lead us to repentance, for they are a neon-sign proof that God exists.

2. Secondly, the working of miracles by the Savior of the world has the result of pressing men to an immediate judgment about the highest logical ultimate, God. Although the ordinary providence of God is sufficient to divide men into parties according to the sincerity of their love for God, miracles hasten the process by setting the heart of man *immediately* over against the heart of God. Since both the true Savior and a pseudo-savior resort to the expediency of miracle-working, decision between these wonder-workers must be made according to what the heart of the recipient loves. "A miracle does not prove the truth of a doctrine, or the divine mission of him that brings it to pass. That which alone it claims for him at the first is a right to be listened to: it puts him in the alternative of being from heaven or from hell."[6]

In deciding between miracle-doers, the antecedent heart-condition of the observer determines whether he shall love or abhor him who does the signs. A man follows that one who speaks words that are most conformable to the major presuppositions of his world-view. "The coming of the lawless one by the activity of Satan will be with all power and with pretended signs and wonders, and with all wicked deception for those who are to perish, *because they refused to love the truth and so be saved*" (II Thessalonians 2:9-10). Jesus thus, when He was about to be stoned by the Jews, said: "I have come in

6. Trench, *op. cit.*, p. 19.

my Father's name, and you do not receive me; if another comes in his own name, him you will receive" (John 5:43). This is in harmony with our suspicion that the reason why men reject the veracity of Christ's miracles is more moral than scientific.

C. *Do Miracles Still Happen Today?*

Whenever Christians gather together to discuss miracles, immediately the burning question arises whether or not we may look for the continuance of miracles in our own day; an issue, as can be seen, which has both practical and abstract implications — practical in that some may wonder if God will still heal their bodies by faith, and abstract in that the continuity or discontinuity of miracles will reflect seriously on one's whole theology.

The safest decision to make is to divide the question, assuming the termination of the *gift of miracle-working,* on the one side, while remaining assured that *God* continues to work wonders for us, on the other.

The gift has ceased because the canon of Scripture is closed. "Since God designed this book to be the sole supernatural revelation to man, and since miracles are needed merely to authenticate such a revelation, there has been no call for special intervention since the canon of Scripture became complete."[7]

---

7. Burtt, *Types of Religious Philosophy,* p. 150. "The canon of revelation is closed; there is no more to be added; God does not give a fresh revelation, but he rivets the old one. When it has been forgotten, and laid in the dusty chamber of our memory, he fetches it out and cleans the picture, but does not paint a new one. There are no new doctrines, but the old ones are often revived. It is not, I say, by any new revelation that the Spirit comforts. He does so by telling us old things over again; he brings a fresh lamp to manifest the treasures hidden in Scripture; he unlocks the strong chest in which the truth has long lain, and he points to secret chambers filled with untold riches; but he coins no more, for enough is done. Believer! there is enough in the Bible for thee to live upon forever. If thou shouldst outnumber the years of Methuselah, there would be no need for a fresh revelation; if thou shouldst live till Christ should come upon the earth, there would be no necessity for the addition of a single word; if thou shouldest go down as deep as Jonah, or even descend as David said he did, into the belly of hell, still there would be enough in the Bible to comfort thee without a supplementary sentence." Spurgeon, *Gems,* pp. 61-62.

The gift of miracle-working among the apostles was for several purposes: (a) to exhibit a validation of the revelation which was brought; (b) to give power and strength to the early church as it struggled for its life against the pagan world; (c) to draw the crowds to the hearing of the gospel, like an accordion at a street meeting.

Lest an unnecessary confusion result, it is vastly important that one comprehend the true meaning of the gift of miracle-working. When one is endowed with the power to work miracles (such as in raising the dead), *he performs these wonders according to his own personal discretion and by a power which, through God, is resident within him.* His working of miracles is systematic, nonchalant, and sure. When Paul healed Eutychus (Acts 20:9ff.), he prefaced it with no extravagant emotional ritual; by powers residing within him he leaned over and brought life back.

No exact time can be set for the termination of the gift of miracle-working. We know from Paul's first letter to the Corinthian church that the various gifts were already falling into decay and corruption (I Cor. 14). Justin Martyr makes mention that the gifts continued for at least fifty years after the death of the Evangelist John. Apparently miracle-working tapered off during an undefined "twilight zone" as the church completed its transition from the leadership of the live apostles to the authority of the words of the apostles in the Bible.[8]

But it would be a mistake to conclude from this admission that God has ceased to perform wonders on behalf of those who believe. This would be repugnant to the spirit of Scrip-

---

8. Some may be disappointed that we do not here actually make good our claim that the miracles of Christ can be established by a study of history, but, obviously, in a volume on apologetics it is impossible to cover the whole gamut of Christian evidences. The reader will have to carry this philosophic setting into those volumes that have been written to show the veracity of miracles, such as Machen's *The Virgin Birth of Christ.* The purpose of the apologete is not to list the data of history that establish the miracles, but, rather to set down a logically defended right for the historian and the archaeologist to go to work. There is little virtue in turning over dirt to locate evidence for Christ's resurrection if Hume has succeeded *a priori* in demonstrating that miracles cannot have happened at all. Philosophy only proves that they can happen; the historian must show that they actually *did.*

ture. It is the firm confidence of every consistent Christian that *prayer changes things.* As is the strength of our faith, so is the mighty working of God. Second causes are directed by God for our benefit, as when a body is healed or a drought brought to an unexpected end. But note: *these acts are not the result of the gift of miracle-working.* The missionary who exorcises a demon does not appeal to powers resident within him. He prays to God, and *God* casts out the demon.

For the sake of accuracy, therefore, one must be very careful how he defines a miracle. Apparently God lavished a power on the apostolic church which he now rations out carefully to those who are living in the Holy Spirit. The Bible seems to suggest that the only person who will have the *gift* of miracle-working in these last days is the *devil.* (II Thess. 2:9-10.)

III. Concluding Difficulties

A. Everything is a Miracle

All reality is a cause for wonder; with what justification, then, do we arbitrarily segregate some of these wonders and label them 'miracles'? Indeed, all *is a cause for wonder,* but a miracle is a *wonderful wonder,* both in that it is wrought by an extraordinary use of secondary means, as in raising the dead, and also in that its peculiar mission is to arouse men to hear and embrace a message from God. All of God's regular use of secondary means is indeed mysterious, but a truly marvelous sign must be infrequent and irregular or it will fail in its mission to bestir us.

B. What of False Miracles?

Since many other religious leaders have made claim to the power of miracle-working, how is Christ's authority any greater than theirs? These miracles, if they are real, fail to sign and seal the truth, and thus are false signs and deceive many. Christ's authority is established in that what He says forms a system of thought which is horizontally self-consistent, and which vertically fits the facts.

C. Puts Christianity at the Mercy of the Scientific Method

If we define our miracles as part of the natural order, the scientist will simply enlarge the borders of his natural laws to include these extraordinary events, and, in so doing, will dispose of Christianity. On the contrary, unless miracles are part of nature, a scientist is under no obligation to account for them, for they are then unknowable. By defining miracles as effects of specific secondary causes, the scientist must explain them. And when he does, he will find that their explanation either requires Christianity or it does not. In either case a service is done. If Christianity is not needed to explain the resurrection of Christ, let it be abandoned; and if it is, then let the scientist repent of his sins and believe. "Let them bring their witnesses, that they may be justified; or let them hear, and say It is truth" (Isaiah 43:9).

Having brought our study to this point, we dare not complete it until we relate the message which the Savior seals in His revelation to one of the most difficult, one of the most pressing, problems that mankind has struggled with since its creation. We have reference to the thorny question, the problem of evil. Let us see if the logic of conservative Christianity can stand up here.

Chapter XVI

The Problem of Evil

For the moment all discipline seems painful rather than pleasant. —*Book of Hebrews*

ONE of the easiest yet surest ways to test a man's allegiance to the Christian faith is to pose one question: What is the relation between God and the process of history? He will either aver that the Almighty originally created the world out of nothing by free, sovereign power, and presently decrees the movement of history according to the counsels of His own will, both majestically to display His infinite perfection and glory, and to bring many sons to salvation through the free grace merited by the redemptive work of His beloved Son, Jesus Christ, or he will not. There is no *tertium quid*. One preserves the freedom of God at *all* points or he loses it at *every* point, for a God that is not absolutely sovereign over history is not sovereign in Himself. As for the Christian, he is quite satisfied to have God absolutely sovereign both in power and in goodness, a God Who made the universe through the freedom of His own will. The Christian teaches that there was no antecedent necessity whatever, either from within or from without God, logical or material, which brought on the divine act of creation *ex nihilo*. "Art not thou God in heaven? and art not thou ruler over all the kingdoms of the nations? and in thy hand is power and might, so that none is able to withstand thee" (II Chronicles 20:6).

As far as the non-Christian is concerned, however, the doctrine of the sovereignty of God blows up in one's face when carried out to its logical conclusions. If God is the Author of *everything,* then He may rightfully be called to account for the present arrangement of things, for the universe seems to spill over at points with mismanagement and bungling. "I confess that, though I believe that the cosmos is a whole and acts as a whole through the multiplicity of histories, I do not understand what sort of a whole it is. It is true that a tree must be known through its fruit. But what is the fruit? I like to dwell on the creation of beauty and order. And there is some beauty and order. But what about the disorder? Perhaps blindness and chance are part of the evolution of order. But there is so much disorder and suffering that seem to lead nowhere."[1] Is it possible that an infinitely good and powerful God could have created *this* universe? Traditionally, the assignment of relating a universe with evil in it to the Author of the universe, Who is supposed to have nothing but good in Him, is known as the problem of evil. We shall hew to that statement of the difficulty.

I. The General Nature of the Problem

Epicurus, Lactantius, and others have given what has come down to us as probably the most succinct statement of the problem of evil yet conceived. Either God wants to prevent evil, and He cannot do it; or He can do it and does not want to; or He neither wishes to nor can do it; or He wishes to and can do it. If He has the desire without the power, He is impotent; if He can, but has not the desire, He has a malice which we cannot attribute to Him; if He has neither the power nor the desire, He is both impotent and evil, and consequently not God; if He has the desire and the power, whence then comes evil, or why does He not prevent it? This statement contains all of the ingredients of the problem, and we can see from it the direction in which we seem to be logically driven. The Christian teaches that God is all-good and all-powerful, yet the empirically observable facts appear to be too ateleological in the few and in the many to bear the weight of this hypothesis. Is it logical to believe that God is sovereign both in goodness and in might, when the universe is of such a character that the righteous suffer while the wicked prosper? when

1. *Twentieth Century Philosophy* (Runes, ed.), p. 104.

the lightning, which is sent by God, seems deliberately to miss the sinner, but strikes upon the saint in prayer? But what shall we say? If we teach that God is not good, we render Him indistinguishable from the devil; and if we say that He is not omnipotent, it may be that He is no longer God. At any rate, we live in a universe where "the organic parts of a flea are marvelously fitted and framed, while human life is surrounded and made restless by the inconsistency of countless disorders."[2]

The first temptation is to say the problem is a mystery, and so turn to another question; but we cannot do so for two reasons. First, we have already limited faith by supposing it to be a resting of the mind in the sufficiency of the evidence, and we cannot back down at this point on our hypothesis that Christianity is systematically consistent. Secondly, the reader, no doubt, has been waiting patiently for the problem of evil to crop up in the book, to see how we would solve it. So, it would hardly be fair to disappoint him. Men of old, perhaps, may have been content to confess that the mystery of evil is inexplicable and ought not to be probed into, but not so with modern man. Men "*will* think on those deep problems which lie at the root of religious belief—on the nature of God, His character, His relations to the world and men, sin, the means of deliverance from it, the end to which all things are moving, —and if Christianity does not give them an answer, suited to their deeper and more reflective moods, they will simply put it aside as inadequate for their needs."[3] Unlike the medieval peasant, the contemporary thinker delights in raising and pressing home all questions which pertain in any remote way to the nature and destiny of man.

Although some exaggerate the problem of evil beyond rational bounds by sentimentalizing the grief of existence every time they see an ambitious robin withdrawing a recalcitrant

2. Augustine, *De Ordine*, I, 1, 2. Soldiers of World War II report the embittering feeling that came from watching the sun rise in the east to shed its light upon the Japanese and German war plants. Which side was God on? The feeling that God was morally indifferent to the situation gave rise to an inexplicable state of heart-wonder.

3. Orr, *The Christian View of God and the World*, p. 21.

earthworm from the moist soil, on the whole, modern man is engaged in a sober piece of calculation on the subject of evil. Through the increase of our technical knowledge, we have become even more sensitive to the organized way in which nature seems ready to crush all human existence. The greater our knowledge of the physical universe, the more clearly it appears that man occupies an irrelevant place; the greater our control of one disease, the more mysterious two others become.

These awarenesses, together with the orgy of two World Wars, have forced the modernists to scrap two fundamental precepts of their faith: the doctrines of the inherent goodness of man, and the inevitability of progress. As long as man seemed to be getting better and better, it was all well and good to suppose that the evil in him was simply a residual sloth which he had carried down from his brute ancestry; but today it is seen that man is getting worse and worse. With things shaping up to a Third World War, only the purblind can say that the evil in man's inner nature is explained by the flimsy arguments of liberalism and its metaphysical optimism. The same is true for the conviction that man is in for automatic growth and progress. Things have not worked out according to plans, for, though man has continued to augment his knowledge of technology, he is morally reverting to the monster. Evil is written so large both in the heart of man and in nature that even human history itself is big with the elements of its own destruction.

This dissatisfaction with liberalism and its tenuous optimism, as shown by the contemporary rise of realism, is symptomatic in a very real sense of a return to that theology of total depravity which conservative Christianity has always postulated as an integral element in its world-view. Yet, from another point of view, the more vivid the problem of evil becomes, the more some minds are convinced that the Christian doctrine of sovereignty is the least likely solution to the riddle of the universe. "In the Old Testament, at least in the older parts of it, the power of God is exalted at the expense of his goodness. For it is simply impossible by any human standard and within any intelligible meaning of the words to regard Yahveh as wholly good. His cruelty is notorious and his capriciousness is that of an Oriental despot."[4] Modern man agrees with Christianity's judgment that there *is* a problem of evil, but he rejects what the latter proposes as a *solution* to that problem. An infinitely powerful, good God cannot be the Author of nature in all of its parts, for "in sober truth, nearly all the things which men are hanged or imprisoned for doing to one another, are nature's everyday performances."[5]

II. The Nature of Evil

Evil is anything which frustrates human values. Basically, there are two types of evil, natural and moral. Let us examine these in turn. Natural evil includes all of those frustrations of human values which are perpetrated, not by the free agency of man, but by the natural elements in the universe, such as the fury of the hurricane and the devastation of the parasite. Psalmist, philosopher, and poet join to lament the curious destinies which are shaped by nature for man. The interest of Asaph is focused on not so much the hideous, the blind, and the maimed, which rush daily out of the womb of time, but, rather, upon the fact that nature seems to play the wrong favorites; since, whereas we praise the good and punish the bad, nature neglects the righteous and lavishes her bounties upon the wicked.

> For I was envious at the arrogant,
> When I saw the prosperity of the wicked.
> For there are no pangs in their death;
> But their strength is firm.
> They are not in trouble as other men;
> Neither are they plagued like other men.[6]

Is God not unfair in His dealings? To this the philosopher adds the fire of sparkling rhetoric: "Killing, the most criminal act recognized by human laws, Nature does once to every being

---

4. Lippmann. *A Preface to Morals*, *p.* 214.
5. Mill, *Three Essays on Religion,* p. 28.
6. Psalm 73:3-5.

that lives; and in a large proportion of cases, after protracted tortures such as only the greatest monsters whom we read of ever purposely inflicted on their living fellow-creatures . . . nature impales men, breaks them as if on the wheel, casts them to be devoured by wild beasts, burns them to death, crushes them with stones like the first christian martyr, starves them with hunger, freezes them with cold . . . All this, Nature does with the most supercilious disregard both of mercy and of justice, emptying her shafts upon the best and noblest indifferently with the meanest and the worst."[7] And who can fail to feel the poet's stinging arrow?

> ..'The Earth, sayest thou? The Human race?
> By Me created? Sad its lot?
> Nay: I have no remembrance of such a place:
> Such world I fashioned not.'—

We would thank death if it would cut down the worthless that live as parasites upon the rich strength of the earth, but such careful selection of victims is quite wanting. "Oh, stay thou, stay thou; spare the righteous, Death, and take the bad! But no, it must not be; death comes and smites the goodliest of us all; the most generous, the most prayerful, the most holy, the most devoted must die."[8] The overt reason why natural evil is peculiarly a *Christian* problem is that Christianity teaches not only that all of nature was originally created by the Almighty and pronounced by Him to be good, but also that the present movement of all things is guided and guarded by the very watchful eye of Him "who accomplishes all things according to the counsel of his will" (Ephesians 1:11). Our children go out in the back yard and cut their feet on glass, not because we foresaw the glass and permitted the injury, but rather because, being finite in power, we did not foresee it. But with God, all things are open and apparent. That is the problem. Can the Christian walk through the crowded corridors of a children's hospital or stumble through the rubble

7. Mill, *loc. cit.*
8. Spurgeon, *Gems*, p. 17.

left by the devastating force of a hurricane, without feeling the force of Job's words? "Surely I would speak to the Almighty, and I desire to reason with God" (Job 13:3).

Moral evil includes all of those frustrations of human values which are perpetrated, not by the natural elements in the universe, but by the free agency of man. Mental evils are worse than physical, though perhaps not as immediately painful; for, though one can move from the path of an impending hurricane, he cannot outrun either the judgment of conscience within or the fear of the course of things without. As to the latter fear, all of our struggles, all of our hopes, seem destined to destruction, and "that which befalls the sons of men befalls beasts; even one thing befalls them: as the one dies, so dies the other; yea, they have all one breath . . . all are of the dust, and all turn to dust again" (Ecclesiastes 3:19-20). Worry causes anxiety, and anxiety brings fear and trouble. These, when they come to fruition, bear the distresses of insecurity, neurosis, and lust. "What causes wars, and what causes fightings among you? Is it not your passions that are at war in your members? You desire and do not have; so you kill. And you covet and cannot obtain; so you fight and wage war" (James 4:1-2). The security of a century's work is dashed by the mad ambitions of a dictator; the retirement money of the aged is lost in a depression; and the institutions in which man has lately put his faith, collapse.

Moral evil is a problem for this reason. Despite the fact that man causes much if not all of the moral evil, the question is why did God, Who could have done otherwise, make us so that we *are* vulnerable to the frets of worry, distress, and fear? "Behold, I was brought forth in iniquity; and in sin did my mother conceive me" (Psalm 51:5). Descartes sagaciously remarked that a proof for his dependence upon God was that if *he* had made Descartes, *he* would have done a different job. But why did not God do that job with us in the first place? We seem able *potentially* to enjoy happiness—why do not we *actually* do so?

III. The Basic Solutions to the Problem

Some receive psychological consolation from meditating upon those meliorating considerations which whittle down the dimensions of the problem of evil. One suggestion is that the problem is overexaggerated. "They think that the whole universe is disarranged if something is displeasing to them, just because that thing is magnified in their perception."[9] If one has a headache, in other words, the whole world looks unworthy to him. Another is the notion that evil's presence is a stimulation to good. Without temptation and danger, all courage and honor would fail. Again, some say that evil is an earthly problem. "Tell me, Alciphron, would you argue that a state was ill administered, or judge of the manners of its citizens, by the disorders committed in the jail or dungeon? . . . And, for aught we know, this spot, with the few sinners on it, bears no greater proportion to the universe of intelligences than a dungeon doth to a kingdom."[10] But these and other like palliatives fail to soothe *our* pain on *this* planet. So long as there is *one* blind person, *one* soul in misery, *one* natural evil to frustrate our happiness, the problem of evil is just as acute as if there were a billion times that much evil present. If *one* righteous person suffers, when God has the power to prevent it and does not, the weight of the problem is fully on us. The *quantity* of evil is an irrelevant contribution to our discussion. Thus, there is nothing left to do, now that we have rejected the suggestion that the problem is insoluble, but to take the bull by the horns and seek for an outright solution. If we are impaled on one of the horns, then let that fate be ours. If there is no rationally verifiable evidence for the Christian doctrine of the relation between God and history, then let faith be abandoned; faith may rest only upon truth.

Roughly speaking, there are only three alternative choices that one may make once he concludes that there *is* a problem of evil which must be faced. The three alternatives are, first,

9. Augustine, *De Ordine*. I, 1, 2.
10. Berkeley, *Works*, Volume II, p. 170.

dispose of the evil by denying its true reality, as in pantheism. Here one defines God as all, and all as God; therefore, evil must be an illusion. Let us call pantheism, then, the philosophy of illusion. Secondly, one can say that evil is real and God is real, and that the two are co-eternal principles that have always struggled against one another and will forever continue so to do, as Plato says. On this view, God is finite, because He was impotent to prevent the entrance of evil, even as He is impotent to decree its exit. We call this approach pluralism, or dualism, for it suggests that there is more than one ultimate principle in reality. Thirdly, one can deny that evil is an illusion; he can reject the notion that God is finite; and he can propose that God sovereignly decreed the present universe, willfully permitting the entrance of evil into it to fulfill those purposes which were elected in His own counsels, as in Christianity. This view is theism, the philosophy which, teaching that God is both transcendent and immanent, declares that from eternity there was only God and no evil. Then, into a good creation, by a willful act of the creature, angel and man brought sin and evil into the world. For the Christian, then, all evil is either sin or punishment for sin. These are the three views. Each has its own peculiar problems; it is the prerogative of a rational man to accept that one which is attended by the fewest problems.

In examining these views, there are at least a hundred approaches we might take. To simplify matters, therefore, we shall hew to the narrow question of the ability of each so to get rid of evil that man can have immortality. Unless evil is put where God wants it, there can be no hope for immortality, for evil may surprise us and triumph at that very point where our immortal life is at issue. With this limitation in mind we may be brief in our observations.

A. Philosophies of Illusion

A sample of pantheism is the modern religious cult, the theology of which is almost too superficial to merit a place in the text, but which is, nevertheless, enjoying unprecedented popularity among the wealthy and socially elite of our day, Christian Science. "Nothing is real and eternal," says the founder, "nothing is Spirit, but God and His idea. Evil has no reality. It is neither person, place, nor thing, but simply a belief, an illusion of material sense."[11] If God is all, then, since He is Spirit, Truth, Life, and Light, all being is Spirit, Truth, Life, and Light. What place, then, is there for evil? Only at that point where men turn to the illusions of the mortal sense and erroneously postulate non-being as enjoying being; the postulation is erroneous because only God has being, and God is all-good. "My discovery that erring, mortal, misnamed *mind* produces all the organism and action of the mortal body, set my thoughts to work in new channels, and led up to my demonstration of the proposition that Mind is All and matter is naught, as the leading factor in Mind-science."[12] Waiving the all-important question, where Christian Science finds evidence for its sweeping, universal definitions, since they are discernible neither in the Bible nor in experience, let us point out, in passing, several surface objections to this species of pantheism.

First, if evil, which is so plain and evident to our senses, is an illusion, then the arguments in *Science and Health* of Mary Baker Eddy, since they are less plain and evident to our senses, are *more* of an illusion. We may discard Christian Science, therefore, for it is an illusion. Shall one trust the reports of his eyes and ears, as he reads and hears the arguments of Christian Science, when these sensory reports are disqualified to relay such overt data as the empirical reality of pain and death? Surely, if one is not able to trust his senses to tell him that *pain* is real, he cannot trust his senses to convey accurately to him those sound and light waves by means of which Christian Science itself is communicated. Secondly, simply

---

11. Mary Baker Eddy, *Science and Health With Key to the Scripture*, p. 71.
12. *Ibid.*, pp. 108-109.

because the *reality* of evil is denied, the problem of evil is not thus solved, for one must now account for the reality of the *illusion*. If all is God and God is all, where, then, has this illusion come from? How did it slip into the picture of a perfect pantheism? Thirdly, either this illusion is ontologically real or it is just a phantom of the mind which has no existence. If the first is true, then Christian Science admits the reality of *an* evil, the evil of the *illusion;* for, whether it be an illusion or no, wherein is the difference when my finger is smashed by a hammer? Whether we see but an illusion when we behold the mangy hands and feet of a leper, or whether we see reality itself, does the poor creature suffer less in either case? What is the difference between the *illusion* of having a leg amputated or experiencing the *real thing?* Illusion must be real, for two things equal to the same thing are equal to each other. If the second is true, then, as Trueblood points out, "if all evil, whether moral, natural, or intellectual is truly illusory, we are foolish indeed to *fight* it; it would be far preferable to *forget* it."[13] But, since the Christian Scientist persists in sending out practitioners to cure these illusions, he must be convinced that the latter are real; otherwise are we not simply shadow-boxing? Christian Science, like all philosophies of illusion, simply changes the name of the entity we struggle to overcome, from 'evil' to 'illusion'; but, as we all know, a rose by any other name—!

B. *Philosophies of Pluralism*

When once a man is assured that evil is real, but that this evil is not to be confused with the being of God, he is forced to set evil over against God, in which case the problem takes a new turn; leaving one with the alternatives, either that God and evil are co-eternal principles, a solution historically known as dualism, or that God existed prior to, and independent of, evil, and presently rules over it with sovereign power, as in Christianity. Let us attempt to show the inadequacies of the

---

13. *The Logic of Belief,* p. 286.

scheme of pluralism before we turn our attention to the difficulties which Christianity must face.

Pluralistic approaches have assumed many different forms in the history of philosophy, such as the struggle between light and darkness in the dualisms of Zoroastrianism and Manichaeism, and the Platonic doctrine of the recalcitrance of the time-space receptacle to yield to the gracious invitations from God to have the Good accurately stamped on it. For Plato, "God is a friend to man and an enemy to evil. Since God is finite, the conflict with evil is real. And since the receptacle is unchanging and timeless, the conflict with evil is everlasting. God takes sides in a battle of which the outcome is not a foreordained victory for his side."[14] We can begin to see the problem which pluralism must face. If the conflict is *everlasting*, what hope is there of ever overcoming evil, and what hope is there of immortality? But let us not anticipate too much. Rather, let us take the best example of the pluralistic philosophies — the doctrine that a God Who is supremely good, but finite in power, is consciously struggling with evil to overcome it and bring us happiness — and see where it leads us. We shall attempt to show that this statement of the problem is attended by greater difficulties than Christian theism.

The doctrine of the finite God is based on the empirical conviction that the world demonstrates sufficient good to grant us the right to postulate an infinite good God as its Author, but that the preponderance of evil which we observe is too evident a datum to warrant the conviction that this postulated God is also infinite in power. A God infinite both in goodness and power could not have permitted such things in nature as the birth of idiots and the unruly massacring of the innocent by natural evil. Presumably, thinks James, the only escape from the reality of both good and evil in a universe that God is somehow responsible for, is "to be frankly pluralistic and assume that the superhuman consciousness, however vast it may be, has itself an external environment, and consequently is finite."[15] "I

14. Demos, *The Philosophy of Plato,* p. 121.
15. *A Pluralistic Universe,* pp. 310-311.

believe that the only God worthy of the name *must* be finite."[16] Professor Brightman, one of the foremost contemporary defenders of the proposition that God is finite, summarizes for us the basic claims of the finitist's position.[17] There is no need to derive basic postulates from ignorance; the surd evils are not ascribed to the will of God; the everlasting distinction between good and evil is maintained; it is an inspiring motive for cooperative moral effort; and finitism is based on empiricism. Let us briefly examine the position.

1. If we are to have immortality, we must at least be assured that God will be able to control evil in the future; otherwise, what value is there in striving? And the finitist assures us that there *is* empirical evidence that God is overcoming evil. The emergence of human consciousness, for example, is a clue to the direction in which reality is moving. Let us first challenge the thought that, upon empirical evidence, we can say that evil may be overcome; then, later, return to show that evil not only may not be overcome, but that on the finitist's premises it cannot.

Since the finitist has rejected the objectivity of Scripture which assures us that God is sovereign both in goodness and in power, he is closed up to present experience for his information as to how the battle between good and evil is coming. The Christian has the sure word of prophecy to assure him that God is going to triumph in the end, but the finitist must keep a pencil and pad handy to add up the daily victories; for, without this infallible word of prophecy, the conviction that God is overcoming evil is just as strong or as weak as the empirical evidence upon which it is founded. Now, granted the very debatable proposition that there is more good in the universe since man has appeared upon the scene than there was before, even so, what assurance have we of *tomorrow*? How can we know from *this* point in history that God may not give the whole affair up as a bad cause one month from now? Even the *rationes,* to which we appealed earlier, provide us with but a God that has sustained the *rationes up to date.* Only Scripture,

16. James, *op. cit.,* p. 125.
17. *A Philosophy of Religion,* p. 314.

not the *rationes,* convinces us that God will sustain them to-morrow. We feel justified, thus, to press home the charge that, if God actually is finite, and if our knowledge of His progress is conditioned to experience, then it is empirically a possibility that God may become exhausted. The proposition, 'A finite God may become exhausted,' involves no logical contradiction, since exhaustion is a possible attribute of any finite being. Why *God* may be exempt from this general rule, is certainly not clear from the data given in the problem. For these reasons we say that a finite God *may* disappoint us, since our only evidence to refute that contention is day-by-day experience. But this is insufficient.

2. Let us now go further and suggest a reason why we think that a finite God *cannot* be relied upon to overcome evil and provide us with immortality. Since evil is eternal, and since God must always have been active in trying to control it, for He is infinitely good, we may safely assume that God has been putting Himself into the fray with His utter might at every point in the whole struggle. With such exhaustiveness, what can inhibit God from realizing His goal? Not Himself, for He is doing all He can every moment. Then another? But what other? Opportunity? Hardly, for in eternity God has had every opportunity. Then evil itself must be the culprit. We must assume therefore either that God has not been inhibited, and evil is presently controlled, or that He has been, and evil is still thwarting Him. If we assume the first alternative, both the problem and this solution cancel out; since the foundation for our whole problem is that evil *is* here and that it must be gotten rid of in a hurry. Otherwise what sense is there in supposing that there are surds in nature, and that we must cooperate with God in overcoming evil? If there is no evil here that is not yet overcome, the whole point of the problem is destroyed and we may turn to a new issue. Let us not forget that the finite-God doctrine is an expediency which is introduced to account for the empirically actual evil which we see about us continually. We can only assume, then, that God, Who has always done His best to get rid of evil, has been

thwarted in His efforts, for evil is still here, after God has had all of the opportunities necessary to dispose of it.

But, if God has been at work getting evil out of the way from eternity, He has already had infinity to prove Himself, *for in eternity all combinations that are realizable will have been realized.* But evil's extermination has not been realized; therefore it cannot have been a possibility. And, since it is not even a *possibility* that evil will be overcome in eternity, how, then, can we avoid the truth of the proposition that God will never *actually* overcome evil with another eternity to work on it?[18]

3. If the finitist interjects a *new factor* into the problem to suggest that, though God may have failed in the first half of eternity—we speak loosely—He will, with this new help, succeed in the second half, difficulties mount rather than diminish. If man, or any other suggested force that may enter the picture to help God, is all that God needed to overcome evil, why is it that God did not resort to the employment of this medium sooner? If God did not discover His need of assistance until late in eternity, He is limited in knowledge as well as in power, in which case two things follow. First, He Himself is no better qualified than we are to know whether evil will be overcome in the end or not. Secondly, revelation from God on the outcome is impossible, and we are left without hope. And if God *did* discover His need at once, then He either immediately resorted to call this help into being, or He did not. If He did, then why is it that man, our presumed paradigm, did not appear on the scene from eternity, and why is not evil, with this new help, exterminated? All the arguments we gave under point two against the possibility of God's conquering evil alone apply here also. And if God did not immediately create man, then He has not always done what He could have against evil, for He was passive when He might have been active, in which case He is guilty of the same charge that is leveled against a sovereign

18. Properly to be labeled 'potentially realizable,' an idea of God, however real, must be one whose externalization God desires. Other ideas are 'potentially realizable' only in a very special sense and do not concern us here.

God. If God is granted the right to be passive at this point, why may He not enjoy the prerogative elsewhere? And, finally, if God eternally has been trying to make man, but has been prevented in so simple an assignment until just recently, such a God is too feeble to merit the appellation, God.

We have called the doctrine of the finite God 'dualism' because we feel that it reduces, in its best elements, to the scheme of Plato where God and evil are eternally at odds. What we must make clear here, however, is that on such a structure one cannot rationally plead the hope for immortal life. God *may* fail us; therefore we are not able rationally to demonstrate that He *will not*. But let us cease airing the soiled linen of Platonism, and turn to the closets of Christianity. Let us see if, with its doctrine of absolute sovereignty, it is able to overcome the embarrassments of pluralism without introducing too many counterbalancing troubles of its own.

Chapter XVII

The Problem of Evil (Continued)

Will you yet say before him that slays you, I am God? but you are man, and not God, in the hand of him that wounds you. —*Ezekiel*

IF the problem of the pantheist is to account for the *presence* of the evil, and if the problem of the finitist is to account for how evil may be *gotten rid of,* the problem of the theistic absolutist is to solve the difficulty of *how evil got here in the first place.* There is nothing fortuitous in the Christian view of God and man. From the dew on the leaf to the motion of the planets in their ponderous courses, all is watched over by the providential eye of Him with Whom we have to do. Unlike pantheism, Christianity has no difficulty in accounting for the present existence of evil, for evil is that which resulted when the creature willfully rebelled against the Creator. Unlike finitism, Christianity has no trouble in getting rid of evil at the end of history, for the atonement of Christ reaches down even to the crushing of death itself. But what Christianity has to explain carefully is how evil found entrance into a universe which was controlled by the sovereign decrees of the Almighty. Let us devote the remainder of our study of the problem of evil to this issue.

I. Christian Theism

Christianity offers no halfhearted philosophy of history; it tells the story of things from the original creation of the world to the marriage feast of the Lamb at the end. It presents a God Who is the sovereign Creator, the sovereign Sustainer, and the sovereign Consummator of all things. By infallible decrees, God called the present world into existence, and by the same infallible power both presently rules and will ultimately call to a finish the process of history.

A. The Beginning of History

The Christian teaches creation *ex nihilo* as the answer to the question how history began. Some object to this by supposing that, since God created the universe, He must have lacked something; from which it follows (a) God is not perfect since He lacks glory; (b) the universe must be eternal, since He always lacked this glory. This argument, however, neglects the Christian teaching on the subject of creation. Creation does not *add* to God's glory; it only *displays* it. Creation therefore fills no lack in God. And as to the question why God did not create sooner, thus to display His glory sooner, the answer is that God elected not to do so. The desire in God to create the world was not eternally fulfilled because the desire to have it fulfilled was not always present. God is not an impersonal rule of changeless logic; He is a Person that makes free decisions. "Thus saith Jehovah, the Holy One of Israel, and his Maker: Ask me of the things that are to come . . . I have made the earth, and created man upon it: I, even my hands, have stretched out the heavens; and all their host have I commanded" (Isaiah 45:11-12).

It is this doctrine of creation that relieves Christianity from an eternal cycle theory in which man's individuality is caught and confused. "Something which is in its principle *new* comes forward, as over against the Greek view of the world . . . Greek science regarded not only the individual man, but also the whole human race, with all its fortunes, deeds, and experiences, as ultimately but an episode, a special formation of the world-process which repeats itself forever according to like laws."[1] Thus the Christian is able to preserve the dignity of man in the process of history by teaching that man was made in the image and likeness of God and is destined for eternal life. There was no antecedent necessity upon the part of God to make man, either for fellowship or to share His love; otherwise, man

1. Windelband, *A History of Philosophy,* p. 255.

would have been made from eternity, since God, Who needed man at one time, would need him at all times; for God is a Being that casts no shadow of turning. The eternal creation of man, however, would return us to dualism and a finite God. The Christian God is without parts and passions; His love flows toward man out of the depths of a divine volition. God is not subject to emotions.

B. The Process of History

God, after His creation of the world, did not leave the stuff and materials to shift for themselves by laws immanent within them. Rather, "He counts the number of the stars; he calls them all by their names. Great is our Lord, and mighty in power; his understanding is infinite . . . Who covers the heavens with clouds, who prepares rain for the earth, and makes grass to grow upon the mountains. He gives to the beast his food, and to the young ravens which cry" (Psalm 147:4-9). Christ's doctrine was that the Father infallibly controls the full course of history, observing the fall of the sparrow and sovereignly ruling over even the hairs of our heads. This high view of providence affords a reason for the Christian to rejoice, since it means that "Jehovah takes pleasure in them that fear him" (Psalm 147:11). It means that "a man's goings are established of Jehovah; and he delights in his way. Though he fall, he shall not be utterly cast down; for Jehovah upholds him with his hand" (Psalm 37:23-24). In a redemptively organized, sovereignly framed universe, the Christian can be assured, "that in everything God works for good with those who love him, who are called according to his purpose" (Romans 8:28).

Into this perfect universe, man and angel brought sin and disruption through their defection from the Divine commands. The *creature,* therefore, not God, is responsible for all of the sin and sorrow which make up both natural and moral evil. The diseases of the body, the fury of the hurricane, the unharnessed belching of the volcano, and even death itself, are the results of the curse which God put on nature because of the sin and rebellion of the creature. "For the creation was subjected to futility, not of its own will but by the will of him who subjected it in hope; because the creation itself will be set free from its bondage to decay and obtain the glorious liberty of the children of God. We know that the whole creation has been groaning in travail together until now" (Romans 8:20-22). Likewise, all moral evils—mistakes in logic, wickedness in the heart, fear and distress, wars and strife, murder and fornication—have come from man's sin. In setting up the problem of evil, therefore, one must remember that it is not accurate to charge God with having originally made an inferior universe. The universe was made absolutely perfect. It is the sin of men and angels which has sullied it.

But Jesus Christ, the Second Adam, covenanted with the Father to be the sin-bearer of all who would trust in His finished work on the cross. "Christ Jesus, who, though he was in the form of God, did not count equality with God a thing to be grasped, but emptied himself, taking the form of a servant, being born in the likeness of men. And being found in human form he humbled himself and became obedient unto death, even death on a cross" (Philippians 2:5-8).

It is well to make it clear that God sovereignly approbated the death of Jesus Christ before the world was made. "He was destined before the foundation of the world but was made manifest at the end of the times for your sake" (I Peter 1:20). This means that God infallibly knew that, if he created man upon earth, man would fall into sin and require the restoring merits of the God-Man, Jesus Christ; and yet He went right ahead and created man in the garden of Eden. The crucifixion, *the worst example of evil,* was not only permitted by God; *it was sovereignly decreed.* "This Jesus, delivered up according to the definite plan and foreknowledge of God, you crucified and killed by the hands of lawless men" (Acts 2:23). And again, "for truly in this city there were gathered together against thy holy servant Jesus, whom thou didst anoint, both Herod and Pontius Pilate, with the Gentiles and the peoples of Israel, to do whatever thy hand and thy plan had predestined to take place" (Acts 4:27-28). The full force of the Christian philosophy of history is now beginning to take shape. Even to suggest that there is any 'surd,' or any 'given,' with which God is struggling, is interpreted by the Christian as a deviation from the pregnant concept of sovereignty that the Bible teaches. "Jehovah has made *everything* for its own end; yea, even the wicked for the day of evil" (Proverbs 16:4). God is an absolute Being. "An absolute being is one that is free, unlimited, independent, and perfect. God is absolute, because He is not dependent for his existence, nature, attributes, or acts, on any other being."[2] In history, then, there is no surd, inexplicable, or antinomy. History is as rational at every point as the rational God Who decrees its movement. There is no strength but what comes from the Strength of Israel; there is no being but what stems from the Almighty.[3]

C. The End of History

Shall not He who brought history into being by sovereign power also declare its conclusion within the framework of that same might? "Tell us, when will this be, and what will be the sign of your coming and of the close of the age?" (Matthew 24:3) asked the disciples of Christ as He sat on the Mount of Olives. And Jesus was not lost for an answer, for He *is* the Logos of history. His answer, which now fills almost fifty verses in sacred Scripture, is an astounding, eschatological document which details the wars, famine, earthquake, suffering, apostacy, infidelity, and the rise of the anti-Christ that will mark off the end of the world's history.

---

2. Hodge, *Systematic Theology,* I, p. 357.

3. Being omniscient, God knew His redeemed from all eternity. "In the very beginning, when this great universe lay in the mind of God, like unborn forests in the acorn-cup; long ere the echoes waked the solitudes; before the mountains were brought forth; and long ere the light flashed through the sky, God loved his chosen creatures. Before there was creatureship — when the aether was not fanned by the angel's wing; when space itself had not an existence; when there was nothing save God alone; even then, in that loneliness of Deity, and in that deep quiet and profundity, his bowels moved for his chosen. Their names were written on his heart, and then were they dear to his soul." Spurgeon, *Gems*, p. 33.

As for man in the end, he will face the judgment of God. "It is appointed for men to die once, and after that comes judgment" (Hebrews 9:27). The final judgment of the souls of men will be made on the basis of what they have done with Him that is called the Christ. Those who are found sprinkled with the blood of Christ, will be rewarded with a felicitous life, while those who are not, will be rewarded with damnation.

> Before Jehovah's awful throne,
> Ye nations, bow with sacred joy.
> Know that the Lord is God alone,
> He can create and He destroy.
>
> His sovereign power, without our aid,
> Made us of clay, and formed us men;
> And when like wandering sheep we strayed,
> He brought us to his fold again.

The two basic presuppositions that the Christian appeals to when unfolding his philosophy of history are, then, the absolute, sovereign goodness and power of the God Who has revealed Himself in Scripture, and the sinfulness and rebellion of the heart of fallen and depraved man. The aggregate movements of history—wars, strife, punishment, etc.—can be explained within the pattern of this movement of God toward man, and the movement of man from God. But let us close this discussion of Christian theism, lest we repeat what we have earlier had occasion to refer to, and turn to an analysis of the fundamental arguments that have been raised against the Christian position. In this way the strength or weakness of Christian theism will be exposed.

II. Objections to Christian Theism

A. Based on an Appeal to Ignorance

Spinoza brands all attempts to solve the problems of life by resorting to the will of God, an 'asylum of ignorance.' Indeed Christianity does appeal to the will of God as the fundamental key to unlocking the mysteries of history, but it denies that there is anything illicit in the practice. What one appeals to as a controlling presupposition in his system is not what determines the validity of the act; rather, granted the starting point, does it produce a system which is horizontally self-consistent and which vertically fits the facts? Spinoza happened to reject the will of God as his logical ultimate, but he appealed to an ultimate, nonetheless. Shall he be granted a right which he denies the Christian? Is not any hypothesis verified when it brings meaning and order to those facts which are under study? As a pantheist, Spinoza can make no place for present moral striving, and *mean anything by it,* while the Christian can. This the latter takes as a real piece of evidence that, by an appeal to the will of God, one is able to locate a principle in relation to which life can be exegeted consistently. If the proof of the pudding is in the taste, the proof of an hypothesis is its ability to support a consistent world-view.

B. Unempirical in Character

Professor Brightman says that the "root of all objections to theistic absolutism is that it is a theory founded in an *a priori* faith, which in turn grows out of desires found in certain types of religious experience . . . Because of his predilection for a few experiences, the theistic absolutist sweeps to one side great masses of empirical fact with the *a priori* faith that some day they will be explained. In this he is unempirical."[4]

The strength of this objection rests upon a misunderstanding of the nature of the evidence for Christian theism. Rather than stemming from religious experience alone, the Christian argues from the knowledge of the self, the *rationes aeternae,* the empirical facts in nature, and the data located in Holy Writ. What does *empirical* mean, save 'being true to all of our experience?' If the data which the Christian appeals to can be relied upon safely to lead him into a system which is horizontally self-consistent and which vertically fits the facts, then he can validly claim to be empirical.

---

4. *A Philosophy of Religion,* p. 313.

C. Obliterates the Distinction Between Good and Evil

Some believe that on the position of sovereignty, the radical distinction between good and evil is lost, for what we may call good, God may call bad, and vice versa. In answer, the Christian points out that changeless criteria of right and wrong, good and bad, cannot be had without the law of God which is above the vicissitudes of time and space. God, Who is the final arbiter in all judgment, infallibly labels sin for us, thus establishing a sure difference between right and wrong, good and evil. Paul stresses this, saying "if it had not been for the law, I should not have known sin. I should not have known what it is to covet if the law had not said, 'You shall not covet' " (Romans 7:7). When God decrees sin to be sin, therefore, *sin is truly made sin.* An *absolute,* then, not a fortuitous distinction, is maintained between good and evil in Christianity.

D. Destroys Moral Struggle

This objection may be stated in two different ways, ways that require two different answers. First, if all is determined by a sovereign God, then evil will be automatically destroyed. Let us then go to the south sea islands to eat bananas and bask in the sun while all things come to pass. There does not seem to be the motive for moral cooperation with God in theistic absolutism that the finitist claims is at hand when one holds to a limited Deity. Secondly, if evil, such as the crucifixion of Christ is decreed by God, all evil must be; what use, then, is there to fight against the Almighty in overcoming it?

Man must fight against evil, not because God is frantically in need of his help; rather, because God has graciously permitted him to be an instrument in its extermination. The Christian struggles against evil, therefore, because God, the perfect judge, has commanded him so to act. God has decreed both the end of the evil and the appointed means for bringing about this end. Such means include the moral struggle of the individual and the preaching of the gospel.

This observation blends into the second. The universe, with all of the evil in it, is the best possible of all worlds, for the very reason that God, the standard of good, has called it good. But it is part of the goodness of this universe that the sin, which God permitted to enter that He might display His grace and love to the sons of men, is to be extirpated by the death of His Son, Jesus Christ. In Christ, God decreed the absolute means that should be used in evil's dissolution. The servants of Christ, therefore, as a proof for their love, carry out the implications of that atonement by seeking to defeat the workers of iniquity on every level of existence. There is no alternative here, for Christ commands that those who love Him follow His words implicitly. "If you love me, you will keep my commandments" (John 14:15). Christianity, therefore, instead of removing the motive for moral struggle, offers the highest reason for exterminating evil. The work of ridding life of evil is exciting, because God, Who could do it alone, graciously condescended to permit us to be "fellow workers in the truth" (III John 8). And the work is inspiring, because it represents a loving response to the commands of Him into Whose hands it is a fearful thing to fall.

If the end of evil were not sovereignly predestined, our labor would be in vain. It is the fact which God has promised us, that "at the name of Jesus every knee should bow, in heaven and on earth and under the earth, and every tongue confess that Jesus Christ is Lord, to the glory of God the Father" (Philippians 2:10-11), which gives us the animus to struggle. If there were the slightest chance that Christ would not put death under His feet, the Christian would know that the atonement was not infallibly consummated, and that he is yet in his sins. If *Christ* fails to put away evil, *a fortiori* where shall *we* stand? Thus, when evil seems to be growing in the world, when Satan seems, as Joad suggests, to be receiving a longer rope than usual, the Christian is not disheartened, for He knows that Christ *will* triumph; there is no if, but, or maybe to the promises of God. Luther expresses this hope classically:

Did we in our own strength confide,
  Our striving would be losing,
Were not the right Man on our side,
  The Man of God's own choosing.
Dost ask who that may be?
  Christ Jesus, it is He.
Lord Sabaoth His name,
  From age to age the same,
And He must win the battle.

And though this world, with devils filled,
  Should threaten to undo us,
We will not fear, for God hath willed,
  His truth to triumph through us.
The prince of darkness grim,
  We tremble not for him.
His rage we can endure,
  For lo! his doom is sure,
One little word shall fell him.

E. *Which of the Gods?*

The Christian supposes that what God rewards is good and what He punishes is evil, but what of all the other religions with their gods that command this or that, too? The answer is, the Christian serves the Almighty. "The gods that have not made the heavens and the earth, these shall perish from the earth, and from under the heavens" (Jeremiah 10:11). The mighty changes not. The petty gods do the will of the Al-gods of the nations come and go, as we daily see, but the Al-mighty God, for they are counted as but a drop in the bucket by Him with Whom we have to do. Thus, when the gods of his land failed Nebuchadnezzar, the latter, because Daniel's God failed him not, testified: "Of a truth your God is the God of gods, and the Lord of kings, and a revealer of secrets" (Daniel 2:47). He who bases his standards of right and wrong upon less than the Almighty, serves not God, but man, for there is but one God, Jehovah. One determines which God is the Almighty by an analysis of truth.

F. Makes God the Author of Evil

A very serious objection to the position that God has foreordained the entire course of events in the world, is that He is the Author of sin. In answer, God is the first efficient cause of everything, but evil has come, not from this first act of creation, but by a second act, an act of creatures. Evil has come from those rebellious acts of angels and men wherein created efficiency was turned from the commandments of God to pride and self-satisfaction. Evil has come, then, not from an act of God, but by a willful rebellion upon the part of created perfection. The energy which the angels used when they left their holiness to turn after sin, came from the Almighty, to be sure, and was thus an act which God permitted as part of His infallibly good universe; but the willful decision for rebellion sprang from the inner intentions of the angels alone. Therefore, God is neither the author or the approver of sin.

This structure is not to be interpreted as an exception to the decrees of God, for there is nothing in heaven and earth which comes to pass without first presenting itself before the Almighty for permission, like Satan did when he was about to tempt Job. But even so, "the sinfulness thereof proceedeth only from the creature, and not from God; who being most holy and righteous, neither is, nor can be the author or approver of sin."[5] God is the author of the author of sin, but He cannot be the author of sin itself, for sin is the result of a rebellion against God. Can God rebel against Himself? Nor are we defending the view that God could not have prevented the angels from willfully sinning, had He so elected to take that course. Such a suggestion would be repugnant to the doctrine of the sovereignty of the Almighty. God allowed the presence of evil in the universe, even though He does not approve of sin, that He might show His providential glory and grace in nature and His saving grace in Christ.

---

5. *Westminster Confession of Faith,* V. 4.

G. Makes God Responsible for Sin

If God is not the author of sin, at least He must be charged with being responsible for sin, for He freely created a universe in which little children starve and lepers suffer, when He could have done otherwise. This sort of question succeeds in impressing us only because it is phrased to suggest that it is meaningful to call the Almighty into court for trial. A little reflection on the subject will show the contradiction involved in charging God with responsibility. Let us ask one question: Responsible to whom, or to what? "Responsibility means to give a response, that is, to be answerable for something; but to be answerable implies that there must be someone to be answerable to. In other words, responsibility implies a superior personal power."[6] But in God's case, who *is* this superior power to whom He submits? Obviously, if we are talking about the *Almighty, He* already is the highest power there is. Therefore, when God decreed this type of universe where Christ was to die for the sins of all who believe, God was responsible to none but Himself.

Should one respond by telling us that, to make a universe where Christ would suffer agony on the cross for three hours, when it was possible to have refrained from so doing, would be a gesture *contrary to the nature of God,* we need only remind the objector that the nature of anything is determined by an analysis of what the thing itself does. We see the nature of the young lion by observing how it differs from the turtle in its actions. We see that man has a sinful nature by observing the manifold deeds of unrighteousness that he does all the day. It is meaningless, then, to appeal to the nature of a thing apart from a careful survey of how that thing acts. The nature of God, likewise, can be known only by observing what God does. But, if Christianity is true, God did freely send His only-begotten Son to die for sinners. God's nature, then, is one which expresses itself in making this kind of world where some men go to heaven for obedience and some go to hell for disobedience.

---

6. Clark, *A Christian Philosophy of Education,* p. 115.

Should one persist in his affirmation that God did not intend to create a world in which sin would emerge, we can only ask where this one has received his information on the subject. Unless he appeals to a private revelation which cannot be checked by the law of contradiction, we know of no source. It does not come from an analysis of history, for history bears out that Christ did die on the cross. If God did not want Him to do so, then we are back on the finite God position and we have no hope. And the Bible certainly does not teach that God was displeased with the death of Christ. On the contrary, "it *pleased* Jehovah to bruise him . . . he shall see of the travail of his soul, and shall be *satisfied*" (Isaiah 53: 10-11). Logic cannot be appealed to, for we have elsewhere shown that it is logical to suppose that God is free to do what He wants without being called into account. What new source, then, does our objector appeal to? Until it is forthcoming, we cannot continue the argument at this point.

The Christian treasures the doctrine that God is responsible to none but Himself, for therein lies the grandeur of His being the Almighty God of heaven and earth, He that received counsel from none and Him to whom all others are responsible. Paul devotes a considerable bulk of the ninth chapter of Romans expressly to make this point so clear that not even the slow of understanding could miss it.

> What shall we say then? Is there injustice on God's part? By no means! For he says to Moses, 'I will have mercy on whom I have mercy, and I will have compassion on whom I have compassion.' So it depends not upon man's will or exertion, but upon God's mercy. . . . You will say to me then, 'Why does he still find fault? For who can resist his will?' But, who are you, a man, to answer back to God? Will what is molded say to its molder, 'Why have you made me thus?' Has the potter no right over the clay, to make out of the same lump one vessel for beauty and another for menial use?[7]

---

7. Romans 9:14-21.

H. Contrary to Social Standards of Right and Wrong

When Bertrand Russell says, "the whole problem of evil is the problem of reconciling divine power with the requirements of what we ordinarily consider to be moral and social standards,"[8] he is introducing an issue which was latent in the above objections, and which, perhaps, is the most stimulating challenge to the logic of the Christian faith that can be made at this point. We have no intentions of minimizing this objection, for, even if we have succeeded in showing that God's will is the standard of right and wrong, our efforts may have been in vain if it can be established that the concepts of goodness and justice which God defends are contrary to those which we have come to regard in society as normative.

The problem is simply this. In society it seems that we punish men who are guilty; in God's economy the innocent are federally united with the guilty, as the infants that were slaughtered when the children of Israel, under orders from Jehovah, killed the Amalekites. The Bible is unequivocally clear on the issue: "Go and smite Amalek, and utterly destroy all that they have, and spare them not; but slay both man and woman, *infant and suckling,* ox and sheep, camel and ass" (I Samuel 15:3). In society we punish the man who does the crime, not his neighbor; but God visited His wrath upon His own innocent Son Who was without sin and guilt. Where, then, is the justice and goodness of God, and how can we tell it from the justice of Satan? God visited capital punishment on a man who was gathering sticks on the sabbath day (Numbers 15:32ff.). He elected Israel and let the other nations go their own way (Deuteronomy 7). He sent Elijah to but one widow when, as Christ Himself admits, there were many that needed help (Luke 4:26). He sent and healed Naaman the leper, when, as Christ again admits, many others were dying (Luke 4:27). He let the tower of Siloam fall upon, and kill, those who were no more guilty than others (Luke 13:4-5). Modernists, seeing this problem in the Old Testament, have

8. *The Philosophy of Bertrand Russell* (Schilpp, ed.), *The Library of Living Philosophers,* Volume V. p. 627.

rushed to the words of the 'gentle Jesus' for comfort; but here no better situation can be discovered. Christ forbade His disciples to give the good news of salvation to those outside of the Jews (Matthew 10:5-6); He intimated that the Syro-phoenician woman, who came begging for crumbs, was a 'dog' (Mark 7:26ff.); He drove out the money changers (Matthew 21:12-13); He preached uncompromisingly the doctrine of eternal damnation (Matthew 10:28); He called the citizens of his day 'sons of the devil' (John 8:44); He approbated John's message which called men a 'brood of vipers' (Matthew 3:7); He heaped scathing invectives upon the Pharisees and Scribes (Matthew 23); He commanded His disciples to buy swords (Luke 22:36); He sent the demons into a herd of swine that belonged to other people (Luke 8:32-33), etc. No, it will do little good to appeal to the 'ethics of Jesus' as over against the supposed 'terrible Jehovah' of the Old Testament. Jesus *is* Jehovah! (Matthew 3:3, for example, "Prepare the way of the *Lord*" is a quotation from Isaiah 40:3. "Prepare ye in the wilderness the way of *Jehovah*.") One must either reject Christianity *en toto,* or struggle with a reconciliation between its message and social decorums.

Legion have been the intellectual leaders who, since the rise of humanism, have taken up the pen to expose the Christian system at this point, but perhaps none have been as successful as William Channing and John Stuart Mill. Channing says: "Now we object to the systems of religion which prevail among us, that they are adverse, in a greater or less degree, to these purifying, comforting, and honorable views of God, that they take from us our father in heaven, and substitute for him a being, whom we cannot love if we would, and whom we ought not to love if we could."[9] To this Mill adds his famous challenge.

> If in ascribing goodness to God I do not mean what I mean by goodness; if I do not mean the goodness of which I have some knowledge, but an incomprehensible attribute of an incomprehensible substance, which for aught I know may be

9. *Unitarian Christianity,* pp. 54-55.

> a totally different quality from that which I love and venerate . . . . To say that God's goodness may be different in kind from man's goodness, what is it but saying, with a slight change of phraseology, that God may possibly not be good? To assert in words what we do not think in meaning, is as suitable a definition as can be given of a moral falsehood . . . . Unless I believe God to possess the same moral attributes which I find, in however inferior a degree, in a good man, what ground of assurance have I of God's veracity?
>
> If, instead of the 'glad tidings' that there exists a Being in whom all the excellencies which the highest human mind can conceive, exist in a degree inconceivable to us, I am informed that the world is ruled by a being whose attributes are infinite, but what they are we cannot learn, nor what are the principles of his government, except that 'the highest human morality which we are capable of conceiving' does not sanction them; convince me of it, and I will bear my fate as I may. But when I am told that I must believe this, and at the same time call this being by the names which express and affirm the highest human morality, I say in plain terms that I will not. Whatever power such a being may have over me, there is one thing which he shall not do: he shall not compel me to worship him.
>
> I will call no being good, who is not what I mean when I apply that epithet to my fellow-creatures; and if such a being can sentence me to hell for not so calling him, to hell I will go.[10]

As a reply to such an outburst against the Almighty, one is tempted simply to quote an appropriate verse of Scripture and pass on. "He that sits in the heavens will laugh: the Lord will have them in derision" (Psalm 2:4). But, since even the validity of that verse is a point which is in question, we shall have to approach Mill's argument on other grounds.

---

10. *An Examination of Sir William Hamilton's Philosophy,* Volume I, pp. 130-131. Mill contradicts himself. If God is *Almighty,* He *will* do everything He desires, even to making Mill, at the day of judgment, willing to worship Jesus Christ. Either, then, Mill is not talking about God, or he must admit the *possibility* of worshipping this God Who can send him to hell.

Before proceeding to an answer, however, let us hear the conservative side of the issue. This will serve to set humanism and Christianity over against each other even more sharply.

> In the first place they inquire, by what right the Lord is angry with his creatures who had not provoked him by any previous offence; for that to devote to destruction whom he pleases, is more like the caprice of a tyrant than the lawful sentence of a judge; that men have reason, therefore, to expostulate with God, if they are predestined to eternal death without any demerit of their own, merely by his sovereign will. If such thoughts ever enter the minds of pious men, they will be sufficiently enabled to break their violence by this one consideration, how exceedingly presumptuous it is only to inquire into the causes of the Divine will; which is in fact, and is justly entitled to be, the cause of everything that exists. For if it has any cause, then there must be something antecedent, on which it depends; which it is impious to suppose. For the will of God is the highest rule of justice; so that what he wills must be considered just, for this very reason, because he wills it. When it is inquired, therefore, why the Lord did so, the answer must be, Because he would. But if you go further, and ask why he so determined, you are in search of something greater and higher than the will of God, which can never be found.[11]

It can be detected from examining Calvin's and Mill's words that we are struggling with the validity of two diametrically opposed world-views: supernaturalism versus naturalism, Christianity versus humanism. Effectively to meet Mill, therefore, one must challenge humanism at its starting point, method, and conclusion. We have tried to do this already by unfolding the logic of conservative Christianity; humanism is a form of empiricism, and empiricism reduces to skepticism. To buttress what has gone before, however, we offer the following suggestions as lines along which the solution to this specific problem lies.

1. The most serious objection to Mill's humanism is, as indicated, that it reduces to skepticism. Having cut itself loose

---

11. Calvin, *Institutes,* III, 23, 2.

from God's law, humanism lacks a fulcrum with which to establish social criteria that are normative for all men everywhere, for from flux only flux can come. While Christianity has difficulties in it, humanism has absurdities.

2. When Mill objects that a God Who sovereignly chose Israel as His bride, passing by the other nations, is not a *good* God, he is committing the same fallacy that thinkers such as Plato and Leibniz did when they supposed that there is some 'good' or some 'law of sufficient reason' over and above God to which He, like ourselves is subject. If God is not free always to do the whole counsel of His will, something antecedent to God is preventing Him from so acting. But anything which is potent enough to be antecedent to *God* is powerful enough to reduce the latter from the status of Almighty to that of a finite Deity. An Almighty God can do anything.[12] But, as Mill supposes, God must do the good exactly as we in society conceive it. God, then, is finite. We have shown before the plight into which the finitist has driven himself. This observation provides additional negative proof for Christianity. Christianity can provide a guarantee for the hope in personal immortality. In considering an hypothesis, remember, one must observe not only what flows from its acceptance, but also what flows from its denial.

3. Let us now go on to show that it is meaningless to say that God must either do the good that we know of in society, or we cannot love Him as our Father. The decalogue certainly is the most sublime, the most catholic, the most socially elevating

12. The Almighty can only be conceived of doing everything that is meaningful. It will do little good to object to our structure by introducing one of those stock illustrations which are supposed to show that God is finite, as, God cannot create a rock heavier than He can lift. Such an example is meaningless because it violates the law of contradiction. God—Who can do everything—is juxtaposed with a rock which does not and cannot exist. The problem is meaningless. It is not the elements in the problem which forbid God from making this proverbial rock; rather, the elements prevent us from understanding the question itself. The problem involves a contradiction in terms and thus cannot be meaningfully commented upon. A meaningless proposition—such as the example in question, or 'fizz woorgv poogmough'—puts one under no obligation to answer because it has no significance.

moral code ever delivered to man, a code to which even the humanist must accede. Let us run through its precepts and see which of its commands can apply to the Almighty. (1) You shall have no other Gods before me. God is the Almighty, and He knows it; He is eternally aware that He can have no gods before Himself, for He is the only God. (2) You shall not make unto you any graven image. God gave this command because He is jealous that no other god receive homage. But is it meaningful to say that God forbids Himself to make an image of Himself because He might be made jealous of Himself? (3) You shall not take the name of Jehovah your God in vain. But may not He Who owns the name use it at His discretion, and will not that discretion always be holy, since God is holy? (4) Remember the sabbath day to keep it holy. God is above time; He is the Author of the sabbath. Furthermore, He did elect to rest, for our example, after the six days of creation. (5) Honor your father and your mother. God is without genealogy. (6) You shall not kill. All life belongs to God; He cannot kill. He merely calls in that which is rightfully His. (7) You shall not commit adultery. God is without parts and passions. (8) You shall not steal. From whom? All belongs to God. (9) You shall not bear false witness against your neighbor. Who is God's neighbor? He is God and He alone. A neighbor is an equal person. Man, thus, is not God's neighbor; man is dust and God is the Almighty. (10) You shall not covet. God is the King. The gamut of reality is His. What is there left to be wanted?

In short, the decalogue is of force only where *sinners* are concerned; but God is the *Holy One*. Of what, then, does Mill speak when He says that God must possess the same moral attributes which one finds in a good man here in society? God cannot be compared to man; it is man that is to be compared to God. Mill fails to realize that there are two orders of being included in this universe of discourse: Almighty God and dust.

4. Next, Mill fails to observe the derivative character of social decorums. Apart from the divinely inspired gospel of

Christ, none of the finer elements of culture have a foundation to rest upon. For example, we are told by the humanist that we ought to love our neighbors as ourselves as a fulfillment of that highest standard of social action, the golden rule. Now, just exactly why should one love his neighbor as himself? The *Christian* has a certain rule: "By this we know love, that he laid down his life for us; and we ought to lay down our lives for the brethren" (I John 3:16). The cross of Christ gave metaphysical significance to the golden rule; men had repeated it for generations, but Christ put some theology into it. He linked it with the Almighty, into Whose hands it is a fearful thing to fall, thus relieving the golden rule from being but a pious piece of pleasant advice.

But why should the non-Christian love his neighbor when he fears no God? He has no judgment to face, and, furthermore, he may at times be benefited by not loving his neighbor. Observe the relative life of ease that Al Capone enjoyed by spending his time systematically defrauding his neighbor. It is normal to love those that do you good, but the point of the golden rule, and the force of Christ's gospel, is that we are to love even our *enemies*. The Christian is to love his enemies because God loved him when he himself was an enemy of God and was estranged from the household of faith; but, again, why is the non-Christian to love his enemy? Is it not more logical to send a bulldog after the neighbor who deliberately dumps ashes in your yard and feeds moldy cake to your children, than to pray for your neighbor's salvation? The humanist has nothing to be saved from, so why pray, anyway? Furthermore, the bulldog brings immediate results.

The whole strength of love, forgiveness, and tolerance as part of a successful social unit is drawn from the metaphysics of the cross. Because Christ died for us, when we were enemies of His cross, we are to engage in brotherly love, to follow personal forgiveness, to turn the cheek, and to go the second mile. These are God's standards: they are what God means by good. If Mill appeals to these standards, then, his whole case collapses, for the God of Christianity is the Guarantor of these values, not the author of their destruction; and if Mill fails to appeal to these standards, he is to be scorned for propagandizing an inferior code of social ethics. Good ethics are derived from God.

5. Since God's standards *are* good, it is well that we point out exactly what the element of univocity is in the propositions, 'What God does is good' and 'What a properly ordered society does is good.' Let us remember that Mill objects to Christianity because he cannot apply the same epithets to God as he can to a worthy member of society. God slays a man for gathering sticks on the sabbath, and that is supposed to be good; while a good man in society forgives his enemies and prays for them that hurtfully despise him.

The solution to the problem is this. The univocal element— and that is all we need to establish to assure Mill that he can mean the same thing by the term 'good' when he says that 'What God does is good' and 'What a properly ordered society does is good'— in both usages of the term 'good' is, 'approbated by the will of the Almighty.' The validity both of God's act of slaying the man who gathered sticks, and of a man's loving his neighbor as himself, is exactly the same. Both are reflections of the one will of God. The ten commandments are good, and damning those to hell who trample under foot the Son of God is good, solely and only because God approves of such acts. Mill, therefore, is attacking a man of straw when he denies that there is a point of univocity in the two propositions, 'What God does is good' and 'What a properly ordered society does is good,' for a society is properly ordered only when it does the will of God.

6. With this in mind we may look for a common thread of method both in God's economy and in man's, since the same will is normative for both. Here are a few examples. First, many object to the fact that God works federally, complaining that it is unfair to be blamed for sins that Adam did. But when a government declares war, are not all of the citizens involved.

whether they have bellicose proclivities or not? And when our ambassador speaks, does he not speak for all? Secondly, many say God is unfair when He passes up those who fail to exercise faith in Christ's saving blood and permits them to go to damnation. How does this follow? If *all* men are unworthy—and they all are—then God is no more unfair to withhold his mercies from some than is a rich man who goes to the slums and gives money to every other person he meets. God is not unjust for not saving all; rather He is gracious to save even some. Thirdly, God punishes His Son, an innocent victim, as a vicarious atonement for the guilty, and the Bible calls this a supreme act of love. And is this not exactly the measure we use, likewise? The soldier who, though not under obligation so to do, throws himself on a live grenade, and dies a vicarious death for his company, is hailed as an illustration of perfect love. Therefore, the fact that Christ was innocent, the fact that He was God, the fact that He willingly gave up heaven's bliss to walk the way of sorrows, are, rather than proofs for the injustice of the cross, sure demonstrations of highest love. Finally, some object to God on the ground that He seems to be whimsical in His dealings. He slew Uzzah, for example, when the man was (apparently) in all sincerity, trying to stay the ark of God when the cart upon which the latter was riding struck a rock (II Samuel 6). The reason why Uzzah lost his life was because he disobeyed the commands of God. Is this unlike society? We make a law that a person who gives away atom bomb secrets shall die. Shall God be denied the same prerogative?[13]

---

13. "Will you call your Maker to the bar, and examine his word upon the accusation of falsehood? Will you set upon him, and judge him by the law of your conceits? Are you wiser, and better, and righteouser than he? Must the God of heaven come to you to learn wisdom? Must infinite Wisdom learn of folly? and infinite Holiness be corrected by a swinish sinner, that cannot keep himself an hour clean? Must the Almighty stand at the bar of a worm? Oh! horrid arrogance of senseless dust! Shall every mole, or clod, or dunghill, accuse the sun of darkness, and undertake to illuminate the world? Where were you when the Almighty made these laws, that he did not call you to his council? Sure he made them before you were born, without desiring your advice! and you came into the world too late to reverse them." Baxter, *A Call to the Unconverted*, pp. 28-29.

From these illustrations, we see that God's economy is not wholly different from the codes which govern society. With this observation, let us turn to a new topic, yet one which carries on our critique of those positions which challenge the doctrine of the primacy of the Lawgiver. This new topic is the problem of ethics.[14]

---

14. Since in our over-all solution to the problem of the one within the many, we appeal to the sovereignty of God, it is incumbent here to make a passing reference to a point which is lucidly clear to the follower of Scripture but which may prove to be a stumblingblock to others. We have reference to the question of the relation between predestination and man's free agency. If God determines the end of history from the counsels of eternity, as the Bible unequivocally avers, then it seems to follow that man is just a puppet in the hands of God. If this is so, all moral responsibility seems to be jeopardized. The Christian responds by pointing out the secondary means through which God brings about His determined ends. These means include man's free decisions. It is through the instrumentality of free, morally-conceived decisions and value-judgments that God superintends history's movement. Let us undertake to illustrate this. The Bible teaches that Judas Iscariot was known in the mind of God as the betrayer of the Messiah. Christ at the last supper prophesied that it was to be through Judas that the betrayal would come. Here are the two elements in the Christian view of history. The Lord was "delivered up according to the definite plan and foreknowledge of God" (Acts 2:23). And yet, Judas acted freely out of motives which appealed to his own ego. So responsible was he for this freely-conceived act of wickedness, that Christ said of Judas, "woe to that man by whom the Son of man is betrayed! It would have been better for that man if he had not been born" (Mark 14:21). God is sovereign and yet man is free. The two are interrelated so magnificently that a cross-section of history at every point reveals both the responsibility of man over against God and the mysterious superintending power of God over against man. Neither cancels out the other. Being made in God's image, man is free; but remaining God's possession while free, man never is so free that he escapes the foreknowledge of God. Man stands responsible for his every act, because God, the final Arbiter and Judge in every dispute, declares that he is. The conscience bears witness to this fact. Our guilt is ever before us. But guilt would be foolishness if there were not responsibility.

For a careful study of the relation between free will and divine determinism, see Augustine, *The City of God*, chapters 9 and 10.

Chapter XVIII

The Ethical One and Many

If my people, who are called by my name, shall humble themselves, and pray, and seek my face, and turn from their wicked ways; then will I hear from heaven, and will forgive their sin, and will heal their land. —*Jehovah God*

If it has not been evident to men before that we must be guided in our social life by universal and necessary ethical rules, it certainly is clear today. With the nations trembling for fear as the west and the east feel each other out for a Third World War; with stock piles of atom bombs being kept in order 'just in case'; with world diplomats vetoing each other out of commission; with starvation, disease, and death marking the aftermath of the recently consummated world-holocaust; and with the threat of economic revolution looming over the entire human race, one can appreciate why even the followers of the scientific method are meeting together in seminars throughout the length and breadth of the country, discussing what can be done to protect civilization from utter destruction in an atom-bomb war. Such discussion is good and necessary, for, if the problem of ethics is carried through to its logical conclusion, one will again be forced to reconsider conservative Christianity, that system of theology which is founded wholly upon the will of the God Who has revealed Himself in Scripture. Let us devote this present chapter to an explanation of how this is so.

I. The Fundamental Problem of Ethics

Ethics is the science of conduct, and the fundamental problem of ethics is determining what constitutes proper conduct.

We can easily see why this is a problem. It is evident that we must act, if we are to remain alive, but we find ourselves in such multifarious circumstances that it is difficult to know at times whether it is better to turn to the right or better to turn to the left, or better not to turn at all. And, before one can choose a direction in which to turn, he must answer the question, better in relation to *what* or to *whom*? In other words, if a man is going to act *meaningfully,* and not haphazardly, he must rationally count the cost; he must think before he acts. Right judgment, then, and proper actions always go together.

Now that the problem of ethics is linked with the problem of thought and predication, we ought not to be surprised to learn that the same criteria which govern true scientific judgments—horizontal self-consistency and vertical fitting of the facts—govern ethical judgments, too. Good judgment must be true judgment, be it mathematical, scientific, or ethical, and truth, we have seen, is that form of meaning which can make peace with two levels of validity: the law of contradiction and the facts of history. Let us carry this pattern of truth through in our study of the ethical one and many.

A. Horizontal Self-Consistency

The law of contradiction requires that one construe his terms consistently throughout a given argument, or given system of thought; otherwise contradiction, the first symptom of error, appears. This is our primary clue for detecting truth in an ethical system: we must see, when the basic postulates of the system are granted, if they cohere together in self-consistency. The alternative to consistency is chaos. One must either obey the law of contradiction in his ethical theory or cease talking about valid rules of conduct altogether.

A very interesting search for consistency in ethics is outlined for us by Plato in the *Euthyphro.* On the porch of the King Archon, Socrates, quester after the truth, meets the youthful Euthyphro, who is confidently on his way to prosecute his father for murder. Socrates is elated to meet such an astounding youth, one who is deeply concerned for the morals of the nation, for alas! perhaps in him he may find that long sought for answer to the problem of virtue. "By the powers, Euthyphro! how little does the common herd know of the nature of right and truth. A man must be an extraordinary man, and have made great strides in wisdom, before he could have seen his way to bring such an action" (4a). So certain is Euthyphro of himself, that he is prosecuting, not a neighbor, but his own father for criminal negligence. The father had taken a slave—who had murdered another hired man while in a fit of drunken passion — bound him, and left him to die in a ditch. At this outburst of piety, Socrates hails Euthyphro as a most remarkable lad. "Rare friend! I think I cannot do better than be your disciple" (5a).

With the stage properly set, Socrates proceeds to apply the law of contradiction to the policies of Euthyphro, for consistency is the first mark of truth. "And what is piety, and what is impiety" (5b)? Confidently Euthyphro responded with the definition, "Piety is doing as I am doing; that is to say, prosecuting anyone who is guilty of murder, sacrilege, or any similar crime—whether he be your father or mother, or whoever he may be—that makes no difference; and not to prosecute them is impiety" (5b). Socrates responds by calling to Euthyphro's attention what one of the basic requirements for giving a definition is. "I did not ask you to give me two or three examples of piety, but to explain the general idea which makes all pious things to be pious" (6b). Socrates wants a connotative definition, one which will give him a standard by which to check the validity of all action. "Then I shall be able to say that such and such an action is pious, such another impious" (6b). To oblige, Euthyphro says that "Piety, then, is that which is dear to the gods, and impiety is that which is not dear to them" (6b). The law of contradiction wrecks this suggestion, however, for even the gods "have differences of opinion, as you say, about good and evil, just and unjust, honorable and dishonorable" (7b). Ah! interjects Euthyphro, grasping for a straw, "I will amend the definition so far as to say that what all the gods hate is impious, and what they love pious or holy; and what some of them love and others hate is both or neither" (9b). Socrates soon explodes this, however, by forcing Euthyphro into the fatal position of admitting that virtue is a rule which the gods do not make, but which they themselves must follow. "And what do you say of piety, Euthyphro: is not piety, according to your definition, loved by all the gods?" "Yes." "Because it is pious or holy, or for some other reason?" "No, that is the reason." "It is loved because it is holy, not holy because it is loved?" "Yes" (10b).[1] This means that all reference to the gods is superfluous, for the pious is something independent of the gods, something which the gods themselves must love; so even if it were discovered that the gods agreed on something, we would not have assurance that what they united upon was that right rule of piety for which we seek, for may the gods not be in error just as ourselves?

Socrates carries on in this way, leading Euthyphro into one contradiction after another, until the latter grows faint-hearted from the ordeal, and turns to pragmatism. "Another time, Socrates; for I am in a hurry, and must go now" (15b). "Alas! my companion, and will you leave me in despair? I was hoping that you would instruct me in the nature of piety and impiety" (15b). The lesson from the *Euthyphro* is that it is a large order to give an *intelligent* answer to the question: Why is murder wrong?[2]

B. *Vertical Fitting of the Facts*

If the first test of a system of ethics is self-consistency, the second is its ability to come right down into the human situation and meet with the actual data of life. Any "philosophy

1. Observe the non-Christian assumption of Socrates. Christianity teaches the reverse. God, not some world of Ideas, is the final standard of all virtue. His law is what tells us what the good is.

2. Note that the Christian can explain the reason why Euthyphro *continued* to prosecute his father, even after he had to admit that he did not have a sure notion of what piety was. Being made in the image of God, Euthyphro was endowed by nature with the *rationes*. Possessing, thus, an inward knowledge of right and wrong, he *knew* murder was wrong, though he was unable to translate that knowledge into compelling propositions.

which, neglecting the real world, takes its start from reason, will necessarily do violence to the reality of life and resolve nature and history into a network of abstractions."[3] Sheer consistency is not truth; truth is *systematic* consistency, *i. e.*, a consistency which makes peace with not only the demands of the law of contradiction, but also the facts of history.

The fundamental datum which every ethical theory must make peace with to merit the appellation of vertical fitting of the facts, is the law of self-preservation. Man is a creature of self-love and self-interests, love and interests which must be placated before man can be persuaded to participate in the more exalted forms of culture. The nature of man includes egoism as part of its endowment from creation.[4] In every ethical decision, therefore, man canvasses not only the consistency of the act, but also how performance or lack of performance of such an act affects his own interests and desires. Such interests may be personal honor, pride, character, or health, but vital interests they are, nonetheless. Every man is an egoist at heart, and an ethical theory, if it is vertically to fit the facts, must reckon with this datum.

C. *Ethical Theory and the Problem of the One Within the Many*

We have pointed out elsewhere what we mean by the problem of the one within the many. The many are those facts or data which wait to be correlated into a coherent pattern of meaning, and the one is the pattern itself. The Christian teaches that the discrete facts of the created world collectively make up the many, while the mind of God is the principle of the one which brings coherence and meaning to the many. In ethics we are faced with the problem of the one within the many in one of its most challenging forms.

The problem is this. The legion of desires which thrust themselves forward in our ego for recognition in ethical situa-

3. Bavinck, *The Philosophy of Revelation*, p. 25.
4. Sin has *metamorphosed* man's egoism into unbridled selfishness, but the self-love which keeps a man from committing suicide is not due to sin. Adam himself possessed an innate rule for self-preservation.

tions are the *many,* and the rule of duty which must bind these desires together is the *one.* Here our elements of truth—horizontal self-consistency and vertical fitting of the facts—meet in a special discipline. The vertical facts, the many, are those attempts of the heart to make all actions terminate upon the ego, while the horizontal self-consistency is that normative principle of duty or right which gives universality and necessity to our ethical decisions. Unless he includes the urges of man, an ethicist is not talking about reality, and without a rule of duty, he cannot avoid skepticism. A man must do the *right* —that is his duty; but he must also be assured that this right is somehow related to his own self-preservation—that is his desire.

D. *The Merger of Duty and Desire*

The problem of the ethicist to reconcile the one and the many on the level of personal actions is known as the merger of duty and desire. Duty without desire cannot stimulate willful action, and desire without duty has no code of direction. One may see that it is his duty to do something, but if he has no way of knowing whether that duty will benefit him as an egocentric individual, the action will probably fail to materialize; and if one has the desire to do something, but has no way of knowing whether the thing desired involves an action which is contrary to duty or not, action may materialize, but it may be unethical.

The ethicist does not have to suggest desires for the heart of man to follow, for they, like the bubbling flux of time and space, are multitudinous in their number, and continuously recurrent in their appearance. The problem of the ethicist is, however, to find a rule of duty which can harness these boundless desires. This duty, when found, must provide at least three things. First, it must give validity to action, *i. e.,* it must make the rules of conduct normative for *all* men, Socrates and ourselves. As all men must use the same rules of logic to *think* alike, so also they must all follow the same rules of duty if they are to *act* alike. Proper action is not a whit less important than proper thought, as a recollection of World War II proves. Secondly, duty must restrain desire. The heart of man is the fountainhead of endless wicked desires; duty must stand guard over the heart. An ethical man learns to say *no* under many circumstances, for the very reason that he discovers a discrepancy between what he desires to do and what he ought to do. So Joseph, when Potiphar's wife tried to lure him into an unlawful sexual act, "left his garment in her hand, and fled, and got him out" (Genesis 39:12). Joseph knew in his heart the law of God, the absolute rule of duty, "for God will judge the immoral and adulterous" (Hebrews 13:4). Thirdly, duty must serve to elevate desires. A pacifist, for example, when he is shown that it is his *duty* to defend with arms the elect of Christ, will turn to the high desire of protecting his nation from the inroads of aggressive unrighteousness, but for the glory of Christ alone. When he sees that an army is, on the level of the international society, what the police force is, on the urban level, an instrument in the hands of the good to keep the evil within those bounds which God has decreed; when he learns that it is his duty at times to sell his staff and buy a sword; then he will make it his *desire* to cooperate in quelling the forces of unrighteousness, instead of sitting passively by while the bride of Christ is raped by lawless men. Proper duty should have the effect of elevating one's desires.

But where shall we locate these rules of duty? *That* is the question! In answering the question, however, one has little latitude of choice. Since duty is proper meaning, and since meaning is a property of either mind or of law, we can expect to locate our rule of duty either in a mind or in a law. Either the law that rules the mind is supreme, or the mind which makes the law is paramount. These fairly well exhaust the possibilities, for, if mind does not make the law, it is law that makes the mind. The Christian will defend the primacy of the Lawgiver; non-Christianity will defend the primacy of the law. Let us consider the latter first, keeping in mind our one question—the solution to the problem of the one within the many.

II. The Primacy of the Law

A. The Arguments for the Primacy of the Law

Kant taught that an action is moral only when it is done out of respect to the right; any searching after reward or personal happiness renders action immoral. Thus, when an ethical situation is faced, man must say: *What is my duty?* never: *What is my desire?* When one acts solely out of rational consideration for duty, he enjoys a good will, a will which is obedient to the law of universal reason. The uniqueness of man lies in the fact that he belongs to two spheres—he is a member of the animal sphere, in that he is subject to desires and inclinations of senuous caliber, and he is a rational being qualified to act upon the basis of that higher law of reason which takes no account of sensibility. The animal is guided by external stimuli; but a rational man must be guided by a consideration of what is right. It is the duty of each man to cultivate an unadulterated reverence for the law of his rational nature, for whenever he yields to inclinations and desires, he forfeits his right to call his act ethical.

And what is this law of rationality which we must follow? It is the categorical imperative: Act as if the maxim of thy action were to become by thy will a universal law of nature. Before acting, then, one must ask himself if he could sincerely will the act itself to be done by all men everywhere. If it cannot, the highest law of reason has not been located. All men are of one nature in that they are rational; hence, when one acts worthily, he conforms his act both to the law of his own nature and to the natures of all men.

This theory of the primacy of law, which has been espoused by no few scholars under the influence of Kant, is known as formalistic ethics. The rights of reason are stressed at the expense of the emotional and sensible, resulting in a 'duty for duty's sake' ethic. Man is distinguished from the lower animals, not in sensibility, but in rationality; so, the formalists contend, an act is not truly human, truly moral, until it grows out of a respect for law alone. Reason is sovereign; sensibility is either outlawed or is relegated to a subordinate place. The virtuous life is the life according to right reason; and the vicious life is the irrational one.

B. The Arguments Against the Primacy of the Law

The richness of this position lies in its enviable ability to achieve universality and necessity in ethical theory. But it achieves this only at a dear price. First, from the fact that rationality is one thing which distinguishes man from the animal, it is falsely inferred that the real man is the rational man. The real man is the *whole* man, intellect, emotions, and will. If we remove the sensible life from man, we remove part of the real man, for there is no activity without sensibility, and no moral life without feelings and desires. Secondly, by dividing man artificially into empirical and transcendental selves, and by putting a warfare between them, Kant removed his ethics from the human path of blood, and sweat, and tears. "The flesh and blood of moral reality come from sensibility. It has been truly said that the movement of the real world is not 'a ghostly ballet of bloodless categories'; no more is the movement of human life."[5] At best, Kant's ethical theory is formalistic; it applies only to the celestial beings that have no bodies. Thirdly, that which unites men together is not the law of contradiction, but the law of love. Reason may outline what we ought to do, but only love, flowing out of a right heart, can supply the power to realize it. "Kill out sensibility, and you not only impoverish your own life, but you separate yourself from your fellows no less thoroughly than if you make your own pleasure your only good."[6]

When one assumes the primacy of the law, as opposed to the Sovereign Lawgiver, he always, if the history of ethics teaches us anything, succeeds in his position only by unnaturally dividing man into two parts, considering that "The part which is immersed in natural process is essentially evil and the part which is subject to reason is essentially good."[7] In such a

5. Seth, *A Study of Ethical Principles,* p. 165.
6. *Ibid.,* p. 167.
7. Niebuhr, *The Nature and Destiny of Man,* I, p. 119.

situation, though he may have achieved that *sine qua non* horizontal self-consistency in his ethical theory, he has failed vertically to fit the facts of real history. A perfect ethical system must preserve the element of self-consistency which Kant defended, keeping ethics a normative science with universal and necessary implications; but it must go on and hook up this validity with the multifarious desires in the heart of man. Whether Kant realized it or not, the real, essential man is first of all an egoistic being.

III. The Primacy of Man as Lawgiver

A. The Arguments for the Primacy of Man as Lawgiver

If the law is not primary, because it is subsidiary to the mind that makes it, it must be that mind is primary. This means that law is displaced from its pedestal place of primacy by the lawgiver; law does not make the lawgiver: the lawgiver makes the law. But who is this lawgiver? Ethicists suggest two answers: God and man. Let us examine the claims of the latter first and then return to establish the coherence of the former.

The most naive union of duty and desire in the mind of a lawgiver is ethical individualism, that state where each man is a law unto himself. The ethical individualist avoids the Kantian deficiency by identifying duty and desire with what he personally elects to do. The worth of an act is considered solely on the basis of personal feelings, inclinations, and intuitions, apart from, and independent of, any factor that any other individuals may contribute.

A higher step is to unite desires, not with duty as each man sees it, but with the mind of a social unit, as in National-socialism under Hitler. If the will of the group is made the operating unit, be it a family, tribe, society, state, or nation, a happy union between duty and desire is found for a larger unit than is located in ethical individualism. Group ethics likewise rejects the dichotomy which Kant set up between duty and desire, but it restricts the coincidence of duty and desire to the mind of a select unit of mankind. National-socialism, for example,

> . . . emphasizes the claim of freedom for the German nation, but rejects it for other nations. It rejects welfare as an unworthy ideal for a heroic nation, and substitutes power and mastery. It rejects absolutely and with abhorrence the principle of equality as an abomination conceived by the French Revolution. It professes a desire for peace—under the supremacy of Germany . . . . Correlated with the doctrine of Aryan or German superiority is the doctrine of racial purity. All racial interbreeding results in degeneracy and has been the primary cause of decline in national power and culture.[8]

The final step in making man the lawgiver is found in certain broad forms of humanism, where an attempt is made to transgress the barriers of individuals and societies, and to unite all men upon the sure basis of those common human decencies which all men must respect if they are successfully to live together. The desire of every man is to live; therefore we must respect the desires of others and let them live. This is our duty. When a man is pledged to the support of universal happiness and well-being of all men, not only is he fulfilling his highest duty, but he is likewise giving expression to what ought to be his loftiest desire, the desire for personal well-being. If a man follows his duty and treats all men as brothers, he himself will benefit in the end because others will do good for him. Contemplation of this long-run service in life shows us our duty; seeing what is ours if we follow this duty reveals to us a reason for desiring to do our duty.

B. *The Argument Against the Primacy of Man as Lawgiver*

The deficiency in ethical individualism is too overt to comment upon. If every man is a law to himself, we have anarchy, not ethics. As for the union of duty and desire on the level of a social unit, two deficiencies are noted. First, horizontal self-consistency is not achieved, for by the very nature of the solution universality and necessity in ethics are ruled out in favor of private group decisions. Observe the present strife which

---

8. *Twentieth Century Philosophy* (Runes, ed.), pp. 31-32.

exists between nations in this postwar period. The Russians, basing their union of duty and desire upon what the *Russian nation* needs and wants, approach every peace conference seeking not the good of all men, but solely their own good. Secondly, vertical fitting of the facts is lacking because the union of duty and desire is enjoyed only by a few. The broad question of the one within the many, therefore, remains unsolved, for only a small selection of the real many has been accounted for. What of the desires of *all* men? Group ethics differs from individual ethics only in that the unit involved is a bit larger; ethical chaos, however, is common to both structures. In the latter it is every man for himself, and in the former it is every nation for itself. Each is a forfeiture of ethics as a normative science. A scientific truth must be true for all, everywhere, not for some, somewhere.

Broad humanism defends a more respectable thesis, but it, too, is impotent to solve the one within the many. First, since humanism is committed to the scientific method in its epistemology, it cannot prove that any norm of ethics, such as the wrongfulness of murder, which might be valid today, will necessarily be wrong *tomorrow*. In an open universe, *i. e.,* a universe without God to keep it regular, not only may doors have one side tomorrow, but also what we value and praise today we may despise and depreciate tomorrow. Through the expedient of a flux-epistemology, it is impossible to relieve human values and human decencies from a moment-by-moment jeopardy. Now, since we cannot know whether any ethical truth which we firmly hold today will be valid tomorrow, it follows that present ethical norms are not really normative at all. Not only are our values contingent to tomorrow's experience, but, also, they wait upon our experience one tenth of a second from now. Therefore, it is impossible to know whether it is better at any one time to turn to the left or to turn to the right, for what may have been the proper course of action yesterday may be the improper one a moment from now. This is ethical skepticism.

Secondly, humanism fails to unite duty and desire in man. There is frequently a conflict between our *personal* desires and the desires of the *group, i. e.,* instances where one will *not* be benefited if he complies with the will of the group. Movie 'stars,' for example, seem to profit by what one has called their 'serial polygamy' even though what they are doing is contrary to the generic will of society that each man have one wife and each woman one husband—till death do them part! And one can only guess how many politicians have defrauded their way to fame and fortune, preferring their own greed and avarice to the will of the people, fabulously profiting by it all of the way, and dying in peace at the end. Humanism denies that there is a God into whose judgment we may fall; consequently, if a man can cheat and lie his way through life, and still be happy and well in so doing, as many seemingly do, humanism can say nothing significant against the practice. This is practical skepticism, for it results in every man doing what he thinks is right in his own eyes.

Thirdly, since humanism follows 'total' evolution, man is but one stage in an apparently endless process. Why, then, are *human* values conceived to be the final and highest stage of things? When Christianity is scrapped, man becomes one minor gear in a mechanical universe; he contributes his little part, just as do mud, hair, and filth. Each is a gear, and each in its own way makes for the smooth movement of the whole. But it is not at all clear that humanity is worthy of any more honor than the other gears in the machine. Why should man be more laudable than, for example, the elephant? Both are doomed to die without hope in a universe which is under the decrees of the second law of thermodynamics, and the animal is bigger than the human. Without God to tell us otherwise, humanity appears to be but a huddling mass of groveling protoplasm, crowded together in a nervous wait for death, not unlike a group of helpless children that aggregate together in a burning building, pledging to love each other till the end comes. But, since we are *all* going to die, and since 'the wages of virtue is dust,' as Sidgwick expresses it, what possible incentive for heroic personal living can humanism proffer? Shall *I* give up *my* own desires to follow some abstractly conceived theory of justice, prudence, and benevolence, when, as a result of *my* lifetime sacrifice, all *I* receive is a dash of dirt? Inasmuch as all men are in the same predicament as I am, and inasmuch as I can be assured of *my* happiness here and now if I do my own, rather than the will of the whole, what reason is there for me *not* to follow my own desires? After all, it is just one gear against another, and may the best gear win.

IV. God as Lawgiver

If we repose ethical standards in pure law, we destroy human nature; and if we place them in the mind of man, we cannot rise out of the flux of history to establish universality and necessity in our rules for conduct. When we have these facts in mind, and see civilization threatened to be destroyed because of poorly conceived ethical systems, we do not think it strange "that many find themselves rather forced back to old fashioned notion of values as subsisting in the mind of God."[9] And, as long as we *are* forced back to an external reference point to give universality and necessity to ethical theory, the Christian suggests that we go all the way and repose in the Almighty, for only under this circumstance will one possess an ethical system which is genuinely horizontally self-consistent and which really vertically fits the facts of history.

A. Horizontal Self-Consistency

The Christian avoids the flux of time and space by appealing to the mind of the God Who has revealed Himself in Scripture. God's judgments are transtemporal and trans-spatial; therefore the law which He commands bears the same characteristics. This law is valid not for one individual, nor for one nation, but for all men everywhere, always; for all men, being made in His image, are perpetually responsible to Him for their conduct. Let us take the case of murder, for exam-

9. *Twentieth Century Philosophy* (Runes, ed.) p. 69.

ple. Willful destruction of life is not culpable simply because it is against society, or because it makes life inconvenient for others, or because one might be killed himself if he takes to killing others; but, rather, because of the worth and dignity of man himself. Man is God's property in a special sense. "And surely your blood, the blood of your lives, will I require . . . at the hand of man, even at the hand of every man's brother, will I require the life of man. Whoso sheds man's blood, by man shall his blood be shed: for in the image of God made he man" (Genesis 9:5-6). All ethicists agree that murder is wrong; Christianity shows how this is so, by laying down ethical rules which possess metaphysical foundations.

God's laws then, define the duty for man. Man is God's property because he is made in the image and likeness of the Almighty. The Christian, therefore, is able to defend as strict an ethical code of duty as either Plato, Aristotle, or Kant, for man cannot be true to his essential nature until he loves God's commandments with all his heart and with all his soul and with all his mind and his neighbor as himself. This duty is imperative! It is objective and changeless, being based upon the nature of the Almighty and communicated in the decalogue.

B. *Vertical Fitting of the Facts*

Because rational man is linked to a sensible nature, the rationalists, to solve the ethical problem, had to *destroy* part of man to give validity to duty. Christianity is not required to do this. It *appeals* to, rather than separates itself from, the law of self-preservation in man. In fact, it makes the highest possible egoistic appeal: *eternal life*. "Fear not, little flock, for it is your Father's good pleasure to give you the kingdom. Sell your posessions, and give alms; provide yourselves with purses that do not grow old, with a treasure in the heavens that does not fail, where no thief approaches and no moth destroys" (Luke 12:32-33). "He who believes in the Son *has* eternal life" (John 3:36). Man naturally loves himself, and it is to this self-love that God appeals in His gospel. If we will confess our sins and believe in the finished work of Christ, instead of facing the fearful wrath of God in judgment, we receive everlasting felicity. Therefore it is safe to say that Christianity and Kantianism are diametrically conceived; for, whereas the latter looks upon motives that appeal to the ego as wholly unworthy and immoral, the former is founded squarely upon an appeal to the ego.

> Ho, every one that thirsts,
> Come you to the waters,
> And he that has no money;
> Come you, buy, and eat;
> Yea, come, buy wine and milk
> Without money and without price.[10]

The preciousness of this approach is that it is founded on a system of objective truth. Christianity not only lists the things that the heart of man dearly wants, but it points out a metaphysically grounded way to show how these things may be realized in the lives of even the weakest. The Almighty, whose word fails not, promises eternal life to the pure in heart, to the meek, to the poor in spirit, to the peacemakers, and to the merciful.

C. The Union of Duty and Desire

Kantian ethical theory destroys the integral unity of the empirical and transcendental egos in man, while Christianity does not. Man is not an angel; he is a rational animal, qualified to worship God, with desires and inclinations of the heart that call for satisfaction. The humanist brought duty down to earth by uniting it with the desires of man, but then promptly lost the normative character of ethics by cutting these values loose from the mind of Christ. Christianity retains the truth of humanism without this attending ethical skepticism. The virtue of Kant is that he saw the necessity of having universality and necessity in ethics if it is to remain a science, and the virtue of humanism is that it sees the real force of

---

10. Isaiah 55:1.

keeping human desires in successful ethics. Each has its merits; only Christianity can unite them.

The duties of man are the objectively revealed commands of God of the decalogue. The first four commandments outline man's relation to God, called the first table of the law, while the last six outline man's relation to man, called the second table of the law. The first table must precede the second table or the latter possesses no metaphysical implications, and thus loses all of its force and meaning. Humanism has tried to float the second table of the law, ignoring the fact that the first table is the hull of the ship of ethics. Duties to men are meaningless until they are first related to our duties to that One Who is higher than man. If man is *not* made in God's image, he is but a more complicated batch of protoplasm than the apes and baboons; why he, rather than they, is the more worthy of our devotion is not easy to see on humanistic presuppositions.[11] And if man *is* made in God's image, it is God, the Maker, not man, that decrees what the relative value of each section of the creation is. *Man,* the Bible informs us, is the crowning jewel of creation (Psalm 8).

God achieves a perfect union of duty and desire by means of a legitimate system of rewards and punishments. The duty of man is to do God's will. The desire is to have happiness and life. In Christianity these are united, for God gives happiness and life to all who do His will. This is the *affirmative* incentive for proper duty to God. Does the ego of man want life? "I came that they may have life, and have it abundantly" (John 10:10). Does the ego want prosperity? "My God will supply every need of yours according to his riches in glory in Christ Jesus" (Philippians 4:19). Does the ego want security? "Jehovah is my shepherd; I shall not want" (Psalm 23:1). Does the ego want recognition? "And when the chief Shepherd is manifested you will obtain the unfading crown of glory" (I Peter 5:4). What else does the ego want? God is

11. "Humanism believes in the importance of man, but a creed which glorifies man by cutting him off from God ultimately causes the importance of man to disappear." Urquhart, *Humanism and Christianity,* p. 54.

able to "do far more abundantly than all we ask or think" (Ephesians 3:20). Next to the ethics of Christ, all other theories seem as weak as the twitter of distant sparrows in competition with the resounding peals of a mighty organ.

The *negative* incentive for proper duty to God is the pain which God inflicts upon all who spurn His offer of reconciliation. If men died under the law of Moses by the word of two or three witnesses, "How much worse punishment do you think will be deserved by the man who has spurned the Son of God, and profaned the blood of the covenant by which he was consecrated, and outraged the Spirit of grace" (Hebrews 10:29)? As we promise spankings to our children who fail to obey what we say is right, so God will punish with damnation all who reject the blood of His Son. "If anyone's name was not found written in the book of life, he was thrown into the lake of fire" (Revelation 20:15). The same Jesus Who beckoned the weary to come to Him for rest also warned those who failed to come that there would be weeping, wailing, and gnashing of teeth at the end of the age for them.

With these affirmative and negative incentives for doing one's duty, the Scripture rightly labels that man who rejects Christ, a 'fool.' A fool is one who chooses a weaker course of blessings and benefits to a stronger one, as the man who spends thousands of dollars to keep his weak body in shape and then rejects the Son of Man, Who alone can give him *eternal* blessedness.

D. God or the Banquet for the Worms

Death is the one sure arch under which all men must pass. But if death ends all—and it very well may unless we have inerrant revelation to assure us to the contrary—what virtue is there in present striving? Job, in his seventh answer, idoneously expressed what is perhaps as realistically conceived a philosophy of life and death as one, in a state of pessimism, can entertain. Man lives as if there is sense to life, but in the end his mortal remains provide but a banquet for the worms, for man dies and "The worm shall feed sweetly on him" (Job

24:20). All our love, all our heroism, all our devotion, may prove in the end to have been but a farce, a futile expenditure of effort. If man, when he is bent low by death, leaves behind him as a monument to his having passed by this way, but a broken, wretched frame, which is ravenously consumed by the maggots, what sense is there to life? "Die I must—this body must be a carnival for worms; it must be eaten by those tiny cannibals."[12] Serious consideration of this futility of life without God is sufficient to sully any real motive for ethical living; why strive at all, if the end of man is but a square meal for the lower animals? Shall *their* welfare stimulate us to live honestly rather than dishonestly? Will it affect their diet any if we commit fornication or if we refrain from it? Will the maggots complain about their menu if we are plunged into an atom war?

The only full relief man can find from the clutches of these 'tiny cannibals' is to locate some point of reference outside of the flux of time and space which can serve as an elevated haven of rest. In Christianity, and in it alone, we find the necessary help, the help of the Almighty, He Who rules eternity: He promises that there is life after physical death, happiness after despair. Relieved by this assurance, the Christian can say with David, "Yea, though I walk through the valley of the shadow of death, I will fear no evil; for thou art with me; thy rod and thy staff, they comfort me" (Psalm 23:4).

> So let me die, let beasts devour me, let fire turn this body into gas and vapor, all its particles shall yet again be restored; this very selfsame actual body shall start up from its grave, glorified and made like Christ's body, yet still the same body, for God hath said it. Christ's same body rose; so shall mine. O my soul, dost thou now dread to die? Thou wilt lose thy partner body a little while, but thou wilt be married again in heaven; soul and body shall again be united before the throne of God. The grave—what is it? It is the bath in which the Christian puts the clothes of his body to have them washed and cleansed. Death—what is it? It is the waiting-room where we robe ourselves for immor-

12. Spurgeon, *Gems*, p. 147.

> tality; it is the place where the body, like Esther, bathes itself in spices that it may be fit for the embrace of its Lord.[13]

Having shown how Christianity achieves perfect horizontal self-consistency and perfect vertical fitting of the facts in its ethical theory, we are now in a position to deal with the last step in the logic of conservative Christianity: the case for personal immortality. But, before turning to this final problem, let us answer two problems that pertain to the Christian ethic.

V. Objections to the Christian Ethic

A. Selfish System of Ethics

Appealing to the ego as a motive for doing one's duty makes Christianity a religion of pure egoism and selfishness. In answer, observe two things. First, the selfish side of Christianity is welded to a perfect selflessness. Paradoxical as it may first seem, God appeals to our selfishness to make us unselfish, for by unselfishly loving Him with all our heart and soul and mind and our neighbor as ourselves, we prepare, in the act, for our own blessings in heaven. Therefore, the more unselfish, the more humble, the more contrite we are, the more we benefit our ego in the long run. "For every one who exalts himself will be humbled, and he who humbles himself will be exalted" (Luke 14:11). Every man is selfish by nature; Christ teaches him how to benefit his egoism by being unselfish. Secondly, if one does not appeal to God and His call to the ego, he loses his hope for personal immortality, and must face a banquet for the worms and a dry dash of dust as the chief end of man. The absurdity of every non-Christian position strengthens the consistency of Christianity. It is no more illicit to be selfish in wanting to avoid hell and to enter heaven by loving God and keeping His commandments, than it is to want to avoid being hit by a bus by jumping out of its way.

---

13. *Ibid.,* pp. 147-148.

B. Leads to a Neglect of Society

If we spend our time trying to get into heaven, we will neglect what one calls the 'real business of living.' We will be more concerned about eternal things than we will be for binding the wounds of the needy and tending to the sick. The hermit and the mystic, who go all out for the other world, are the logical conclusion to Christianity's theory of heaven-striving.

This objection is naive. On any other position than Christianity there is no motive for social action. The only really convincing reason why one should sell all that he has and give the receipts to the poor is that Christ, Who loved him and died for him on the cross, asks him in love to take up his own cross and follow Him; for, in so doing, he will store up treasure in heaven where there are no moths and thieves to rob him of his wealth. In love to Christ, then, Christians should be good humanists, for they prove their love to God only as *do* they love one another. "If any one says, 'I love God,' and hates his brother, he is a liar; for he who does not love his brother whom he has seen, cannot love God whom he has not seen. And this commandment we have from him, that he who loves God should love his brother also" (I John 4:20-21).

Chapter XIX

Resurrection and Immortality

For we know that if the earthly tent we live in is destroyed, we have a building from God, a house not made with hands, eternal in the heavens.—Paul

THE Christian now may cash in on a benefit which has accrued to his system of philosophy: namely, the guarantee of personal immortality and the resurrection of the body from the grave. With the one major premise, the existence of the God Who has revealed Himself in Scripture, the Christian is assured of the rationality of the universe, a basis for changeless truth, *and a firm foundation for hope in personal immortality.* In fact, the whole point to the Biblical solution of the one within the many is to lead men into that peculiar relationship to the Almighty which establishes immortal felicity to all who embrace the implications of the covenant with saving faith.

I. The Problem of Immortality

A. The Meaning of Immortality

The only species of immortality worthy of discussion is *personal* immortality, that state of being in which individual centers of consciousness are preserved in endless existence after the shock of physical death, as opposed to such substitutes as 'impersonal' immortality—the return of the elements of the body to the supposed eternally sustained energy of the universe; 'biological' immortality—the hope that one's life will continue in his children; 'sociological' immortality—the persistence of one's life in the memory of his friends; and 'metaphysical' immortality—the absorption of the self into some higher Self. Each man is a living soul whose being is controlled by the dictates of the law of self-preservation. Therefore, man demands eternal, personal felicity as a prerequisite for complete happiness. The felicity must be eternal, for any end to life is death; and the felicity must be personal, for each man eagerly craves to have his own, as well as his neighbor's soul, saved. *Personal* immortality, therefore, is what man seeks after.

B. *The Verification of Immortality*

Men certainly need immortality. Yet how can it be proved that they actually will enjoy that state? In chapter six we learned that there are two general ways to prove a proposition: formally, by mathematics and logic, and through probability, by systematic consistency. Now, since immortality is a question which lies outside of the pale of formal logic, it may be proved only by coherence. *But it must be proved.*

We stress the fact that hope in immortality and rational coherence must go together because the recurrent temptation among philosophers at this point is to turn poetic, supposing that, since it would be 'religiously distressing' not to have a ground for immortality, immortality must be a legitimate hope. But let us not be deceived. If wishing for a pot of gold at the end of the rainbow does not make it so, neither will wishing for immortality make that so. If there is no immortality, then there is no immortality. It is better for a rational man to be sad and honest, than to be happy and deceived.

II. The Arguments for Immortality

Although not exhaustive by any means, the following arguments represent a typical cross section of the main philosophic attempts to establish the coherence of immortality. Let us examine these views and see how they fare.

A. *Inductive Science*

Some say that science, since it has already succeeded in making pills that increase the present life span of man a few years, must be looked to, to give us immortality. However, the one method that we can dismiss immediately as quite impotent to deal with the problem of our immortality (since we have no present guarantee of eternal life by science's manipulations), is the narrowly conceived scientific method. Immortality deals with the unseen and the eternal; science is limited to the observable here and now.

B. *Arguments of the Mystics*

Mystics, through their presumed 'inward vision,' claim to have seen that both the existence of God and the immortality of the soul are realities. Shall their testimonies go unheeded? The mystic's testimony is worthless in the present discussion, for, by definition, it is ineffable, while the *sine qua non* for all evidence in any philosophic argument is the rational proposition to which the law of contradiction may be applied.

C. *Man is Conscious of the Eternal*

The soul, as Plato and many others taught, knows the *rationes aeternae;* therefore it is related to eternity in some real sense. But must not the soul itself be eternal to participate in the eternal? Hardly. Because we are able to know God, we do not have a right rationally to conclude that somehow we must be God. From the datum that we are qualified to think of the *rationes aeternae,* we may logically conclude only that finite creatures are capable of thinking of the *rationes aeternae,* that and nothing more.

D. *Man is Endowed to Enjoy Eternity*

A variation of the above is the argument that, if man is thought of as but an animal of time and space, when, *de facto,* he is capable of living forever, he is unaccountably and mysteriously over-endowed. Again, all we can conclude from this is that man is *capable* of enjoying eternal life, not that he actually *will.* Many of the lower animals are endowed more highly than utility requires, as the large horns on certain northern deer, which, instead of being a stimulus to longevity, have brought extermination.

E. The Pragmatic Argument

Some claim that, despite the fact that there may be no scientifically verifiable evidence for immortality, we may still believe that it is real because of the pragmatically measurable peace and blessings that it adds to our character. "Tried by the pragmatic test, whether applied by the psychologist, scientist, or prophet or Christian believer, our faith in immortality stands justified. Without its vision the highest and finest life would perish."[1] This is incredibly naive. Is a rational man (and we are here talking about men and not animals) justified to believe that the law of relativity is another name for pumpkin pie, that two and two are three, and that roots grow up, not down, just because it improves his character? In a rational universe, character must be related to truth, not fancy; otherwise, perhaps, some might claim that their character would be improved if they could feed arsenic of lead to all government workers. If there is no immortality, there is no immortality; that is all there is to it. To say that there is, when there actually is not, either to build character or anything else, is but deliberately to speak a falsehood.

F. Argument from Evolution

What has nature been trying to do throughout evolution save produce human beings, her highest fruit? A process is known by its fruit, and this fruit is man. Human beings "are the crown of creation; no mother could insist that her babe is worth more than all the Alps with greater assurance than reason insists on evaluating personalities above unconscious and unmoral rocks and stars. And now when the universe has so achieved a creature in whom evolution has ceased being physical and has become psychical, in whom exhaustless possibilities are at last begotten, does the universe in utter unconsciousness of her achievement toss the potentialities of mind and spirit into Sheol with the refuse of the flesh, and caring no

---

1. Snowden, *Can We Believe in Immortality?* p. 111. "We have seen what assurance of eternal life means to character." Fosdick, *The Assurance of Immortality,* p. 139.

more for one than for the other, bring all alike to a dismal and inconsequential end?"[2] Observe the movement of the argument: *man* is what nature is striving to produce; therefore, we cannot but assume that nature, after having gone to this Herculean effort, will continue to preserve these 'crowns of creation' forever. There are several weaknesses in this argument, however.

First, by what criterion do we assume that man, rather than the tadpole or the weasel, is the highest form in the *present* stage of evolution? High or perfect or advanced in relation to what, or to whom? The Christian, appealing to God, can show that the fact of man's rational nature is enough to relieve him from being included in the baboon category, but to what can the empiricist appeal? Perhaps man is but a sport, a mutation, a wild mass of uncontrolled flesh, a monster that nature abhors and is struggling frantically, though with little present success, to recall. Furthermore, is it likely that nature would deliberately make a creature that would turn around and destroy nature herself through its wars and other acts of violence?

Secondly, by what criterion do we assume that man is the true goal of evolution? Since we are part of that process which seems to be without end, it may be that man is just being prepared as fodder for some future ten-headed personality-eating freak. There is no compelling reason from available scientific facts to assume that evolution is at an end, now that man is at last here. If one is committed to the non-Christian assumption of 'total' evolution, as opposed to what we have called 'threshold' evolution, he cannot disprove the hypothesis that there may emerge a creature who is to man as man is to the slime. Who then would be the end of evolution? Or would not it still be meaningless to speak of 'ends' at all, when the process is eternal? Can we detect from the first ten blows of the stonecutter's chisel what the completed statue is like? In like manner, since we are in the process of history and have

---

2. Fosdick, *op. cit.*, p. 111-112.

no revelation (on the evolutionist's position) to tell us otherwise, today's king may be tomorrow's knave. In any case, the more we observe the out-of-place-character that human personality has in a universe which is under the decrees of the second law of thermodynamics, the less plausible does it seem that *man* is the end of creation. Furthermore, is it not suspicious that man chooses himself as the end of evolution? We feel with assurance that an ape, could he talk, would be convinced that he, not man, is the end of things. He is stronger, hairier, and, according to his own standards, much better looking than man, not to mention the fact that he does not commit those sinful atrocities all the day that man, his supposed higher cousin, does.

G. Argument from the Rationality of the Universe

Another argument which grows out of this same erroneous conviction that human values are the highest things going, is the supposition that, since the universe is rational, man, being so valuable, must live forever; it would be mad to destroy him. "When, therefore, we assume, as science always does in the physical realm, that this is a reasonable world, we have a positive and assuring argument for immortality. Of course, this may be an utterly erratic universe, not in the least to be depended on to furnish reliable clues to truth, but such a conception makes science as impossible as it makes immortality unlikely."[3] This is a classic piece of *non sequitur* reasoning.

Fosdick correctly believes that the "fundamental assumption of all science is that the universe is truly a universe, consistent in its regularity of procedure, not erratic and whimsical, but uniform, dependable and law-abiding,"[4] but he is quite wrong when he supposes that upon this piece of evidence a basis for immortality is established. All that science understands by the rationality of the universe is that it is regular and predictive. If it is part of the regularity of this universe that men die without hope, are eaten by the maggots, and that

3. Fosdick, *op. cit.*, p. 113.
4. *Ibid.*, p. 99.

is their end, such data, as long as they are regular, do not impinge on the hypothesis of the rationality of the universe. It only means that the universe expresses its regularity and rationality by promptly and orderly exterminating all men at the end of their three score years and ten. Fosdick unwarrantedly leaps from his definition of rationality, 'in accord with human values,' to the scientist's definition, 'predictive,' when, as a matter of philosophic fact, there is no relation between them.

H. The Justice and Goodness of God

Although the literature on the subject of immortality is immense, most of the arguments on the question simmer down to what amounts to a deep sigh and a committal of the issue to the 'justice and goodness of God.' Fosdick is convinced that a God Who would make human personalities only to destroy them again, is but a half-witted artist Who amuses Himself with tasks that have no meaning.[5] Emmet is confident that the "Good Shepherd who seeks for the lost sheep will not rest until he has saved the goats."[6] Trueblood is morally assured that "If God is the author of evolution and if men are, as Jesus taught, God's children, creatures toward whose existence the long effort of creation has been pointing, then we may rest secure about our futures."[7]

Contrast these optimistic opinions with the severe judgments of the Son of Man. "And do not fear those who kill the body but cannot kill the soul; rather fear him who can destroy both soul and body in hell" (Matthew 10:28). "And if your eye causes you to sin, pluck it out; it is better for you to enter the kingdom of God with one eye than with two eyes to be thrown into hell, where their worm does not die, and the fire is not quenched" (Mark 9:47-48).

Once more we view an example of that conflict which exists at every point between the Christian view of God and the

5. Fosdick, *op. cit.*, p. 113.
6. *Immortality*, p. 217.
7. *The Logic of Belief*, p. 320.

world, and the non-Christian. The latter teaches, with Plato, that the gods must do the good, while the former affirms that the good is what God does. The latter assumes that God is good and just only when he preserves human values, while the former is assured that God is under no antecedent obligation whatever to save as much as one hair on the head of the most righteous. The latter thinks the universe is in operation to augment human values, while the former teaches that the *raison d'etre* of the world is a display of the glory and power of God. The latter claims that the *summum bonum* is human life, while the former preaches that the *summum bonum* is the will of God.

This conflict is an old story to us by now; it is the finite God, the God that *must* preserve human values, versus the Almighty that sovereignly rules heaven and earth. Believing that the latter is a tyrant unworthy of our love, modern man has rejected Jehovah, and, in His place, put another God in heaven, one that suits the temper of a scientific age. Let us now show that, on the view of either the finite or the infinite God, it is impossible by an appeal to the 'justice and goodness of God,' to establish our hope for personal immortality.

If God is the Almighty, and if the good is what He does, then, obviously, one can measure what the good is only by observing what God does. On this position, God, Who received no counsel in making the human race, seeks no counsel in disposing of it. In perfect goodness and justice, therefore, not only can He send some men to hell, but He can send them all. Where, then, is our hope for felicity?

And if God is not the Almighty, but a finite deity Who is committed to preserving human values, come what may, our immortality cannot even then be assured; for, though God may be quite well-meaning in His intentions to save us all, it cannot be known but what He is too impotent to make these intentions good. He may be like the man sitting on the chair, with his arms tied, watching a little girl drown, desiring oh so much to save her; but, because he lacks the power to save her, the girl drowns just as surely as if he were not there to sympathize with her. We *appreciate* God's sympathy, but will that give us immortality?

Here is the dilemma again. If we make God *omnipotent,* then we give Him power and authority to damn us in hell if He so elects. And if we hold back some of His power, and keep God limited in what He can do, then we leave open the possibility that God is impotent right at the very point where we need Him most to give us immortality. Choose your alternative; it makes no difference. In neither case can you establish proof for our immortality from the 'goodness and justice of God.'[8]

I. The Argument from Grace

Assured that Jehovah is God and He alone, the Christian makes no claim to any law of sufficient reason or standard of goodness and justice which may serve as a big stick to make God perform and give man immortality: for Jehovah is the *Almighty.* "I am Jehovah, and there is none else. I form the light, and create darkness; I make peace, and create evil; I am Jehovah, that doeth all these things" (Isaiah 45:6-7). Instead of teaching that man is of such infinitely incontestable value, that God, to be worthy of His name, must preserve him immortally, the Christian follows Paul's judgment that there is none righteous, no not one (Romans 3:10). Man, then, deserves *death,* not life. The Christian cannot appeal to the rationality of the universe, for all rationality is from God. He cannot claim an independent rule of goodness and justice to assure him of life, for all goodness and justice flow from God. In short, the Christian knows that man, a vile, wretched, filthy sinner, will receive immortal life solely and only by God's grace; man neither deserves immortality nor is worthy of it.

8. If one is to appeal to God at all here, the least he can do is produce evidence for his right to do so. Fosdick says that a "just and fatherly God cannot have brought into being children capable of endless growth, aspiring after perfect knowledge and character, only to toss them one by one into oblivion, until at last, tired even of the house he built for them, he burns it up" (*op. cit.,* p. 115), but one is at a loss to know where he received his information for this conviction. The Bible does not teach it and there is no evidence from science.

Unless He that made man sovereignly elects to give him salvation and life, by grace and not by works, man is absolutely without hope. Man came into this world naked and it is certain that he will depart in exactly the same manner; and He Who gave life in the first place can also recall it either to damnation, blessedness, or annihilation.

The Christian, therefore, prostrate before the Almighty, cries for helping grace, not unlike a man in a burning building that offers no way of escape from death. "For by *grace* have you been saved through faith; and this is not your own doing, it is the *gift of God*—not because of works, lest any man should boast" (Ephesians 2:8-9),

Not the labors of my hands
  Can fulfill Thy law's demands.
Could my zeal no respite know,
  Could my tears forever flow,
All for sin could not atone;
  Thou must save, and Thou alone.

Nothing in my hand I bring,
  Simply to Thy cross I cling;
Naked, come to Thee for dress,
  Helpless, look to Thee for grace;
Foul, I to the fountain fly,
  Wash me, Savior, or I die!

The trouble with the modern man is that he has such a good opinion of himself. Failing to see that he is a lost sinner and that he is under the fearful wrath and judgment of God, he toys with God as if playing with a piece of string, not realizing that in his very attitude he is displaying the fruit of an arrogant, sinful heart. Thus, while the non-Christian claims self-sufficiency at every point, the Christian repudiates it at every point. "For what is more consistent with faith than to acknowledge ourselves naked of all virtue, that we may be clothed by God; empty of all good, that we may be filled by him; slaves to sin, that we may be liberated by him; blind, that we may be enlightened by him; lame, that we may be guided; weak, that we may be supported by him; to divest ourselves of all ground of glorying, that he alone may be eminently glorious, and that we may glory in him?"[9]

The argument from grace takes its place in a system of thought which is horizontally self-consistent and which vertically fits the facts of life. Through the expediency of the one hypothesis, the existence of the God Who has revealed Himself in Scripture, the Christian places immortality in as secure a position in the framework of his world-view as any other judgment which terminates upon reality. Immortality is absolutely guaranteed by the God to whom we have appealed as a solution to the one within the many. "Truly, truly, I say to you, he who believes *has* eternal life" (John 6:47). There is no if, but, or maybe to the promises of God. "I am the resurrection and the life; he who believes in me, though he die, yet shall he live, and whoever lives and believes in me shall never die" (John 11:25-26). If one is to reject the Christian doctrine of personal immortality, he must also reject the entire Christian revelation, in which case he must start *ab ovo* from the flux of time and space to solve the problem of the one within the many. And if he is consistent in this little assignment, he will learn that any alternative to a supernaturally conceived universe is a naturalistically conceived one. But naturalism, when carried to its logical conclusion, leads to skepticism, for from flux only flux can come. A world-view, as we have indicated, like water, cannot rise above its source. If we begin with God in our theory of values, we end with a God Who provides immortality for man; if we begin with man in our theory, we end with neither God nor immortality, but with pessimism and despair only.

If Christianity could but make personal immortality secure, it would have done enough to assure it a place in the philosophic hall of fame; but when Christianity goes on and guarantees, not only personal immortality, but the resurrection of our own bodies, then it has done something that none of the ancients even dreamed could be incorporated in a rational world-view. But this is the very hope of the Christian, that,

9. Calvin, *Institutes, Dedication,* pp. 23-24.

since Jesus Christ rose from the grave, he will rise also! With this doctrine of the resurrection we find the final and perfect solution to the soul-sorrow of man which we plotted in chapter one. The primary source of soul-sorrow, we learned, is the fear of death. Christ has destroyed death in His atonement. The next source is the union of the body and soul in man, the union of the real and the ideal. Man's body is too fragile to bear up the ideals of the soul, in order that man may enjoy perfect well-being in the whole man. Christianity assures us that the body which man now has is a sinful, carnal frame, one that is under a curse; for this reason it is unable to bear up the ideals of the soul. In the resurrection, however, our present body will be exchanged for a new one. "It is sown in dishonor, it is raised in glory. It is sown in weakness, it is raised in power. It is sown a physical body, it is raised a spiritual body" (I Corinthians 15:43-44). Here is the end of a truly worthy philosophy of life: the resurrection of the body and the purification of the soul, united together perfectly to enjoy eternal blessing and happiness. Fully to assure this felicity, God will prepare a setting commensurate to our new state, an environment where the second law of thermodynamics is wholly out of order, for in heaven "God himself will be with them; he will wipe away every tear from their eyes, and death shall be no more, neither shall there be mourning nor crying nor pain any more, for the former things have passed away" (Revelation 21:3-4). Through faith in Jesus Christ, believers find at last a perfect solution to the practical human predicament!

O happy retribution!
  Short toil, eternal rest;
For mortals and for sinners,
  A mansion with the blest!

III. Objections

A. Heaven Would be Boring

Some say they would not even want the Christian heaven, even if they could have it, for it would be boring to play harps and sing Psalms all day. In answer, not to mention what a privilege it would be for any mortal being to play before the Almighty, heaven is a place of *perfection,* and perfection is that state in which there is no room for improvement. If a man wants *anything,* therefore, he should want heaven, for heaven is the good of anything augmented to the *nth* degree. If a man does not want what God prepares for him, he evinces the fact that he does not love God and is a fool, for God knows what is good for him better than he himself does.

B. Resurrection based on a Faulty Induction

"If the Resurrection actually occurred," says Trueblood, "it would seem to be not so much evidence of immortality in general, but rather of Christ's uniqueness. It is an indication, not of what occurs in the lives of other men, but of what does *not* occur in the lives of other men."[10]

The *meaning* of the resurrection, not simply the empirical fact, is what the Christian appeals to, for others besides Christ were raised from the dead and yet are not thought of as being the basis for Christian theology. Not any resurrection will do. In Christ's resurrection the *God-Man* destroyed death, and so proved that all men who trust in Christ would likewise rise from the grave at the last day. Death can no more hold them than it could hold Him Who holds the keys to death. *Who* rose and for *what reason* is the Christian appeal; not simply that *a* resurrection occurred.

C. Christianity is Nicer, not Truer

Suppose that Christianity succeeds in its doctrine of the resurrection; it just makes it an *aesthetically* nicer world-view than that system which cannot figure the resurrection in. This is false. What is truth but proper meaning? And if it is part of proper meaning to affirm the reality of the resurrection, then Christianity *is* truer as well as nicer. Also, let us not be deceived by the boldness of the objection. If one system is as true as another, plus being nicer, a rational man, unless he has

---

10. *The Logic of Belief,* p. 312.

lost his sense of values completely, will elect the former every time.

D. Hell is Irrational

The Christian teaches the doctrine of eternal damnation on the ground that "If sin be such an evil that it required the death of Christ for its expiation, no wonder if it deserve our everlasting misery."[11] But to the self-righteous, modern man, the doctrine of hell is obnoxious. Pratt, for example, questioned a number of people and discovered that "the old ideas of golden streets and of fire and brimstone seem to have been pretty generally given up . . . Only a small proportion of my respondents believe in anything like the old-fashioned hell."[12]

We settled this issue when we dealt with the problem of evil in chapters sixteen and seventeen; so we will not take it up again, save to ask where one finds his evidence for the conviction that hell is irrational. If earth would be a chaos without penal institutions, why should the wicked and the righteous mingle together in eternity? One may not personally care for the argument in the Bible for eternal hell, but personal disgruntlement cannot replace good argument. Where is there a basis for the conviction that hell is irrational? The Bible does not teach it. From logic? An Almighty God can do anything He elects. From experience? Impossible! Has any competent observer died and come back to report on conditions in the judgment? From the goodness and justice of God? If God is infinite, He does the whole counsel of His will; the good and the just are what He chooses, even to damning men that reject the Son of God and count the blood of His covenant an unworthy thing. And if God is not infinite, He is finite; in which case hell is still a possibility, for God's power may fail Him right at that point where hell is to be prevented.

---

11. Baxter, *A Call to the Unconverted*, p. 29.

12. *The Religious Consciousness*, p. 224. When will men learn that truth cannot be decided by counting noses?

The Bible teaches that when we face God ***we face Him in judgment.*** Now, a judgment is the result of a mental act, and in the final judgment, God, the Supreme Court of heaven and earth, judges. Therefore, since God's mind is infallible, His judgment is incontestable, and cannot be appealed. And if God's judgment decrees men to be worthy of damnation, then worthy of damnation such men are. Do some yet object? "But, who are you, a man, to answer back to God" (Romans 9:20)?

CONCLUSION

Chapter XX

Conclusion

This is the end of the matter; all has been heard: Fear God, and keep his commandments; for this is the whole duty of man. For God will bring every work into judgment, with every hidden thing, whether it be good, or whether it be evil.—Solomon

I. Summary and Recapitulation

BECAUSE man is both body and soul, he is a creature which is subject to perennial frustration and fear. The soul, limited in its soarings only by the law of contradiction, dreams of those reposes of bliss and happiness which it should like to enjoy, only to be crushed to earth at the end of its venture because it is united to a frail body which cannot support these dreams and ideals which the soul sets before itself. In addition to this problem of soul and body, man struggles to relate himself, a personal being, to an ostensibly impersonal universe. The more man meditates upon the incompatibilities which exist between what he might be and what he actually is, the more sorrowful his soul becomes. Man wants life, but he is offered death; he wants peace, but strife and friction are his lot.

And what shall he do about the situation? He may either commit suicide; or ignore the problem; or admit the problem and make the best of it; or challenge the whole interpretation of nature itself, to see if there is not rational meaning to the basic movement of things. It is this last course that the Christian has elected to take. He has seriously set out to see exactly what comprises the real nature and destiny of man.

The fundamental barrier to understanding what the whole universe is about, the Christian soon learns, however, is the problem of the one within the many, the many being the discrete facts which make up the bubbling flow of time and space, of which man is a part, and the one being the thread of meaning or co-ordination which runs through the many to give them significance. The problem of the one within the many is intensified by the fact that, if a man draws too close to the many, as in scientific empiricism, he will inevitably, if he is consistent, be driven to skepticism, for from the flux of history only flux can be abstracted. And if one withdraws too far from the universe and becomes completely absorbed in the one, as in mysticism, he is so far from real history that his world-view does not apply to *this* universe.

But by the one assumption, the existence of the God Who has revealed Himself in Scripture, the Christian finds that he *can* solve the problem of the one within the many, and so make sense out of life. Jesus Christ, eternally very God of very God, and, in virtue of His incarnation, true man, is discovered to be the solution for which the Christian had long sought. Christ, as Creator, is the Author of the many, and, as Logos, is the principle of the One, the Author of the meaning of the many. "All things were created . . . through him and for him. He is before all things, and in him all things hold together" (Colossians 1:16-17).

Seeing this connection between Christ and the one within the many, the Christian is immediately in possession of a basis for truth and faith. Truth is propositional correspondence to God's mind and the test for truth is systematic consistency. Christ *is* the truth, for He is the Logos, the synthesizing principle and the true meaning of all reality. And when a man sees and embraces this truth with a cordial trust, he has proper faith, for generic faith is but a resting of the heart in the sufficiency of the evidence. In a cordial trust the heart of the Christian is united to the heart of Jesus Christ, for, in possessing truth, the Christian possesses the Christ Himself. Being united to Christ in faith, the Christian then turns to the Bible even more eagerly to see what attending blessings and privileges are his in special revelation.

When pressed to give a reason for his right to appeal to the Bible as his epistemological major premise, the Christian points to the fact that all life, all science, and all philosophy are possible only because the mind makes judgments; and all judgments are hypotheses, for an hypothesis is a pattern of meaning which the mind of man advances to cover a certain area of fact. The Christian, therefore, claims as much right to advance the hypothesis of the Bible's inerrancy as the scientist has when he appeals to the law of gravity, for each is an inference based upon the observation of specific facts.

But how does the Christian *prove* the validity of the Bible? He does it in the same way that the scientist proves the law of gravity. He shows that, granting the hypothesis of the existence of the God Who has revealed Himself in Scripture, he can produce a system of philosophy which is horizontally self-consistent, *i. e.,* which makes peace with the law of contradiction, and which vertically fits the facts of life. Having fulfilled these two standards, the Christian is assured that there is enough rational evidence for him to believe in a supernaturalistically ordered universe.

Rejecting the Thomistic doctrine that there is nothing in the intellect which was not first in the senses, the conservative Christian turns to inward illumination to establish a synoptic starting point for his philosophy of life. A knowledge of God's existence is found from an analysis of the *cogito,* the finitude of the self, and the *rationes aeternae.* But even with this, the Christian has not begun to exhaust the resources of his major premise, for he is privileged to appropriate all of the benefits which are found in special revelation. In the Bible, the Christian is accurately instructed about the nature of God, the relation of God to the process of history, the relation of God to the *rationes aeternae,* and the relation of God to soteriology. In Holy Writ, the Christian has learned of Jesus, the lover of man's soul, and he says with Wesley,

Other refuge have I none;
Hangs my helpless soul on Thee;
Leave, ah, leave me not alone,
Still support and comfort me.

All my trust on Thee is stayed,
All my help from Thee I bring;
Cover my defenseless head
With the shadow of Thy wing.

When he appropriates the implications that are found in the Bible for life's meaning, the Christian solves the problem of common ground, the relation between science and theology, the problem of miracles, the philosophy of history, the problem of evil, the ethical one and many, and the hope of immortality and the resurrection. Upon every important theoretic problem of life, the Bible has reliable, logical judgment to offer, judgment which, when accepted by the whole heart and soul, yields a system of thought which is horizontally self-consistent and which vertically fits the facts of life.

Coupled together with the theoretic virtues of the Christian system are the imposing affirmative and negative practical incentives which God sets before man to woo the latter into obedience and service. Affirmatively, God promises life and peace to all who will leave their sin, take up their cross, and follow Christ. "For God so loved the world that he gave his only Son, that whoever believes in him should not perish but have eternal life" (John 3:16). And negatively, God promises death and damnation to all who reject the blood of Christ and trample under foot the finished work of His cross. "He who does not believe is condemned already, because he has not believed in the name of the only Son of God" (John 3:18).

Even as Christ concluded His discourses by giving an invitation to all His hearers to believe and so be saved, so we here plead the same. Is the servant greater than the Master? "Oh taste and see that Jehovah is good: blessed is the man that takes refuge in him" (Psalm 34:8). "Jehovah is nigh unto all them that call upon him, to all that call upon him in truth" (Psalm 145:18). But if a man rejects the solution to the riddle of the universe that Christ offers, and if he cannot believe in a system of philosophy which at least *professes* to answer the question of the rationality of the universe, to solve the dilemma of truth, and to provide a basis for personal immortality, how shall he answer Peter's question, "to whom shall we go?" (John 6:68)?

II. Pascal's Wager

As a final attempt to show both the futility of atheism and the logical probability of theism, let us detail the famous argument of Pascal, called the 'Wager.' Although this argument does not depend for its success upon any specific proposition which we have defended in the logic of conservative Christianity thus far, it is, nonetheless, completely in harmony with the Christian conviction that he who leaves revelation for empiricism is left with a universe in which there is no meaning, for there is always a 50/50 chance of anything, or its contradiction, happening.[1]

"If there is a God he is infinitely incomprehensible, since, having neither parts nor limits, he has no proportion to us; we are then, incapable of knowing either what he is, or whether he is. This being true, who will dare to undertake to resolve this question? It is not we, who have no proportion to him.

"Who, then, shall blame, as not being able to give a reason for their belief, those Christians, men who profess a religion for which they can give no reason? They declare, in exposing it to the world, that it is a folly, *stultitiam;* and then you complain that they do not prove it! If they proved it, they would not keep their word: it is in lacking proofs, that they do not lack sense. Yes; but though this may excuse those who offer it such, and take away the blame for producing it without reason, this does not excuse those who receive it. Let us examine this point then, and say: God is, or he is not. But to which side shall we incline? Reason cannot decide it at all. There is an infinite chaos that separates us. A game is being

1. The text of the Wager is found in the *Pensées,* chapter XI.

played, at the extremity of this infinite distance, in which heads or tails must come up. Which will you take? By reason you can wager on neither; by reason you can hinder neither from winning.

"Do not, then, charge with falsehood those who have made a choice; for you know nothing about it.—No: but I blame them for having made, not this choice, but a choice; for, although he who takes heads, and the other, are in the same fault, they are both in fault; the proper way is not to wager.

"Yes, but you must wager: this is not voluntary, you are embarked. Which will you take then? Let us see. Since a choice must be made, let us see which interests you the least. You have two things to lose, the true and the good; and two things to stake, your reason and your will, your knowledge and your beatitude; and your nature has two things to shun, error and misery. Your reason is not more wounded, since a choice must necessarily be made, in choosing one rather than the other. Here is a point eliminated; but your beatitude? Let us weigh the gain and the loss, in taking heads that God exists. Let us weigh these two cases: if you gain, you gain all; if you lose, you lose nothing. Wager then that he is, without hesitation.—This is admirable: yes, it is necessary to wager; but perhaps I wager too much.—Let us see. Since there is equal hazard of gaining or losing, if you had to gain but two lives for one, still you might wager. But if there were three to gain, it would be requisite to play (since you are under the necessity of playing), and you would be imprudent, when you are forced to play, not to hazard your life in order to gain three in a play where there is equal hazard of loss and gain. But there is an eternity of life and happiness. And this being true, even were there an infinity of chances, only one of which might be for you, you would still be right in wagering one in order to have two, and you would act foolishly, being obliged to play, to refuse to play one life against three in a game where among an infinity of chances there is one for you, if there was an infinity of life infinitely happy to gain. But there is here an infinity of life infinitely happy to gain, a chance of gain against a finite number of chances of loss, and what you play is finite. This is quite settled: wherever the infinite is, and where there is not an infinity of chances of loss against the chance of gain, there is nothing to balance, we must give all. And thus, when we are forced to play, we must renounce reason in order to keep life rather than to hazard it for the infinite gain, as ready to come as the loss of nothingness.

"For there is no use in saying that it is uncertain whether we shall gain, and that it is certain that we hazard; and that the infinite distance between the certainty of what we risk, and the uncertainty of what we shall gain, raises the finite good which we risk with certainty, to an equality with the infinite which is uncertain. It is not so: every player hazards with certainty to gain with uncertainty, and nevertheless he hazards certainly the finite to gain uncertainly the finite, without sinning against reason. The distance is not infinite between this certainty of what we risk and the uncertainty of gain; this is false. There is, in truth, an infinity between the certainty of gaining and the certainty of losing. But the uncertainty of gaining is proportioned to the certainty of what we hazard, according to the proportion of the chances of gain and loss; whence it comes that, if there are as many chances on one side as there are on the other, the game is playing even; and then the certainty of what we hazard is equal to the uncertainty of the gain: so far is it from being infinitely distant. And thus our proposition is of infinite force, when there is the finite to hazard in a play where the chances of gain and loss are equal, and the infinite to gain. This is demonstrative; and if men are capable of any truths, this is one of them."

(FINIS)

Glossary

Index of Scriptural Passages

Index of Proper Names

Index of Subjects

Glossary

(The terms contained in this section are defined only in that narrow sense in which they are used throughout this volume. The glossary, therefore, is not to be thought of as a substitute for the standard philosophical and English dictionaries. Rather, it is included here solely and only for the purpose of making the reading of this book possible for those who have no access to the more authoritative sources.)

ABSOLUTE: Being uncaused, unconditioned; free from external limitations.

ABSTRACT: Either a quality or attribute considered in isolation from the subject in which it inheres, as 'whiteness.' Or a theory considered apart from any concrete application, as 'abstract' truth.

ABSURD: Logically contradictory, as a triangle with two sides.

ACCIDENT: That property of being which may be destroyed without changing the essence of the being itself, as the color of a book.

ACQUAINTANCE, KNOWLEDGE BY: Immediate insight into nature by perception, as contrasted to conceptual knowledge or knowledge by description.

AD HOC HYPOTHESIS: Pertains to one case alone and cannot be tested by being put into new situations. Disconnected hypothesis, unrelated to the other hypotheses in the system. Mark of weakness in a world-view.

AD HOMINEM (to the man): Either appealing to passions or prejudices rather than the intellect, or using a premise which your opponent is responsible for to aid in refuting the opponent himself.

AD INFINITUM: Without limit or end. Carry on forever.

AESTHETICS: Science of the beautiful. Art.

A FORTIORI: All the more, as, if a large man can safely cross a bridge, with how much more probability can a small one.

ALLEGORY: A sustained or prolonged metaphor.

ANALOGIA ENTIS: Analogy of being. Scholastic concept. Device to unite the eternal realm of being and the temporal in significant predication.

ANALOGY: Similarity of two things in relation, as an ocean liner is like a floating city.

ANTECEDENT: Going before. Prior, preceding. As the egg to the chicken.

APOLOGY: Formal vindication of a hypothesis or conviction.

A PRIORI: Known by reason alone, prior to sense experience, as the knowledge of the *rationes aeternae*.

ASSUMPTION: Presupposition or postulate. The taken or the posited in a given argument.

ATELEOLOGICAL: Having no purpose. Opposed to teleological.

ATHEISM: Not believing in the existence of a personal God.

AUFKLÄRUNG: The 17th and 18th century movement in German philosophy which attempted to rid the mind of man of extraneous prejudice, authority, convention, and tradition. Known as the 'Enlightenment.'

AUTONOMY: Self-governed. Refusing to be governed by the law of the Almighty.

AXIOLOGY: The science of values.

AXIOM: A self-evident truth, as the law of contradiction.

BECOMING: Any being, the characteristic of which is change and flux.

BEING: The existent. In Parmenides, the real, that which is not subject to change, flux, and motion.

CALVINISM: That theology, stemming from the fundamental postulates of the sovereignty of God and the absolute authority of Holy Writ, which is detailed in the Gallican, Second Helvetic, Dort, and Westminster Confessions of Faith.

CATEGORICAL IMPERATIVE: "Act on that maxim whereby thou canst at the same time will that it should become a universal law." Ethical maxim of Kant.

CAUSE: That which occasions or is the necessary condition to a given effect.

CHRISTIAN: Any one, being regenerated by the Spirit of God, who, upon the occasion of faith, has had his sins atoned for by the blood of Jesus Christ, the incarnate God-Man.

COGITO ERGO SUM: 'I think, therefore I am.' Argument of Descartes.

COHERENT: That condition of a philosophy of life in which the major postulates are horizontally self-consistent and vertically fit the facts.

CONCEPT: Idea; the meaning which the mind gives to a universal term, as the concept of 'bookness.'

CONSERVATIVE: One who follows the hypothesis that there is a true God; this God is triune; this God has revealed Himself in Scripture; and Scripture constitutes the only rule of faith and practice. Broadly, one who has faith in the shed blood of Christ as an atonement for his sins.

CONTINGENT: Dependent, fortuitous, accidental.

CONTRADICTION, LAW OF: A proposition cannot be and not be true at the same time. The same attribute cannot at the same time be affirmed and denied of the same subject.

CORRELATIVE: One thing which stands in reciprocal relation to another, and depends upon this other for its meaning, as father and son, truth and error.

COSMOLOGICAL ARGUMENT: An attempt to prove the existence of God from the empirical fact that things exist. Being contingent, the universe requires the existence of the non-contingent, God.

COVENANT OF GRACE: That agreement in the counsels of God whereby the Father chose the Son to serve as the reconciling party in restoring sinful man to favor with God. The parties of the covenant were the Father and the Son; the Father represented God and the Son represented sinful man. The condition of the covenant was that Christ perform as the Second Adam what the first Adam failed to do. The promise of the covenant was life to all who believe.

CRISIS THEOLOGY: see neo-orthodoxy.

CRITERION: A standard or norm in relation to which things are judged.

DATUM: The given or the offered in an argument or system of thought.

DEDUCTION: Passing from the general to the particular.

DE FACTO: Actually. As a matter of fact.

DEISM: Theology which denies the immanence of God in history, while holding to the transcendence of God above history.

DEMIURGE: Plato's intermediary maker of the universe. Assisted in creation.

DIALECTIC: The art of drawing out truth by leading hypotheses to their logical conclusions.

DIALECTICAL THEOLOGY: see neo-orthodoxy.

DING AN SICH (thing in self): Reality in itself, as opposed to appearance, or the phenomenal (in Kantian sense). Used by Kant.

DUALISM: World-view which teaches the existence of two metaphysical ultimates.

EINHEITLICHE WELTANSCHAUUNG: Unified world-view.

EFFABLE: Capable of being expressed in words. Contrasted to ineffable.

EMPIRICISM: Form of epistemology which, accepting *tabula rasa,* claims that all data for knowledge come from sense experience.

EPISTEMOLOGY: The science of the origin, structure, limits, and validity of knowledge. Answers question: How do we know?

EQUIVOCATION: Using a term with two meanings as if it had one. Ambiguity.

ESCHATOLOGY: Science of last things to happen in the universe.

ESSENCE: The sum total of those attributes which cannot be removed from a being without destroying the being itself, as rationality in man.

ETHICS: Science of conduct. Answers question: What is the right?

EVIL: Either frustration of human values, or, if sin, any want of conformity unto, or transgression of the law of God. All evil is sin or God's punishment for sin.

EX CATHEDRA: Literally, "from the chair." Refers to the pope in his official office as head of the church. When the pope speaks ex cathedra, his judgments in matters pertaining to faith and practice are assumed to be infallible.

EX NIHILO: Describes God's act of creating the world. 'Out of nothing.'

EXCLUDED MIDDLE, LAW OF: A is either B or it is not B; no tertium quid.

FACT: Any unit of being which is capable of bearing meaning.

FAITH: (a) Generic faith: A resting of the heart in the sufficiency of the evidences; (b) Saving faith: A whole-person trust in the person and work of Jesus Christ. Saving faith is formed of three parts — knowledge (*notitia*), assent (*assensus*), and cordial trust (*fiducia*).

FALLACY: Mistake in relating, inferring, or concluding, while reasoning.

FINAL CAUSE: The end reason for a process, as the purpose which God had in mind in creating the universe.

FINITE: Having specific limits or boundaries. Opposed to infinite.

FLUX: Change, becoming, movement, as a flowing river.

FORMAL: Pertaining to theory or validity. Not material or concrete.

FUNDAMENTALIST: A conservative.

GENERIC: General.

GENUS: A general class of objects which possess the same qualities, as 'lamp.'

GOD: A Being, infinite, unchangeable, and eternal in His wisdom, justice, goodness, and truth. Creator of the universe. The Absolute. The Trinity.

GOOD: That which God approves or rewards.

HORIZONTAL SELF-CONSISTENCY: Freedom from contradictions. That state in which propositions can make peace with the law of contradiction.

HUMANISM: That philosophic-religious system which has as its central controlling interest the values of man.

HYPOTHESIS: A judgment which the mind entertains to explain an area of reality.

IMMANENT: Dwelling within, as God's presence in the universe.

IMMEDIACY: Directness, freedom from mediation or intervention.

IMPLICIT: Involved in or capable of being construed from, as the oak is implicit in the acorn.

INDUCE: To reason inferentially from the particular to the general.

INEFFABLE: Incapable of being expressed in words.

INFINITE: Without limits or external boundaries. Applies to God alone.

INNATE IDEA: Knowledge which is part of the mind's endowment at birth.

IN RERUM NATURA: In the nature of real things. Objectively real.

IPSE DIXIT: Literally, "He said it himself." Pertains to belief of something on the mere assertion of a person. A dogmatic utterance, unfortified by proof.

IRRATIONAL: Contrary to reason.

IRRELEVANT: Having no bearing on the subject, unrelated to issue at hand.

JUDGMENT: As act, the making of hypotheses, the relating of subject and predicate. As result of act, the proposition or hypothesis which the mind advances to explain a specific area of reality.

LIBERAL: A Modernist.

MEANING: Connotation, sense, significance of a thing. Fruit of the mind's evaluation of fact.

METAPHYSICS: Science of ultimate being. Answers question: What is the nature of being *qua* being?

MIRACLE: An extraordinary visible act of divine power, wrought by the efficient agency of the will of God, through secondary means, accompanied by valid, covenantal revelation, and having as its final cause the vindication of the righteousness of the triune God.

MODERNIST: One who, rejecting both the theology of conservative Christianity and its attending metaphysics, accepts the general plan of epistemology outlined by Kant, 'total' evolution, higher criticism of Scripture, and the fruits of comparative religion as detailed by science, and who teaches a loosely knit system of ethical postulates that are based on the words of Jesus, the doctrine of the brotherhood of man and the fatherhood of God, the inherent goodness of man, and the inevitability of progress, and who subscribes to the hypothesis that the Bible is but the record of the religious experiences of men in a certain age.

MYSTIC: One who claims to know God immediately through a form of spiritual inwardness, as against knowing through sensation or ratiocination.

NATURALISM: World-view which denies all supernaturalism and teleology in favor of the hypothesis that the universe is self-operating, self-directing, and self-explanatory.

NATURAL THEOLOGY: That science which seeks to demonstrate the existence of God from an examination of the content of sense experience.

NEO-ORTHODOXY: That contemporary theological movement, being called 'crisis theology' on the continent and 'Realism' in America, which, rejecting the immanence theology of modernism, has attempted to restore the validity of faith in a transcendent God, in order that an optimistic faith in eternity might be preserved over above a pessimistic view of man and history. The device resorted to, to preserve the relation between time and eternity, is referred to as 'the dialectic.'

NIHIL EST IN INTELLECTU NISI PRIUS FUERIT IN SENSU: There is nothing in the intellect which was not first in the senses. A presupposition followed by the empiricists, Aristotle, Aquinas, and Locke, but which was rejected by the rationalists, Plato, Augustine, and Leibniz. The mind is *tabula rasa.*

NON SEQUITUR: Fallacy of drawing a conclusion which does not follow from the premises given in the problem.

NORM: Criterion, standard, rule of evaluation.

OBJECTIVE: That which exists in its own ontological rights, independent of an evaluating mind, as the being of God. Opposed to subjective.

ONTOLOGY: The science of the essential properties, nature, and relations of being as such. Metaphysics.

PAGAN: One who rejects the Christian faith or one outside of that faith.

PANTA REI: "All flows." The doctrine that the universe is constantly changing, taken from the philosopher, Heraclitus.

PANTHEISM: That world-view which, denying the transcendence of God, identifies God with the world and the world with God. Thorough-going immanence.

PERCEPT: An impression received through sense experience. Opposed to concept.

PETITIO PRINCIPII: Begging of the question. Using as one of the premises in an argument, the conclusion which is being established.

PHENOMENON: Either any conceivable fact or thing, any item of reality; or the appearance of things as opposed to the things in themselves.

PHILOSOPHY: That science which attempts to give a rational explanation for the whole of reality.

POLYTHEISM: Belief in the existence of a plurality of gods. Against monotheism, the belief in the existence of but one God.

POSITIVISM: Any philosophy which, repudiating the possibility of a theological or metaphysical explanation of reality, confines verifiable knowledge to a description of phenomena.

PRAGMATISM: That philosophy which makes the test for truth the observed practical consequences which are seen to follow when a given hypothesis is led down into concrete experience.

PREDICATION: That act of mind in which a subject is related to a predicate. The act of making judgments. The formation of propositions.

PROCRUSTEANIZE: To force facts into one's hypothesis regardless of their suitability.

PROPOSITION: The lowest unit of knowledge to which the law of contradiction, the test for self-consistency, may be applied, and of which the questions of truth and error may meaningfully be asked. That form of language which may be analyzed into subject, predicate, and copula.

PRO TANTO: Literally, "for so much." To a certain extent.

QUA: In so far as, or in the capacity of.

RATIONES AETERNAE: The changeless criteria which give trans-temporal, trans-spatial significance to knowledge, as the norms of logic, ethics, and aesthetics.

REALISM: see Neo-orthodoxy.

REIFY: To materialize, to give concrete existence to.

RELATIVE: Existing in relation; contingent.

SKEPTICISM: The denial that changeless truth can be known.

SCIENCE: Systematically classified knowledge.

SINE QUA NON: An indispensable condition. That without which a thing cannot enjoy existence. As, a *sine qua non* for life is food.

SOTERIOLOGY: The science that answers the general question: What must I do to be saved?

SUBJECTIVE: Related to the thinking subject. That which exists only when it is apprehended by an active mind, as a mirage on the desert or snarks on Mars. Lacking objective ontology.

SUMMUM BONUM: The highest or supreme good. For the Christian: possession of God.

TABULA RASA: The theory that the mind, before receiving impressions, is a smoothed tablet, *i.e.*, is completely without innate ideas. From Locke.

TELEOLOGICAL: Having or related to a purpose or a designated end.

TELEOLOGICAL ARGUMENT: An inductive argument from the presence of purpose in the universe to a Designer behind the universe.

TERMINUS A QUO: A point of starting. A point at which measurement begins.

TERMINUS AD QUEM: A point of ending. A point at which measurement ends.

TERTIUM QUID: A third somewhat. A mediating alternative which one may choose when pressed into a dilemma.

THEISM: The belief in the existence of a personal, infinite Creator Who is both immanent in His creation and yet Who is wholly transcendent above it. God as Creator is transcendent—He is other than the world. God as Sustainer is immanent—He is the final reason for the power of everything in the world.

TOTO CAELO: Diametrically. Differing even to the extent of the whole heavens.

TRANSCENDENT: In God: existing prior to, independent of, and exalted over, the time-space universe.

TRUTH: Correspondence with the mind of God. Test: Systematic consistency.

UNIVERSALITY AND NECESSITY: Qualities of truth. Universality: truth under all conditions, regardless of contingencies of time and space. Necessity: true by force of compulsion in the light of the facts. Opposed to esoteric or relative.

UNIVOCAL: Having one meaning only, contrasted to equivocal, having two or more meanings.

VALID: Consistent.

WELTANSCHAUUNG: World-view.

WORLD-VIEW: A systematic philosophy of, or insight into, the movement and plan of the entire universe Philosophy of reality.

VALUE: Anything regarded with worth. Anything prized because it contributes to our well-being.

INDEX OF SCRIPTURAL PASSAGES

INDEX OF PROPER NAMES

INDEX OF SUBJECTS